IRANIAN INTELLECTUALS AND THE WEST

IRANIAN
INTELLECTUALS
AND THE WEST

*The Tormented Triumph
of Nativism*

Mehrzad Boroujerdi

Syracuse University Press

This book is part of the Mohammed El-Hindi Series on Arab Culture and Islamic Civilization and is published with the assistance of a grant from the M.E.H. Foundation.

The paper used in this publication meets the minimum requirements of American National Standard for Information Sciences—Permanence of Paper for Printed Library Materials, ANSI Z39.48-1984. ⊚™

Library of Congress Cataloging-in-Publication Data

Boroujerdi, Mehrzad.
Iranian intellectuals and the West : the tormented triumph of nativism / Mehrzad Boroujerdi. — 1st ed.
p.   cm. — (Mohamed El-Hindi series on Arab culture and Islamic civilization)
Includes bibliographical references (p.   ) and index.
ISBN 0-8156-2726-2 (alk. paper). — ISBN 0-8156-0433-5 (pbk. : alk. papaer)
1. Iran—Intellectual life—20th century.   I. Title.   II. Series.
DS316.4.B67   1996
955.05—dc20   96-27371

Manufactured in the United States of America

*To my mother and the memory of my father
for teaching me the meaning of
fidelity and fortitude*

Mehrzad Boroujerdi is assistant professor of political science at the Maxwell School of Citizenship and Public Affairs at Syracuse University.

The history of thought and culture is, as Hegel showed with great brilliance, a changing pattern of great liberating ideas which inevitably turn into suffocating straightjackets, and so stimulate their own destruction by new, emancipating, and at the same time, enslaving conceptions. The first step to understanding of men is the bringing to consciousness of the model or models that dominate and penetrate their thought and action. Like all attempts to make men aware of the categories in which they think, it is a difficult and sometimes painful activity, likely to produce deeply disquieting results.

—Isaiah Berlin
"Does Political Theory Still Exist?"

Contents

Illustrations

Prologue

THE IRANIAN REVOLUTION of February 1979 was undoubtedly a seismic political event that heralded the return of religious revolutions to the annals of modern history. The rapid downfall of a mighty autocratic regime, the use of religion as the primary agency of political mobilization, the tremendous level of animosity displayed against the West, and the establishment of a theocracy in the later decades of the twentieth-century presented serious questions for social scientists to ponder. In the seventeen years that have elapsed two dominant schools of thought have emerged on the causes of this popular, turbulent, and controversial revolution. The first approach views the revolution in terms of socio-economic factors related to Iran's rapid and uneven economic development. The second emphasizes cultural and ideological factors, notably the rise of politicized Islam, Iranians' disenchantment with the West, and their search for a new cultural identity.

Having wrestled for more than one decade with the considerable task of investigating the theoretical orientation and social function of modern Iranian intellectuals, I have come to appreciate both schools of thought. The political economy and the culturalist perspective by themselves, however, only capture fragments of the complicated reality of the Iranian scene. A more profound understanding of the genesis and trajectory of this revolution requires an epistemological bifocality that makes allowance for cross-fertilization and thereby makes one privy to their combined wisdom. I am well aware that this type of eclecticism does not suit all tastes and that one can be dragged into a deadly scholarly quagmire. Yet Goethe's maxim, "All theory, dear friend, is gray—the Golden tree of life is green," convinces me to take the risk nonetheless. My goal is not so much to foster a compromise but to open a space for dialogue by demonstrating the insufficiencies of the two approaches. In this book I demonstrate how Iranian intellectuals responded to the cultural, socioeconomic, and political transformation within their society from the early 1950s to the mid-1990s. The time interval under consideration is of utmost importance because it marks an era of tremendous socioeconomic upheaval and political metamorphosis.

I have confined my theoretical investigation of contemporary Iranian intellectual history within a cultural triangle: the impact of Western culture and civilization; Iran's (pre)Islamic heritage; and the intellectuals' estimate of the latter two. The importance of the first lies in the fact that Western philosophical, scientific, economic, and military prowess have irrevocably affected the day-to-day way of life and thinking in contemporary Iran. The second is significant because it constitutes Iranians' primary source of cultural and intellectual identity. The third is crucial because in their capacity as creators and narrators of culture, intellectuals have played a vital role in mediating the encounter between Western culture and Iran's (pre)Islamic heritage. Within this cultural triangle a set of problems have surfaced: What is the West? How should it be approached? What comprises Iranian identity? What is the proper relationship among religion, science, and philosophy? Is religion an anachronism for a "developing" society such as Iran? Should modernity and secularism be viewed as universal principles or as Western intrusions that are incompatible with Iranian culture? In the pages that follow I analyze the methods of formulating such questions and the responses of Iranian intellectuals. I pursue this task by critically examining intellectuals' discursive practices relative to the state and the West.

In light of the revolution's outcome a goodly number of scholarly books on Shiʿism and Iranian clergy have proliferated.[1] Relatively little has been done, however, on the contributions by nonclerical religious intellectuals.[2] Still less attention has been devoted to analyzing the thoughts and actions of secularized intellectuals, who have been treated mostly as marginal actors.[3] Unlike in most other modern revolutions, Iranian secular intellectuals did not climb to the top of the revolutionary movement that came to power in 1979. Nonetheless, it would be a grave mistake not to study the crucial role they played in the political and ideological dress rehearsals that led to the revolution. It is impossible to understand the genesis of the Iranian revolution without referring to the theoretical reflexes and the political struggles of secular intellectuals. That in modern Iranian intellectual history Hegel's Owl of Minerva (symbolizing wisdom or historical understanding) has brought

1. For some of the best examples see Akhavi 1980, Amir Arjomand 1988, Bayat-Philipp 1982, Enayat 1982, Fischer 1980, and Mottahedeh 1985.

2. For a number of competent examples see Abrahamian 1989, Chehabi 1990, and Dabashi 1993.

3. For three hitherto unpublished works that treat the historical plight of Iranian secular intelligentsia see Gheissari 1989, Kia 1986, and Shahdadi 1982.

something different from the customary unfolding of secularization makes an examination of lay religious intellectuals a necessity.

With these points in mind I deal in this study primarily with the ideas and practice of secular and lay religious intellectuals. It will be argued that what abounded in the Iranian intellectual circles in the years leading to the revolution was a nativist discourse that was much more corpulent, encompassing, and ubiquitous than Shiʿa Islam. It is true that Shiʿism is an integral part of the Iranian political culture, and it is equally valid to maintain that political culture is the background against which the drama of politics is enacted. Yet the argument that Iranian political culture is Islamic in a sui generis fashion does not pass close scrutiny. My study of the cognitive map, nomenclature, and discursive practices of the modern Iranian intellectual elite demonstrates that the ideology of the revolution was not ab initio Islamic. In other words, Shiʿism was a key, but not the sole, ideological component of the revolution. What motivated or dragged many of Iran's intelligentsia to join the revolutionary tide was more than religious sentiments. Religion might have been more a surrogate for Iranian nationalism. It was a rallying cry for those who had been adversely affected by the course of economic and social metamorphosis experienced in the country in prior decades.

In line with the theoretical disposition of the present work I present an integrated analysis of the last five decades of intellectual production in Iran by providing both a glimpse into the socioeconomic ambiance of the country as a whole and by furnishing a synoptic discussion of ten leading intellectuals. The criterion used to select the intellectuals is not public fame but substantive theoretical contribution. Whereas some of the thinkers examined in this book can be considered leading personalities of the 1979 revolution, I include also those hitherto unknown to non-Persian—speaking audiences and, alas, also to many Iranians. By uncovering the ideas and texts of these neglected authors, past and present, I draw attention to the remarkable continuity in Iranian thought before and after the 1979 revolution.

The theoretical predilections of this study are set forth in chapter 1, wherein the central concepts of *other-ness, orientalism, orientalism in reverse,* and *nativism* are discussed. An understanding of these ideas is crucial for making sense of the chapters that follow. In chapters 2 and 3 I examine how the secular Iranian intellectuals of the 1950s, 1960s, and 1970s confronted a dual sense of other-ness with the state and the West, which, respectively, resulted in dissent and nativism. The second chapter begins with an examination of the term *intellectuals* and proceeds to demonstrate how the "rentier" nature of the Pahlavi state brought about its crisis of legitimacy, which, in turn, was exploited by secular militants and literati committed to political activism. In chapter 3 I deal with the second type of other-ness confronting Iranian intellectuals, the other-ness of the West. The latter group's search for self-identity is deconstructed through the literary, political, and philosophical texts of three important intellectuals: Seyyed Fakhroddin Shadman, Ahmad Fardid, and Jalal Al-e Ahmad. In chapter 4 I present an account of the changing nature of the clergy's philosophical and political discourse. In chapter 5 I investigate the discursive practices of a newly emerging class of lay religious intellectuals whose vision of cultivating an "Islamic alternative" led to cries for "authenticity" and calls for a "return to the self." First, to provide an account of the intricate process through which these Muslim intellectuals contributed to the formation of the religious subculture, I present a case study of the holy city of Mashhad. I then examine the writings of two more influential thinkers, Ali Shari'ati and Seyyed Hoseyn Nasr, as well as the Mojahedin-e Khalq guerrilla organization. Combined with chapter 4, this chapter completes the discussion of how the ascendancy of political Islam became possible. In chapter 6 I explain how the Iranian academia contributed to the articulation and further popularity of the nativist discourse by looking at the works of Ehsan Naraqi, Hamid Enayat, and Daryush Shayegan. In the final chapter of the book I elucidate the range of problematics and challenges facing the postrevolutionary intellectual elite in Iran by critically scrutinizing three consequential sets of debates involving Reza Davari and Abdolkarim Sorush.

Acknowledgments

THIS BOOK BEGAN as a doctoral dissertation completed at the American University (Washington, D.C.) and recognized by the Foundation for Iranian Studies as the best of its kind in the Field of Iranian Studies in 1990. In the years that have ensued it has undergone a metamorphosis both in content and in style. A fair amount of the revisions were carried out during my stays at Harvard University (1990–91) and the University of Texas at Austin (1991–92) where I was, respectively, a Postdoctoral Fellow and a Rockefeller Foundation Resident Fellow in Humanities. I thank all of my colleagues at the Middle East Centers of these two fine institutions, in particular Roy Mottahedeh and Fedwa Malti-Douglas, for enabling me to enjoy two efficacious and remunerative years of research and writing. My interactions with peers and students at Syracuse University since September 1992 have allowed me to reflect upon and refine further some of my earlier arguments.

I have been the recipient of numerous intellectual loans from the following mentors, colleagues, and friends who each kindly read parts or all of this work and made numerous suggestions for its improvement, not all of which I have had the forte or wisdom to include: Ervand Abrahamian, Shahrough Akhavi, Reza Alavi, Mehdi Aminrazavi, Ahmad Ashraf, G. Matthew Bonham, Houchang Chehabi, Anna Enayat, Faridoun Farrokh, Traci A. Fordham, Valerie J. Hoffman, M. R. Ghanoonparvar, Naeem Inayatullah, Ahmad Karimi-Hakkak, Şerif Mardin, Ali Mirsepassi, Nicholas G. Onuf, Abazar Sepehri, Mohamad Tavakoli-Targhi, and Prodromos Yannas. In addition, I thank many of the scholars cited in this book who generously shared with me in lengthy interviews their experiences and thoughts on the intricacies of Iranian intellectual life. Needless to say, the responsibility for all the shortcomings of this book rests on my shoulders alone. The list of individuals who helped me compile the data for the appendix over the last decade is too lengthy to summon here. I thank every one of them. I also thank the Routledge and E. J. Brill publishing houses for their permission to use materials from chapters 3 and 6 of the present book that were previously published in Boroujerdi 1992; 1994b. Similarly, I thank all the staff of Syracuse University Press and, in particular, the executive editor, Cynthia Maude-Gembler, for grace, serenity, professionalism, and efficiency.

I am grateful to my colleagues in the political science department of Syracuse University for inhibiting me from turning the present manuscript into yet another penultimate version of that "ideal" first book of which so many young scholars innocently dream. On a higher plane, I hope that members of my immediate family accept this labor of love as a token of my sincere gratitude for all that they have endured in the course of the last two tempestuous decades. Finally, as a father, I take solace in the thought that this book may help my son, Mateen, better understand the nature of a revolution that robbed him, rather unfairly, of a wise and affectionate grandpa.

A Note on the Text

THIS BOOK EMPLOYS the transliteration system laid out by Nasser Sharify in *Cataloging of Persian Works* (1959). To make the book more accessible to the general reader I have modified Sharify's system in three ways: (1) with the exception of the *ayn* and *hamza* all diacritical marks for Persian and Arabic terms have been dispensed with, (2) diacritical marks have been omitted in the initial position, and (3) deference has been accorded to contemporary/popular rather than classic/scholastic Persian pronunciations. Anglicized names found in *Webster's Third New International Dictionary of the English Language* have been granted preference where appropriate. Finally, in the materials quoted from English and French language sources, the respective authors' preferred spelling of names has also been listed.

For dates I have pursued the following format. For material originally published in Persian the bibliography provides both the Muslim solar (Hijri Shamsi) calendar years and the equivalent years in the Christian Era, respectively. In the body of the text and the notes, however, I only provide the Christian Era dates. In March 1976 a new calendar system, which dated back to the establishment of the Achaemenid Empire by Cyrus the Great in 558 B.C., was instituted in Iran. According to this imperial calendar, the Iranian solar year 1355 (equivalent to year 1976 in the Gregorian calendar) became the year 2535. Between 1976 and 1978 all books and official documents published in Iran were dated according to this imperial calendar.

Because the number of Iranian intellectuals cited in this book is large, I give all biographical information on them as part of the Appendix. Finally, unless otherwise indicated, all translations from Persian and French are my own.

IRANIAN INTELLECTUALS AND THE WEST

1

Other-ness, Orientalism, Orientalism in Reverse, and Nativism

> Contact between cultures always makes for drama: an ontological, communal drama of human differences or an existential, intellectual drama in the life of an individual. Superficial contact creates a feeling of strangeness; more profound encounters risk bringing on the dissolution of the self, the shattering of its coherence, the end of certitude, and a traumatic challenge to one's values.
>
> —Hichem Djaït, *Europe and Islam*

On Other-ness

MOST STUDENTS OF PHILOSOPHY AGREE that the René Descartes (1596–1650) "I think, therefore I am" statement helped usher in a new era in human history. The rationalistic premise of this short sentence constitutes a decisive break with premodern thought. Since then, the Cartesian *I,* or the *thinking ego,* has become an indispensable centerpiece of Western philosophy by presenting itself as the subject (or agent) of knowledge, ethical responsibility, and change. "With the Cartesian 'I think,' an egoity appeared and became the established definition of humanity. The I provided an origin from which a certain but egocentric and dualistic universe was secured for Western experience" (Liberman 1989, 127).

A compatriot of Descartes, the philosopher and historian of thought Michel Foucault (1926–1984), engaged in a lifetime quest to understand how the Western self develops knowledge about itself. Studying the genealogy of human sciences in the period since the eighteenth century, Foucault maintained that these sciences managed to articulate a new and positive definition of *self* that was radically different from Christianity's notion of self-renunciation. He maintained that the human sciences' construction of this new self came about through the constitution of an *other*. That is, self-knowledge develops through a knowledge of the other. To demonstrate this issue he mined the genealogy and archaeology of various modern scientific disciplines such as biology, medicine, penology, psychiatry, and demography.

Foucault identified four technologies that human beings use to understand themselves: technologies of production; technologies of the sign system; technologies of power; and technologies of the self (Foucault 1988, 18). Whereas Marx was concerned with the technology of production, Foucault was preoccupied with the technologies of the self.[1] Understanding the genealogy of knowledge is not possible without comprehending the ties between power and knowledge. Foucault was concerned with how the *other* disappears into the singular *I* and into the collective *we*. Thus, he began his intellectual odyssey into the margins of selfhood and of society. He studied the "madman," the "deviant," the "prisoner," the "delinquent," the "murderer," the "hermaphrodite"—in short, internal "others."[2] Foucault charged that these others have been created by *discourses*[3] harnessed to powerful social forces and institutions. It is not objects that create discourses but the reverse because language antedates and constructs subjectivity. Furthermore, through their linkage to the dominant power structures and in the name of scientific objectivity the discourses of the human sciences have come to constitute "regimes of truth" (Gregory 1989, xiv). These regimes of truth perform a "policing function" whose imperative is to "establish boundaries between regulated and unregulated domains of human activity, which creates a mentality that interprets such activity in terms of binary oppositions: sanity and insanity, health and sickness, legitimate and criminal behavior, lawful and illicit love" (Hutton 1988, 126). Foucault was intent on proving the arbitrariness of these categorizations. In *Madness and Civilization* he untangled psychiatric discourse, demonstrating how perception of the insane changed from one of eccentric behavior in the Middle Ages to embarrassing behavior in the sixteenth century and, finally, to intolerable behavior in the eighteenth century. He per-

1. He writes: "Technologies of the self permit individuals to effect by their own means or with the help of others a certain number of operations on their own bodies and souls, thoughts, conduct, and ways of being, so as to transform themselves in order to attain a certain state of happiness, purity, wisdom, perfection, or immortality" (Foucault 1988, 18).

2. See Foucault 1965, 1975, 1979a, and 1980.

3. Foucault considers discourse as a conceptual terrain where knowledge is produced. This knowledge and its corresponding suppositions, rules, and agendum, however, are socially and politically constructed. In other words, bodies of knowledge are not independent intellectual structures but also are cites of power where power and knowledge freely intermingle with one another.

formed a similar deconstruction on the "discursive practices" of a variety of other disciplines.[4] He charged that by inventing or reactivating a set of rules these disciplines came to constitute a system of control in the production of discourses. Discourses, thus, became "assets" for which different social forces compete in a discursive economy.

Foucault's "genealogy" centered around the problematic of power-knowledge and the triangle of power, right, and truth in the age of modernity. He contended that "the exercise of power itself creates and causes to emerge new objects of knowledge and accumulates new bodies of information. . . . Conversely, knowledge constantly induces effects of power" (Foucault 1977b, 51–52). The manifold relations of power in any society "cannot be established, consolidated nor implemented without the production, accumulation, circulation and functioning of a discourse" (93). He further maintained that "there can be no possible exercise of power without a certain economy of discourses of truth which operates through and on the basis of this association" (93). The association was, thus, centered on a triangle composed of rules of right, mechanisms of power, and the effects of truth.[5]

By questioning whom discourse serves Foucault supplemented Marx's question of whose interest the relations of power support. Whereas Marx looked at the means and modes of production, Foucault's critical sequel interrogates the means and modes of representation. Both thinkers, however, were preoccupied with the processes of exploitation and alienation whereby the human subject leaves the authentic state of being in order to become an other.

Foucault's work also called into question the central tenets of phenomenology, which holds the sameness of self and the other as a basic prerequisite of mutual interpersonal understanding, communication, and relations. For Foucault other-ness is not just a question of difference but also one of hierarchy, because the other is not one with whom we identify, but instead one whom we perceive to be either superior or

4. Foucault defines a *discursive practice* as "a body of anonymous, historical rules, always determined in the time and space that have defined a given period, and for a given social, economic, geographical, or linguistic area, the conditions of operation of the enunciative function" (Foucault 1972, 117).

5. Foucault, however, was also cognizant of the resistance potential imbedded within discourse as he wrote: "Discourses are not once and for all subservient to power or raised up against it, any more than silences are. We must make allowance for the complex and unstable process whereby discourse can be both an instrument and an effect of power, but also a hindrance, a stumbling-block, a point of resistance and a starting point for an opposing strategy. Discourse transmits and produces power; it reinforces it, but also undermines and exposes it, renders it fragile and makes it possible to thwart it" (Foucault 1980, 100–101).

inferior to us. Foucault also parted ways with structuralists, who are more concerned with delineating the stable structures and continuities of history than with showing its irrationalities and discontinuities.

Foucault's criticism of the totalizing master narrative of Western modernity and his deconstruction of its ensuing forms of representation and superimposition constitutes the bulk of his intellectual contribution. Hence, one can summarize his accomplishments in three tiers: bodies of knowledge are always tied to power and systems of social control; Western civilization does not constitute a well-defined and homogeneous entity; and by committing violence (hindering, misconstructing, precluding) toward an other, "we" are, in fact, damaging our own sense of self-identity.

Foucault's ground-breaking work on other-ness inspired numerous scholars to apply his genealogical methodology to different subject matters, disciplines, geographical entities, and historical settings. Two areas that proved receptive to this line of inquiry were feminism and racism. The feminist literature on other-ness has demonstrated how the gender-coded, bifurcated modern society functions. In so doing it has informed us of the mechanisms through which "the man" is perceived as the absolute self and "the woman" as the inferior other: of how the "wife" develops to be the persistent, naturalized, and the internal other of the "husband," while "she" is all along the "other of phallocentric discourse."[6] Similar works on the history of racism have also demonstrated how ethnic Indians become the "strangers" of European immigrants to America, black slaves the "inferiors" of the white masters, and Jews the "subversive enemies" of fascism and Nazism. Perhaps the most challenging types of deconstructive work have emerged, however, in such fields as history and anthropology, which, among other things, share a common subject matter (other-ness); are both concerned with the text and context of actions rooted in time and place; are concerned with the acts of translation, understanding, and explanation; and report results in a literary form (Cohn 1980, 198–99).

The development of secularism, along with the appearance of a "colonial" discourse in the late seventeenth and eighteenth centuries, reinforced the dichotomous mind-set of the West. The appearance of terms such as *civilization* in the middle of the eighteenth century and the *West* in the mid-nineteenth century necessitated the positing of "Barbarians" and "Orientals" as the antithetical "Others." As such, the dichotomies of civilization/barbarism, and West/Orient easily replaced the Christen-

6. For some feminist works on the problematic of "other-ness" see Felstiner 1980; Lloyd 1984.

dom/Muslim dyad prevalent in the Middle Ages. The development in the nineteenth century of anthropology as an intellectual endeavor came against such a background. From the beginning anthropology was a discipline defined by James Clifford as a "salvage paradigm," a geopolitical, historical paradigm that has organized Western practices of "art- and culture-collecting" (Clifford 1987, 121). The "salvage" paradigm represents the white man's burden of attempting to subjugate the "savage," "heathen," "beast," or "barbarian" while desiring at the same time to rescue their "fossils," "authenticity," and "tribal culture." This relationship obviously is not one of parity because non-Westerners are always regarded as dispensable marginals incapable of realizing the importance of preserving the well-being of their own objects. Hence, it is the white man's burden to "salvage," "rescue," "save," and "preserve" their artifacts. As Clifford points out, it is not a coincidence that connoisseurships, art collection, the rise of public museums, the scramble for ethnographic artifacts, and the emergence and popularity of world fairs all occurred simultaneously with the development of anthropology in the nineteenth century. Thus, the West came to define the standards of authenticity while anthropology worked to justify its right of entitlement. The latter decided to ignore the fact that "others" were in a significant way an artificial creation of the West's own discursive practices (Friedman 1987, 165).

In *The Conquest of America* writer and critic Tzvetan Todorov demonstrates how the history of cultural confrontations can be demystified and rewritten if one were to take cognizance of the presence of the other. One can read Todorov to be reexamining the "discovery" paradigm of European historiography in light of the Spanish conquest of Central America in the sixteenth century. Like the "salvage" paradigm of anthropology, the "discovery" paradigm of intercultural confrontation reifies the people and cultures that it studies but fails to treat them as subjects of history. Todorov suggests that the problematic of alterity can be placed upon at least three levels: the axiological level, involving a value judgment (the other is good or bad); the praxeological level, involving a rapprochement or distancing in relation to the other (embracing the other's values or identifying the other with yourself); and the epistemic level, involving knowledge or ignorance of the other's identity (Todorov 1984, 185). Although interested in all three, Todorov pays particular attention to the second axis of assimilation and identification. He maintains that since the time of the conquest, Western civilization has employed this axis in order to assimilate the other into its own domain and, indeed, has in great part succeeded. Todorov refers to the science of ethnology, this "child of colonialism," as one of the processes through which the assimilation of the other became possible. As he shows in the case of the Spanish conquistadors, the epiphany of the other can also be imaginatively constituted whereby instead of uncovering an objective other we discover our very own subjective cognition. Hence, Columbus's "discovery" of the Americas in 1492 was not so much the beginning of the modern era but a rediscovery of the European self vis-à-vis a newly found other in the wonderlands of Mexico and the Caribbean.

On Orientalism

One of the first and most promising attempts to systematically apply Foucault's genealogical method to a new subject matter came with the publication of Edward W. Said's *Orientalism* (1978). Like Foucault, Said was interested in the machinery of representation, of how an other comes to be constituted. Said's subject matter was the Orient, an exotic spatial and cultural configuration, which had succeeded for centuries in captivating the attention and fomenting fears and passions among Europeans. Said's "Orientals" resemble Foucault's insane, perverts, and criminals in a number of ways. All are subjects of prevalent institutional discourses and narratives who are identified, analyzed, and controlled but never allowed to speak. All share a condition of other-ness arising from their perceived difference with respect to what is accepted as "normal," "true," and "right."

Through an examination of scholarly writings, diplomatic archives, travel memoirs, and literary volumes Said demonstrates how the Orient was first appropriated "textually" by Europeans in the post-Enlightenment period. According to Said, all societies acquire their identities through a juxtaposition to another: an alien, a foreigner, or an enemy. A schematic glance at the spectrum of political cultures around the world substantiates Said's claim that the dichotomizing technique of differentiation between "us" and "them" is an important component of any organized system of political thought. Politics both as a discipline and a vocation classifies people on the basis of supporter or opponent, companion or rival, and, most importantly, friend or foe.

Said contends that this appropriation was made possible through a discourse of difference that he designated as *orientalism*. He defines orientalism as "an enormously systematic discipline by which European culture was able to manage—and even produce—the Orient politically, sociologically, militarily, ideologically, scientifically, and imaginatively during the post-Enlightenment period" (Said 1978, 3). According to Said, orientalism as a body of knowledge and system of representation succeeded in portraying the Orient as modern Europe's silent "civilizational other." The line that was drawn somewhere between present-day Greece and Turkey to separate Orient and Occident was not so much a fact of nature but an invention of European "imaginative geography" (Said 1985, 2). He writes:

> We must take seriously [Giambattista] Vico's great observation that men make their own history, that what they can know is what they have made, and extend it to geography: as both geographical and cultural entities— to say nothing of historical entities—such locales, regions, geographical sectors as "Orient" and "Occident" are man-made. Therefore as much as the West itself, the Orient is an idea that has a history and a tradition of thought, imagery, and vocabulary that have given it reality and presence in and for the West. (Said 1978, 4–5)

Because the self is invariably linked with the other, it was in opposition to this designated entity that Europe was able to create and maintain its own identity. Among the countries of the Orient China represented the ultimate exotic other because of its geographical remoteness and historical isolation. India, long the crown jewel of British colonial acquisitions in the subcontinent, was the next candidate for other-ness, becoming more important with the rise of the Romanticist Movement in the nineteenth century. The only remaining candidate tailored to serve Europe's need of a quintessential other was the Muslim world. The Islamic East was regarded as close to, yet different from, the totality of Western civilization. As a Semitic religion, Islam shared many of Christianity's theological axioms. Yet its geographical proximity and confrontational attitude, which had led to the conquest of European lands in the Middle Ages, along with its demonstrated political unity under the Ottoman Empire, established it as Europe's great cultural and political adversary. Until the eighteenth century Islam was viewed as a perversion of Christianity and the Muslim world as the province of the Antichrist. With the coming of the rationalist and humanist philosophy of the Enlightenment, the Islamic world came to be perceived as the embodiment of all that was recently left behind in Europe: an all-encompassing religion, political despotism, cultural stagnation, scientific ignorance, superstition, and so on.

Hence, the Islamic Orient became Europe's collective nightmare, a world prone to exotic and erotic fantasies. For Western thinkers, the "Orientals," who include the Muslims, Arabs, Turks, and Persians, were only occupying a "discursive space." They served as Rousseau's ideal type of "noble savage" and as Montesquieu's fictitious travelers to Paris in *Lettres persanes*. The former viewed them nostalgically as the representatives of a bygone age in harmony with nature, whereas the latter used them as a symbolic mouthpiece for his criticism of European life at the time. In both cases they served as the metaphorical reflections of the occidental self upon itself.

Thus, as Said has rightfully argued, "the relation between Orientalists and Orient was essentially hermeneutical: standing before a distant, barely-intelligible civilization or cultural monument, the Orientalist scholar reduced the obscurity by translating, sympathetically portraying, inwardly grasping the hard to reach object" (Said 1978, 222). The Orient and Orientals could only serve in the capacity of "communities of interpretation," always represented yet never representing. The Orientalist was always present while the Orient was routinely absent. The Orient and the Orientals served as real and imaginary "texts" and "subjects" for European authors. The world of Western writing and oriental silence made it possible to represent and label a variety of things "oriental." Such terms as oriental *corruption, cruelty, despotism, essence, mentality, mysticism, sensuality, spirit,* and *splendor* soon entered the everyday discourse of European observers. The Orient thus came to epitomize not just a surrogate idea but an ontological other that was discovered, confined, salvaged, and "civilized."

This paradigm of difference was maintained through the discourse of orientalism, which was rooted in the rationalism, secularism, and universalism of the eighteenth century and the romanticism, positivism, and colonialism of the nineteenth century. Deeply grounded in the political culture of their time, orientalist scholars came to rely on such diverse disciplines as biology, anthropology, philology, and lexicography to justify the paradigmatic dominance of the Occident. Academic orientalism soon became a school of interpretation and a source of knowledge about the Orient. The accumulated lineage of this cultural tradition facilitated the West's self-appointed mission to transform the world into its own image. Responding to Foucault's knowledge/power maxim, Said discloses the conscious and the unconscious collaboration between Orientalists and the colonialist powers whereby the former apprehended the Orient intellectually while the latter appropriated it physically. Thus, since the eighteenth century, positive knowledge expedited the process of power and capital accumulation.

What made this cooperation possible, according to Said, was the common ethnocentric and imperialistic beliefs of the academic Orientalists and the colonialist politicians. The religiously inspired racial prejudices of the Middle Ages were the historical antecedent for the biological and geographical racisms of the post-Renaissance era. The passage from the feudal system to a capitalist mode of production, with the subsequent requirements of capital accumulation, directed Western powers to dispatch their troops to all corners of the underdeveloped world. The most influential factor of all, however, was the Eurocentric culture of modernity.[7] Orientalism was, first and foremost, the manifestation of modernity and its political stepchild, colonialism. Modernity claimed a universal mandate and a scientific mantle. The universalist thrust of the European idea of progress, which viewed humanity in a permanent drive forward, could not look favorably upon the nonsynchronous experience of the Orient. The land of antiquity and metaphysics could only be abandoned if the cherished goal of progress were to be attained.[8] Despite their "oriental" pedigree, Europeans appropriated Hellenism and Christianity as the constitutive elements of their own particular heritage.

It was from the position of this borrowed identity that they paternalistically took it upon themselves to represent and judge the Orient as the depository of the archaic past and eternal stagnation (Amin 1989, 100–101). Hence the "oriental" world was demarcated not as a neutral other but as an entity over which power had to be exercised.

Both Foucault and Said were learned critics of representation who were concerned with deconstruction of the prevalent ways of thinking. Their aim was to resurrect the forgotten presence of the subaltern and marginal others. Although sharing Foucault's general line of reasoning, Said differed from him in a number of ways. First, whereas Foucault attempted to particularize European culture within its own self-defined boundaries, Said ventured into the more contested terrain of questioning Western claims to truth. Second, Foucault and Said differed in how they viewed the relationship between individual texts and authors and collective formations and discourses. In Foucault's encyclopedic macroanalysis of the genealogy of various institutions, individual texts and writers do not count much, whereas in Said's microanalysis they are of primary interest. On this difference Said writes: "Yet unlike Michel Foucault, to whose work I am greatly indebted, I do believe in the

7. In his consequential book Marshall Berman has interpreted the four major features of modernity: (1) that modernity is a uniquely European phenomenon; (2) that it transformed the premoderns' traditional polarity of an illusory compared to a real world; (3) that by unveiling religious and political illusions the bourgeois revolutions "uncovered and exposed new options and hopes"; (4) that the bourgeoisie not only brought forward a free economic market but also provided for a freedom "to shop around and seek the best deals in ideas, associations, laws and social policies, as well as in things" (Berman 1988, 13–36, 105–14).

8. Said notes that "Oriental history—for Hegel, for Marx, later for Burkhardt, Nietzsche, Spengler and other major philosophers of history—was useful in portraying a region of great age, and what had to be left behind" (Said 1985, 5).

determining imprint of individual writers upon the otherwise anonymous collective body of texts constituting a discursive formation like
Orientalism" (Said 1978, 23). The third discrepancy between the two
thinkers manifests itself in their attitudes toward power. Foucault is
more concerned with the technologies and manners of realization of
power, whereas Said is preoccupied with resistance to it. Whereas
Foucault remained a critic of humanism throughout, Said is a passionate
defender of it. Spatially speaking, one can say that whereas Foucault's
normative considerations usually stay in the background, Said's valuative
beliefs are always at the very forefront of his writings. Whether deplor-
ing Orientalists or defending the plight of his Palestinian compatriots,
Said's normative predilections can be easily detected. In short, Said is
convinced that to deconstruct (à la Foucault) is to challenge but not to
empower an alternative. In the absence of a challenger a power structure can be thoroughly discredited and yet remain in power.

On Orientalism in Reverse

Toward the end of *Orientalism* Said raises the following questions:
"How does one represent other cultures? What is another culture? Is
the notion of a distinct culture (or race, or religion, or civilization) a
useful one, or does it always get involved either in self-congratulation
(when one discusses one's own) or hostility and aggression (when one
discusses the other)?" (Said 1978, 325). These questions are, obviously,
of paramount theoretical and political significance for the scholars of
international and intercultural relations. Furthermore, epistemologists
are also concerned with this issue because it consequently poses other
questions: Can representation and imagery, as acts of other-ing, ever be
undistorted?; Can such acquired knowledge thus be viewed as objective?
Said's poststructuralism compels him to answer these questions with an
unequivocal no.

> The real issue is whether indeed there can be a true representation of
> anything, or whether any and all representations, because they are repre-
> sentations, are embedded first in the language and then in the culture,
> institutions, and political ambiance of the representor. If the latter alter-
> native is the correct one (as I believe it is), then we must be prepared to
> accept the fact that a representation is eo ipso implicated, intertwined,
> embedded, interwoven with a great many other things besides the
> "truth," which is itself a representation. (Said 1978, 272)

Considering the above, several questions immediately come to mind.
Is Said's own representation of orientalism true and accurate? and Can

the Orientals' representation of their own others, the Occidentals, be less flawless than occidental writings on the Orient? Said was not initially concerned with the latter question. For him there was no such equivalent to orientalism as occidentalism because the Orientals neither talked about themselves nor the West, nor did they have the institutions to do so if they had so desired. Yet Said must have become alarmed at the prospect of a "reverse discourse"[9] because he concluded his book with the following plea: "I hope to have shown my reader that the answer to Orientalism is not Occidentalism. No former 'Oriental' will be comforted by the thought that having been an Oriental himself he is likely—too likely—to study new 'Orientals'—or 'Occidentals'—of his own making" (Said 1978, 328).

In a critique of Said's book the contemporaneous Syrian philosopher Sadik Jalal al-Azm (1934–   ) implicated Said on these same grounds.[10] Al-Azm disagrees with Said's assertion about the malevolent intentionality of studying different societies. For him the desire to study cultures and societies that differ from one's own is only a general human tendency shared by nearly all societies. He further maintained that it is a universal tendency to fabricate self/other dichotomies because the fundamental premise of other-ness is grounded in an imaginative exteriorization. In other words, the mental image one has of any other culture cannot but be culturally and politically motivated. Al-Azm went on to argue that despite Said's "important warning to the subjects and victims of Orientalism against the dangers and temptations of applying the readily available structures, styles and ontological biases of Orientalism upon themselves and upon others," this has now become a fairly wide-scale practice (al-Azm 1981, 19). He called this phenomenon "Orientalism in reverse."

Orientalism in reverse is a discourse used by "oriental" intellectuals

9. Foucault (1980, 101) acknowledged the possibility of the "reverse discourse" as a recalcitrant practice. Speaking of homosexuality as one such discourse he wrote, "It began to speak in its own behalf, to demand that its legitimacy or 'naturality' be acknowledged, often in the same vocabulary, using the same categories by which it was medically disqualified."

10. Al-Azm was educated in the Arab world and in the United States. He graduated from Yale University in 1961, having completed a dissertation on the moral philosophy of Henri Bergson. After teaching in Lebanon and Jordan, he returned to Syria where he has been a professor of modern European philosophy at the University of Damascus since 1977. Al-Azm is a former editor of *Arab Studies Review* and author of such books as *Al-naqd al-dhati ba'd al-hazimah* (Self-criticism after the defeat); *Naqd al-fikr al-dini* (Criticism of religious thought); *Dirasat yasariyah hawl-al-qadiyah al-Filastiniyah* (Leftist studies on the Palestinian problem); and *The Origins of Kant's Arguments in the Antinomies* (1972).

and political elites to lay claim to, recapture, and finally impropriate their "true" and "authentic" identity. This self-appropriation is almost invariably presented as a counterknowledge to Europe's oriental narrative.[11] Far from rendering a post-mortem on orientalism, however, it has come to share much of its ontological and epistemological axioms as in all inversions. First and foremost, orientalism in reverse uncritically embraces orientalism's assumption of a fundamental ontological difference separating the natures, peoples, and cultures of the Orient and the Occident. Orient and Occident are depicted as essentialistic geographical, historical, and cultural entities asymmetrical to one another. Each is supposed to possess its own distinct and easily identifiable history, imagery, tradition of thought, mode of discourse, ethics, and culture. Implicit in this abstractness that construes Orient and Occident as the irrevocable others of one another is an assumption about the homogeneous compositions of the so-called East and West. The proponents of each view talk and think about each other's inhabitants and territories as if they are all concrete, conscious, and undifferentiated totalities and terrains. The Occident plays the same role of alter ego (for the proponents of orientalism in reverse) that the Orient has traditionally performed for the Orientalists. Stanley Diamond has argued that Western culture could only conceive of itself through reference to the invented primitive (Diamond 1974). It is relative to the native, the barbarian, the underdeveloped, and the non-European that Western identity, civilization, and heroism is defined. The same logic seems to persist in the case of orientalism in reverse because the oriental "we" is always constructed relative to the (not "we"), *Homo Occidentalis*.[12] Considering the historical and theoretical impregnation of this discourse by colonialism and the normative angst of this belated discourse, the infatuation with the dominating other (the West) makes absolute sense. The other always functions for both sides as a hypothetical viewer, or what Jacques Derrida (1982) has referred to as a "culture of reference."

Considering that the West serves as the navel of the world (as a result

11. I prefer the term *orientalism in reverse* or *reverse orientalism* to *"occidentalism"* for two reasons: (1) instead of abandoning the ontological, methodological, and epistemological doctrines of orientalism proper, the term is an inverted use of these same apparatuses; and (2) its point of departure is primarily introverted (concerned with understanding its "own" Orient) and only secondarily extroverted (concerned with understanding "the other's" Occident.)

12. One sees a conscious attempt to throw off this mental construct, albeit with mixed results, in the works of the Egyptian philosopher Hasan Hanafi (1991) and the Indian thinker Ashis Nandy (1983).

of its omnipresence), orientalism in reverse is forced to borrow its icon-oclasm from its very subject. Thus, even in their newly acquired capac-ity as speakers, authors, and actors the "Orientals" continue to be overdetermined by the occidental listener, text, and audience. Belea-guered Orientals come to wage their "war of position" within the terri-tory of the contestant. Threatened by the superior arsenal of the adversary in this cultural war, many marginalized intellectuals of the Orient appropriate nationalism, the ideological paradigm of the enemy. Reminiscent of Marx's assertion that the proletariat would commandeer the means of production to combat the bourgeoisie's hold over power, the "Third World" intelligentsia comes to appropriate another nine-teenth-century Western doctrine (nationalism) to challenge the latter's imperialism.

Despite its surreptitious retainment of much of the theoretical infra-structure of orientalism, orientalism in reverse does not constitute an exact antithesis of orientalism. Like orientalism, orientalism in reverse is premised upon exteriority, yet it is more concerned with representing (or "big brothering") its own domestic constituency than with under-standing and dominating the exotic other. As a postcolonial discursive formation, the dialogue of orientalism in reverse is concerned primarily with its own constituents and only secondarily with its occidental adver-saries. Orientalism in reverse also differs from orientalism in terms of its knowledge/power configuration. Like orientalism, orientalism in re-verse is a discourse of power. Yet, instead of articulating the views of the victors, it claims, often successfully, to (re)present the aspirations as well as the frustrations of the disenfranchised. Orientalism in reverse does not match orientalism's grounding in the two pillars of academic and institutional support, nor does it enjoy the latter's universalism, prestige, or voluminous investigations. It is more dispersed, elusive, dis-articulated, and fragmented than orientalism. Orientalism in reverse does not follow orientalism's heavy reliance on such sciences as biology and anthropology. Instead, it bases its claims to truth on such norma-tive fields as theology, mythology, mysticism, ethics, and poetry.[13] In short, orientalism in reverse neither claims the universalist and scientific mantle of orientalism proper nor is powerful enough to superimpose a totalizing identity or ideology upon its non-oriental others if it so desires.

13. Al-Azm points out that one area in which the proponents of the two discourses share a common interest is in the analysis of language, texts, philology, and related subjects.

One can argue that in the postcolonial milieu, the colonial masses responded to their previous condition of *subalternity* by embarking on the practice of "other-ing the self."[14] Orientalism in reverse is a prime example of this other-ing of the self. To (re)present the Orient it became necessary to indulge in its further orientalization. The prerequisite for delineating the Orient was to reinforce particularity, worship difference, and emphasize its other-ness from the paragon. The essentializing categories of Orient and Occident allowed for "imaginative geography" to operate in reverse. The "West" was thus viewed symbolically, semantically, or substantively as "the other" or more narrowly as "the enemy." In short, orientalism in reverse represents a discourse bent on manufacturing difference, a self-validating and closed discourse that emphasizes other-ness to account for the uniqueness of the East. The essentialization of the West helps to nurture nativist and nationalist sentiments.

On Nativism

The popularity of orientalism in reverse among Third World politicians and intellectuals is part and parcel of the ubiquitous presence and seductive lure of nativism. In its broadest sense nativism can be defined as the doctrine that calls for the resurgence, reinstatement or continuance of native or indigenous cultural customs, beliefs, and values. Nativism is grounded on such deeply held beliefs as resisting acculturation, privileging one's own "authentic" ethnic identity, and longing for a return to "an unsullied indigenous cultural tradition" (Williams and Chrisman 1994, 14). Nativism stands in the same relation to orientalism in reverse as Eurocentrism does to orientalism proper. Both nativism and Eurocentrism provide an ontological and epistemological umbrella under which it becomes possible to develop a theory of history and a political platform. Whereas Eurocentrism advocated such ideas as the uniqueness and superiority of the West and its unequivocal manifest destiny, nativism champions the cause of abandoning, subverting, and reversing these same metanarratives and master codes. Nativism was born of the lamentable circumstance of colonialism and the agonizing milieu of the post–World War II period of decolonization. It represents a cultural reflex on the part of many Third World intellectuals from Southeast Asia to the Caribbean eager to assert their newly found identities. The proponents of nativism were adamant about ending their

14. Fredric Jameson, a prominent American Marxist literary critic, has defined *subalternity* as "the feelings of mental inferiority and habits of subservience and obedience which necessarily and structurally develop in situations of domination" (Jameson 1986, 76).

condition of mental servitude and their perceived inferiority complex vis-à-vis the West.

Relinquishing these psychological yokes of colonialism was a prerequisite for obtaining an *authentic identity*. Psychologists maintain that at times of crisis the quest for *identity*—whether at the individual or collective level—becomes a self-conscious and necessary problematic. This "crisis" emerged in the aftermath of World War II when the old colonial empires were replaced by a new hegemonic geometry of power. The previously bare colonial subjugation of much of the world at the hands of European powers gave way to a more subtle form of imperialism. The former "colonies" became new "nation-states," or what Benedict Anderson has more aptly phrased new "imagined communities" (Anderson 1991). With the onset of political decolonization in much of Asia and Africa in the 1950s and 1960s, nationalism became the primary ideological formation and the mobilizing political force of this era. Many Third World nationalist leaders and thinkers such as Yasir Arafat, Ahmed Ben Bella, Steven Biko, Houari Boumedienne, Amilcar Cabral, Fidel Castro, Aimé Césaire, Frantz Fanon, Paolo Freire, Ernesto Guevara, C. L. R. James, Gabriel Garcia Marquez, Albert Memmi, Mohammad Mosaddeq, Gamal Abdel Nasser, Jawaharlal Nehru, Pablo Neruda, Kwame Nkrumah, Walter Rodney, Léopold Sédar Senghor, Sukarno, and Mao Zedong came to dominate the terms of discourse, narrative, imagery, and rhetoric as well as the aspirations of millions of their respective peoples.

The calls of nationalist leaders and thinkers for political independence, cultural authenticity, and knowledge indigenization were mostly rooted in a preoccupation—at once real and imaginary—with the other. The reality of nationalist rhetoric is based on the apprehensible colonial vicissitudes of the not-so-distant past. At the same time, this nationalism's imaginariness emanated from the practice of readily applying the mental frameworks and categorical dualisms of the former masters upon themselves. In addition to nationalist leaders and liberation movements, the bilingual intelligentsia, the migrants, the travelers, the Western-educated students, and even the masses began to talk and write about themselves and the Western world from the vantage point of difference.[15]

Of all the post–World War II thinkers who wrote on behalf of Third

15. One should also bear in mind that it was during this period that numerous organizations devoted to advancing the cause of Third World people and states emerged. Among these were the Non-Aligned Movement, the Arab League, Organization of Petroleum Exporting Countries (OPEC), Organization of Islamic States, and Organization of African States.

World intellectuals, Frantz Fanon (1925–1961), the psychiatrist and revolutionary activist from the island of Martinique, was, perhaps, the most original. In many ways he can be credited with having inaugurated the counterdiscourse designated here as *nativism*. Fanon's *Wretched of the Earth* (1979) changed the terms of discourse; for the first time the West, and not the native, was defined as other. As Suha Sabbagh (1982, 3) has put it, this constituted "a resolution to the colonial problem on the level of the text." Fanon addressed himself to the issue of how Third World natives could resist becoming cognitively colonized by the West. Through a poetic style Fanon not only incriminated the colonizers but also criticized the colonized for having internalized the others' depiction of them as "inferiors." For Fanon this greatest moment of colonization led to an eradication of indigenous intellectual traditions. What ensued was a psychological condition in which the colonized could only imitate, yet never identify with or away from, the dominating "they."

According to Fanon, liberation could not be attained until this subservient consciousness was first relinquished. Ending this condition of liminality requires iconoclasm and a counternarrative (in addition to political resistance) to redefine the boundaries of the colonized self and the colonialist other. Fanon believed political liberation could not be secured through Western benevolence because independence must be obtained, not granted.[16] Correspondingly, the wretched of the earth could not alter their condition of intellectual dependency if they were not to abandon entirely Western definitions, descriptions, and vocabularies. The first concern led Fanon to participate in the Algerian revolution; the second led to the writing of *Black Skin, White Masks* (1967) in which the narcissism, emulative behavior, and servile social consciousness of the natives came under relentless critique. In both cases Fanon tried to resurrect the historical attendance of the native *I* by reverberating its marginalized voice, thus elevating it from its state of introvert quietism to an extrovert outspokenness.

Fanon believed that the way to bring natives out of their sense of inferiority to the West was through the praxis of "writing back" at it. The means toward regaining "true identity" was first to reclaim it textually by acquiring the right of narrative voice. If the natives were to abandon their internalized inferiority complex, they also had to challenge the strategy of mimicry and the counterfeit modernism of the native colons (or as Fanon put it "walking white lies"). Thus, *nativism*

16. In *The Wretched of the Earth,* Fanon argued that for the colonized people violence (which can also take a symbolic form) can be psychologically liberating because it is a "cleansing force" that frees natives from their inferiority complex and from a sense of despair.

should be considered a response to Eurocentrism and colonialism both at the level of text and at the level of political consciousness. In other words, nativism is not just the manifesto of Third World intellectuals' resistance but also the very discourse for which their struggle is waged.

From its very inception nativism presented itself as more than a mere political response to colonialism. As the embodiment of postcolonial cultural nationalism(s), nativism also strived toward an epistemological counterforce to Eurocentrism. Critiques of imperialism and colonialism paved the way for indictments of Western social science theories. These critiques challenged Western social sciences' nominally universal notions, assumptions, and language. It was argued, rightfully and forcefully, that social scientific research in the non-Western world had to be "indigenized" by generating and employing concepts and theories that take into account the sociohistorical contexts, cultural practices, and worldviews, as well as the intellectual traditions and scholarship of these societies.[17] In short, the proponents of nativism questioned the historicity, the prefabricated nature as well as the self-universalizing and self-congratulatory truth claims of the Western social sciences in the name of authenticity and indigenization. They cautioned that one needs to adopt a vigilant attitude toward Western, camouflaged as macrocosmic, ideas, concepts, and theories in the social sciences.

These attempts to delimit and decenter Western modes of knowledge and thought were (and still are) extremely important. Cosmopolitan and acculturated Third World intellectuals most often respond to nativism with myriad deprecatory comments or disparaging jeers. Neither strategy, however, has proved particularly effective in discrediting nativism. The appeal of nativism has to do with two facts. First, the globalization of capitalism and modernity in this aging century has problematized, as well as adversely affected, the "life-worlds" of various social stratas who feel that their traditional familial, tribal, ethnic, and national identities and attachments are being eroded. Second, the entry and incorporation of new popular classes (the nouveau arrivé migrants, guests/seasonal workers, first-generation city dwellers, etc.) into the political scene has ensured nativism of a steady stream of adherents, benefactors, recruits, and instigators. As such, and contrary to popular stereotypes, nativism is not tantamount to ignorance of modernity. Instead, it should be viewed as a modern phenomenon in as much as the "be yourself" aphorism of authenticity is itself a handiwork of the age of modernity. To consider modernity as an in toto holistic enterprise, and not an abstract construct is to realize that the nativist claim for cultural authenticity has

17. For one good example see Alatas 1993.

already been historically molded and mythicized by a hazardous appropriation of modernity.

Ascertaining the positive attributes of nativism, however, should not lead one toward an uncritical embracement of it because nativism has many epistemological and ethical flaws.[18] First, the essentializing and foundationalist ontology of nativism, which sees everything in the context of the binary opposition between the "authentic" and the "alien," often leads to a sweeping rejection of all "non-indigenous and non-traditional vocabularies as alien and dangerous" (Moghadam 1989, 87). The nativist "cult of authenticity" often leads its partisans to develop a compulsive tendency to fetishize and celebrate difference. Considering nativism as an infantile stage of cultural nationalism or, as he puts it, "a besetting bobble of most so-called postcolonial, subaltern works," Edward Said criticizes the nativist proclivity toward historical amnesia by writing: "Nativism . . . has often led to compelling but demagogic assertions about a native past, narrative or actuality that stands free from worldly time itself. One sees this in such enterprises as Senghor's *négritude,* or in the Rastafarian movement, or in the Garveyite back to Africa project for American blacks, or in the rediscoveries of various unsullied, precolonial Muslim essences" (Said 1993, 228). Said continues to criticize the nativist flight from history with the following:

> To accept nativism is to accept the consequences of imperialism, the racial, religious, and political divisions imposed by imperialism itself. To leave the historical world for the metaphysics of essences like *négritude,* Irishness, Islam, or Catholicism is to abandon history for essentializations that have the power to turn human beings against each other; often this abandonment of the secular world has led to a sort of millenarianism if the movement has had a mass base, or it has degenerated into small-scale private craziness, or into an unthinking acceptance of stereotypes, myths, animosities, and traditions encouraged by imperialism. Such programs are hardly what great resistance movements had imagined as their goals. (Said 1993, 228–29)

Nativism can also be criticized for its high-pitched polemic that often traps Third World intellectuals in the marshlands of an insular, obscurest, nostalgic, jingoistic, and particularistic mind-set. Xenophobic nationalism, a conspiratorial mind-set, a garrison-state mentality, and unqualified anti-Westernism are some of the end products of the nativist discourse. Needless to say, these tendencies along with nativism's

18. As Maxime Rodinson has nicely put it, one should not assume that "all foes of the powerful were pure heroes, all their ideas the unalloyed truth, and all their deeds paragons of virtuous action" (Rodinson 1980, xiii).

uncritical exaltation of the past and the indigenous can have dire consequences for progressive projects.

The combination of textual, metaphysical, and deep-rooted sociopolitical and economic rhetoric of blame against the West, local elites, and the status quo have provided nativism with powerful ideological instrumentalities capable of mass mobilization. In the following chapters I continue to remind the reader that nativism should be understood in the dual context of the internal politics of the societies in which it emerges and from the process of (cross-)cultural encounter with the West. I show how, in the context of the Iranian intellectual scene, nativism became a convenient foil for middle-class intellectuals who were witnessing the social disruption and normative torsion of their society and how this discourse was put to use by various dissident and establishment intellectuals in a strategic tug-of-war over hegemony. The rationale for concentrating on intellectuals has to do with the fact that the quest for an authentic identity is mostly undertaken by intellectuals who, by definition, are engaged in a quest for meaning and wholeness.[19] Furthermore, I elucidate the extent to which Iranian nativist thinkers have been conversant in Western philosophy and successful in criticizing it.

19. As Foucault (1977a, 124) has put it, "The function of an author is to characterize the existence, circulation, and operation of certain discourses within a society."

2

The Other-ing of a Rentier State

> The combination of Socratic alienation and Platonic hope
> gives rise to the idea of the intellectual as someone who is
> in touch with the nature of things, not by way of the opin-
> ions of his community, but in a more immediate way.
> —Richard Rorty, "Solidarity or Objectivity?"

On Intellectuals

PROVIDING A DEFINITION of an *intellectual* that is satisfactory to most
people is a formidable task. One wishes that it were possible deliberately to avoid such a quibble. The task is doubly hard when one tries to
come up with a working definition for this nebulous strata in the so-
called developing world. Following Socrates and Plato one can regard
intellectuals as the critical conscience of every society. The need to seek
the truth and distinguish between knowledge and opinion necessitates
the presence of a group who see things with the eyes of a stranger
(Rorty 1985, 4). These permanent strangers who float freely among
society often concern themselves with the issues of how identity, value,
and culture are created and transmitted from one individual or collectivity to another. Max Weber defined intellectuals as a group of people
"who by virtue of their peculiarity have special access to certain achieve-
ments considered to be 'culture values' and who therefore usurp the leadership of a 'culture community'" (Weber 1981, 176). Similarly, Karl
Mannheim considered intellectuals as a socially unattached, "classless" social stratum that claims a cultural mandate.[1] Edward Shils has defined intellectuals as those who concern themselves with ultimate values and live in a
"wilder universe." Alvin Gouldner considers intellectuals as a "speech com-

1. Intellectuals often justify this claim on the basis of their higher education, professional expertise, and greater degree of mental labor as they predominantly support
themselves through employment in such institutions as universities, research centers,
the civil service, newspapers, and commercial enterprises.

20

munity" that promulgates a culture of critical discourse. Finally, Edward Said defines an intellectual as "an individual endowed with a faculty for representing, embodying, articulating a message, a view, an attitude, philosophy or opinion to, as well as for, a public" (Said 1994, 11).

The first question we need to ask is whether intellectuals in the non-Western world have the same demarcated functions and the corollary social status of their Western counterparts. How do they compare to the traditional elite of their own societies? An observer of Middle Eastern social thought once asked, "In the contemporary Muslim-Arab societies, does the function of the intellectual recall that of the classic scholar, at once counselor of the great people, honor of the city or of the village, and regulator, through the culture, through judicial consultation or through the education, of social life?" (Charnay 1973, 40). Perhaps, the answer is a qualified no. In the contemporary Middle East the intellectual does not enjoy the power, status, or popularity of the traditional notable, the military officer, the clerical leader, or the nouveau riche bourgeois. They neither have the ingrained organic knowledge of the traditional notable nor the economic or military might of the respective capitalist or military officer. Yet it can scarcely be disputed that with the onset of modernity intellectuals (as a social stratum) have managed to encroach upon or delimit the social space of these more powerful contenders. For example, today in most Middle Eastern societies, the intellectuals have undermined the inexorable monopoly and sacerdotal makeup of the traditional elites. The clerical caste, who were the intelligentsia of these traditional societies, are no longer considered the sole proprietors of knowledge. These intellectuals have managed to secure for themselves such new roles as "interpreters of the world," "producers of the collective conscience," and "conduits of secular and progressive change." The ideological and political handiwork of these intellectuals can no longer go unnoticed. They have, among other things, articulated powerful ideologies (nationalism, Marxism, and Islamicism), organized political parties, won parliamentary seats or cabinet posts, and have augmented the intellectual stock of their respective societies. Moreover, if not as plenipotentiaries, they have come to serve as crucial intermediaries and interpreters between their own culture and that of the West. The surge in the number of secular educational institutions along with the qualitative and quantitative expansion of the middle class and media of mass communication in addition to governments' need for a class of Mandarins to supervise the machinery of the state have guaranteed a secure pool of recruits, sympathizers, and audiences for intellectuals. In short, economic development makes the numerical expansion of the intellectuals both possible and necessary and by extension accords them a greater degree of legitimacy.

Intellectuals can generally be grouped into two grand clusters: the socially engaged visionaries and the instrumental-bureaucratic functionaries and professionals. The first group uses critical discourse to echo and instigate demands, question and criticize social problems, and, finally, lead and represent the discontented masses. The ever-present need of ruling elites to get the services and, more importantly, the approbation of intellectuals enables a second group of these individuals to become careerists or ideologues. The primary task of these "experts in legitimation" (to use the words of Antonio Gramsci) is to oversee gradual and orderly change and to legitimize the authority of political elites.

This study is primarily concerned with the ideas and functions of the members of the first group in Iran. As a much politicized stratum with a strong sense of political mission, an overwhelming number of Iranian intellectuals have proven their commitment to the articulation of alternatives by questioning the past and the present and by espousing new visions for the future. Indeed, these intellectuals have been more inspired by the uncharted possibilities of the future than by the realities of present. As such, they have been among the most concerned, searching, reflective, and attentive observers of Iranian cultural transformation. They have also been some of its most vociferous participants. As active culture bearers, their narration of Iranians' past and present history and their interpretation of Western culture has, no doubt, affected the outlook of Iranian masses toward such issues as nationalism, modernity, secularism, democracy, and humanism. Examining the theoretical content of these intellectuals' thought is, therefore, one way of reflecting on the experience of recent generations of Iranians and the 1979 revolution.[2]

Embarking upon further discussion of Iranian social thought necessitates a number of conceptual clarifications. In the early 1940s the Iranian Academy coined the Persian term *rowshanfekr* to replace the Arabic-sounding term *monavvarolfekr,* which itself was the equivalent for the French terms *les eclaires, clairvoyance,* and *libre penseur.* This term soon found its proper place within the political parlance of modern Iranians. The plural term *rowshanfekran* was hence used as the Persian equivalent of the French *intellectuels,* the Russian *intelligentsia,* and the English *intellectuals.* This equivalency, however, can be somewhat misleading because *rowshanfekr* developed a more generic connotation than its French, Russian, and English counterparts. The latter terms, which were all coined in late-nineteenth-century Europe, had rather concrete connotations. In

2. As Said (1994, 10–11) has aptly put it: "There has been no major revolution in modern history without intellectuals; conversely there has been no major counterrevolutionary movement without intellectuals. Intellectuals have been the fathers and mothers of movements, and of course sons and daughters, even nephews and nieces."

France, the term *intellectuels* was used to refer to those thinkers who were advocates of deism, scientific rationalism, and ideology. The Dreyfus affair in 1894 helped to consolidate further the social identity and collective responsibility of the intellectuels as such thinkers and artists as Emile Durkheim, Anatole France, André Gide, Claude Monet, Marcel Proust, Romain Rolland, and Emile Zola came to defend him publicly. The Russian intelligentsia referred to that class of Tsarist elites who had undergone European education, and who had vowed to act as committed and revolutionary agents of cultural transformation. In Iran it was this Russian definition of the intellectuals as agents of progressive and radical change that was popularly circulated until the early 1960s. From that point on, however, with the extension of scientific and technical structures, the term underwent a qualitative transformation as a class of educated and professional Iranians came of age. The category of rowshanfekran was hence used in a broader sense to refer to both the intellectuals and the intelligentsia or, in general, all those who, in one way or another, were associated with modern education and modern professional skills. Thus, groups such as writers, poets, literary critics, artists, teachers, students, professors, researchers, translators, publishers, and journalists, along with lawyers, judges, engineers, doctors, and managers were all categorized as intellectuals. To borrow a phrase from Richard Hofstadter, the term *intellectual* was no longer the sole designation of one who "examines, ponders, wonders, theorizes and imagines."[3] In this study, however, it is indeed those with Hofstadter's qualifications with whom I am predominantly concerned. Neither the professional bureaucrat segment of the intelligentsia nor the veteran politicians figure prominently in my investigation. Instead, it is the literati, the academics, the philosophers, the establishment ideologues, and the political activists who interest me.[4]

3. Richard Hofstadter, *Anti-Intellectualism in American Life* (New York: Knopf, 1963) as quoted in Bill 1972, 57.

4. I am well aware that using such an all-inclusive definition of an "intellectual" exposes me to the charge of conceptual ambiguity and confusion. I believe, however, that the attempts made so far to draw delicate conceptual distinctions between the "intelligentsia" and the "intellectuals" still leaves much to be desired (for an admirable endeavor, nonetheless, see Sadri 1992). This problem is further complicated by the ideological and political predisposition of various individuals. For example, some of the antiestablishment ideologues examined in this book did not consider their pre- or postrevolutionary establishment counterparts worthy of such a designation as an "intellectual." Furthermore, a number of the antimodernist thinkers analyzed here took exception to characterization of themselves as "intellectual" since they believed the term was too gravely (and unjustly) imbued with liberal or leftist connotations. I do not deny the subjectiveness of my definitional choice.

I have had to use a more elastic definition of *intellectuals* to allow for the fact that the clerics have historically acted as the organic representatives of the traditional intelligentsia in Iran. As men of learning, they have appeared in such diverse capacities as teachers, writers, translators, judges, court consultants and ideological functionaries. In fact, a substantial fraction of the philosophical, literary, and intellectual stock of Iran throughout the ages has resulted from the cumulative efforts of men of religion. To deny the proper place of Sunni and Shi'ite theologians and scholars and Sufi mystics and poets in the annals of Iranian history leads to a distorted intellectual historiography. After all, an intellectual does not necessarily have to be an iconoclast, a heretic, a liberal, a revolutionary, or a secularist. This designation can also be bestowed upon a conservative conformist, a carrier of tradition, a partisan of the status quo, or even a guardian of faith.

Besides these conceptual clarifications, any study of Iranian intellectuals must also account for a number of historical and social peculiarities. A brief comparison with other Asian countries helps to demonstrate these distinctions. First and foremost, the fact that Iran was never officially colonized by European powers meant that its intelligentsia never became bilingual or linguistically bicultural as did their counterparts in India, Pakistan, Algeria, Morocco, and Tunisia. Second, in comparison with their Ottoman colleagues, Iranian intellectuals had a belated acquaintance with Western philosophy; they only began to consult original European sources toward the end of the nineteenth century. Much of what they knew about European schools of thought before then was transmitted to them through Ottoman and Indian translations. It should not come as a surprise that twentieth-century Iranian intellectuals could not outdo their Turkish counterparts in their commitment to secularism.[5] Third, Iranian secular reformers were not able to follow the example of their Russian counterparts who had developed a forte for Enlightenment thought as early as the eighteenth century and later managed to elevate such European ideologies as Marxism and anarchism to new pinnacles.[6] Finally, the Iranian intelligentsia did not exhibit the same degree of stamina as the Japanese intellectuals of the nineteenth century and the Indian intellectuals of the twentieth century, who translated thousands of books from European languages and proceeded to assess critically various facets of their societies' relationships with the West.[7]

5. For two treatments of secularism and secularization in Turkey see Mardin 1962; Berkes 1964.

6. For two treatments of Russian intellectual thought see Berlin 1978; Walicki 1979.

7. See Blacker 1964; Mehta 1985.

Within the setting described concern with the content of Iranian social thought is limited to three sets of questions. How did modern Iranian intellectuals view their state? How did they view the West? What constituted their response? Examining these questions provides insights into the political praxis and mental travails of successive generations of modern Iranian intellectuals.

The Legitimation Crisis of a Rentier State

In the aftermath of World War II Third World societies, in general, and Middle Eastern countries, in particular, confronted the essential dilemma of socioeconomic change. In a region characterized by the rapid transformation of its economic infrastructures and the instability of political institutions, the search for appropriate models of development became a constant preoccupation. The outbreak of World War II had put an end to the autocratic leadership (1925–1941) of Reza Shah in Iran. The reign of his son, Mohammad-Reza Pahlavi (1941–1979) was characterized by a return to autocracy after an initial period—two decades, in fact—of power consolidation. In the early 1960s the Shah inaugurated an agrarian reform program that in spite of its many shortcomings supplemented the state's policy of import-substitution industrialization by providing it with the requisite labor force. The massive infusion of new wealth generated from the export of oil enabled this undertaking. Furthermore, because the state no longer had to rely on agricultural surplus for capital accumulation, it embarked on a fast-paced modernization process. The result of this process was the transformation of the Iranian economy from one based on agriculture and commerce to a one-product economy based on oil.[8] Mohammad-Reza Shah's regime was viewed throughout by most Iranian and Western observers as modernizing, secular, and stable. Yet at its hour of destiny it collapsed swiftly at the hands of a political adversary. Its demise once again exposed the fragility of stability and of the claims to legitimacy emblematic of most Middle Eastern ruling classes.

The state's increasing reliance on petro-dollar revenues made Iran a textbook example of a *rentier state,* a state that derives a substantial portion of its revenue on a regular basis from payments by foreign concerns in the form of rent. The rentier state is in itself a subsystem of a *rentier economy,* an economy "substantially supported by expenditures [of] the state, while the state itself is supported from rent accruing from abroad" (Beblawi and Luciani 1987, 11). In Iran government revenue

8. Oil was first discovered in Iran in 1908, and its extraction began in 1911.

from oil increased from $555 million in 1963–64 to more than $20 billion in 1975–76 (Abrahamian 1982, 427). Oil revenue as a percentage of total government revenue jumped from 11 percent in 1948 to 41 percent in 1960 and up to 84.3 percent in 1974–75. By this time oil revenue comprised 45 percent of Iran's Gross Domestic Product (GDP) and 89.4 percent of its foreign export receipts (Amuzegar 1977, 63). Thanks to accumulating oil revenue, Iran's Gross National Product (GNP) grew at the annual rate of 8 percent in 1962–70, 14 percent in 1972–73, and 30 percent in 1973–74. Between 1972 and 1978 Iran's GNP grew from $17.3 billion to an estimated $54.6 billion, giving it one of the highest GNP growth rates in the Third World (Parsa 1989, 64). From 1954 to 1975, however, the total percentage of direct taxes levied by government on salaries, real estate, private, and state corporations only rose from 5 percent to 10 percent (Najmabadi 1987, 215).

Sudden economic gains in a traditional society such as Iran had both advantages and drawbacks. First, these rapid economic gains enabled the quick launching of public works projects, but without the taxation, drastic deficits, or inflation that usually plague developing countries. Because oil revenue increased at a faster rate than the GNP, the public sector expanded rapidly. The fortuitous oil transformed the embryonic Iranian state of the early 1900s into a form of *etatisme*. The government became the dominant actor in the economy. As Theda Skocpol has put it:

> The state's main relationships to Iranian society were mediated through its expenditures—on the military, on development projects, on modern construction, on consumption subsidies, and the like. Suspended above its own people, the Iranian state bought them off, rearranged their lives, and repressed any dissidents among them. The autonomy of the state from a taxation base, and its desire to disentangle itself from its civilian constituency gradually eroded any linkage between the state and civil society. The Shah who viewed himself as the "Great Benefactor" did not rule through, or in alliance with, any independent social class. (Skocpol 1982, 269)

Instead, by intervening in all significant decision-making policies and demanding absolute loyalty the shah stripped the state of any corporatist potential. Hence, oil revenues helped to establish a patron-client relationship and a *neopatriarchal* state.[9] The elitist, imperial nature of the state precluded the state from becoming an effective intermediary be-

9. Hisham Sharabi has defined *neopatriarchal* as "an entropic social formation characterized by its transitory nature and by the specific kinds of underdevelopment and non-modernity visible in its economy and class structure as well as its political, social, and cultural organization" (Sharabi 1988, 4).

tween the court and the citizenry. Thus, by default, the state contributed to the further alienation of the latter from the former. In this neo-patriarchal rentier state, or what Homa Katouzian (1981, 213–255) has called a "petrolic despotism," monological speech dominated all levels of sociopolitical discourse. The subjection of the Iranian economy since the mid-1950s to the expenditure shocks of rapidly increasing oil reve-nue resulted in severe economic discrepancies, social dislocation, and political tensions. First, economic development tended to be confined to certain enclaves within the rent parameters. This condition led to major geographical disparities and produced a process of uneven devel-opment. Second, the repercussions of oil expenditures were not uni-form in all sectors of the economy. While the service and industrial sectors were developing immensely, agriculture was stagnating. The per-centage of the labor force employed in nonagricultural sectors increased from 54 percent in 1966 to 66.1 percent in 1976 (Nazari 1989, 36). Correspondingly, the share of the agricultural sector in the total GDP dropped from 28 percent in 1962 to 9.3 percent in 1977 (Pessaran 1982, 505). Third, the concentration of vast external rents in a few hands created inequities in income. In 1973 the wealthiest 10 percent of the urban households captured 38 percent of spending, whereas the poorest 30 percent accounted for only 7 percent (Looney 1977, 47). As a result, class disparity between the rich minority who were benefiting from the oil boom and the poor majority who were still suffering great deprivation was increasing at an alarming rate.

Fourth, because of the concentration in the 1960s and 1970s of wealth and development projects (construction) in metropolitan areas, Iran witnessed a massive migration from the countryside to urban mu-nicipalities. Iran's urban population increased from 38 percent in 1966 to 47 percent in 1976. Sixty-three percent of these newly urbanized citizens settled in thirty large cities (Nazari 1989, 178–79). The former landless peasants became seasonal laborers and construction workers. Unable to meet the high rents in Tehran and other major cities, they created shantytowns on the outskirts of the major metropolitan centers and joined the ranks of the urban poor. Their material condition as rural uprooted or evicted peasants along with their religious convictions and cultural alienation in the cosmopolitan surroundings of urban cities proved too volatile to restrain. As the course of future events demon-strated, these groups came to play an instrumental role in the overthrow of the shah's regime.[10]

10. For two studies of the living conditions and the political psychology of the urban poor before the revolution see Kazemi 1980; Banu'azizi 1983.

Fifth, the windfall profits generated from the export of oil and natural gas were not saved or used efficiently. Huge sums were lavished on the latest military technology. In the 1970s nearly one-third of the total budget was regularly allocated for military expenditures. "The annual military budget increased from $293 million in 1963 to $1.8 billion in 1973, and after the quadrupling of oil prices, to $7.3 billion in 1977" (Abrahamian 1982, 435). The luxury goods imported by the government and by the elites only added to the burden. The result was inflation and import dependency. By 1974–75 imports were increasing at an annual rate of 77 percent while non-oil exports were actually falling by 8 percent (Issawi 1978, 166).

If one were to use Max Weber's definition of *legitimacy* as any transformation of authority that is generally accepted and obeyed without frequent resort to coercion, one realizes that political legitimacy has more often than not been a mere phantom in Iran. The annals of Iranian history are, alas, a tragic testimony to the violent nature of political change marked by the despotic reign of kings and the tumultuous mutinies of the opposition.

Iran's history during the reign of Mohammad-Reza Shah was no different. Being reinstalled to power through a CIA-supported coup in 1953 and, therefore, having little political legitimacy, the shah increasingly had to resort to violence to subdue his opponents. The only other way the state could have compensated for its dire lack of political legitimacy was by providing for the welfare of its citizenry, particularly for the emerging new middle class. As political economists have repeatedly reminded, however, economically interventionist states run the risk of forfeiting their legitimacy if the economy goes bad. Because in rentier economies like Iran the state is the dominant economic actor and all strata rely on its directives and allocations for services, employment, and privileges, economic crises tend to translate rapidly into political crises. To make matters worse, the historical weakness of the indigenous Iranian bourgeoisie forced the "state" to fulfill yet another function as the agent of capital accumulation and industrialization (Ashraf 1970). Needless to say, this duty only added to the burden of the state because it had to play a dual role. First, the state was the prime agent responsible for capital accumulation and allocation and economic development. Second, the state had to act as the hegemonic machinery of the Iranian ruling class. As one observer put it by the end of the shah's rule, "The state had become the largest wealth holder, industrialist, and banker in the country" (Parsa 1989, 63). The peculiarity of Iran's development path can be summed up in the context of three trends. First, the growth of the social forces of capitalism (bourgeoisie and modern petty bourgeoisie) was happening concurrently with the growth of their more traditional counterparts (commercial bourgeoisie and traditional petty bourgeoisie). Second, the development of modern capitalism did not discredit traditional ideological and cultural structures and values (religion, patriarchal relations). Third, the implementation of the supposedly "new" strategy of industrialization was to leave traditional and archaic political structures (monarchical despotism, the nonexistence of democratic institutions) intact.

In short, the shah's regime combined the universal vulnerabilities of a rentier state with the peculiar weaknesses of the Iranian domestic bourgeoisie. Although economic windfall and land reform had lent token legitimacy to the state, subsequent events proved these to be inadequate stock in the unstable market of Iranian politics. A leading authority on rentier state, who also happened to be a former deputy director of the Division of Economic Affairs of Iran's Plan and Budget Organization, foretold the shah's predicament accurately in 1970:

> A government that can expand its services without resorting to heavy taxation acquires an independence from the people seldom found in other countries. However, not having developed an effective administrative machinery for the purposes of taxation, the governments of Rentier States may suffer from inefficiency in any field of activity that requires extensive organizational inputs. In political terms, the power of the government to bribe pressure groups or to coerce dissidents may be greater than otherwise. By the same token, this power is highly vulnerable since the stoppage of external rents can seriously damage the government finances. (Mahdavi 1970, 467)

By the mid-1970s this possibility had become a reality. As a result of the dramatic rise in oil prices in 1973, the government doubled its expenditures, lifted all foreign exchange controls, and implemented selective liberalization of foreign trade. These policies added to the existing disparities and injustices of the shah's hasty industrialization program. By the mid-1970s the state's cumulative expenditures caught up with its financial resources. In addition, by 1975–77 world demand for Iranian oil contracted. The result was the abrupt termination of many industrial projects, which, in turn, precipitated massive unemployment. Combined with the corruption and conspicuous consumption of Iranian high society, the preexisting sense of deprivation among urbanites became magnified. Rapid economic growth had fostered an even more rapid growth in expectations. The rentier economy had produced a *rentier mentality* in which the sacred neoclassical work-reward theorem (which was supposed to generate a strong work ethic) was obsolete. The public viewed reward and windfall gains as based on situational or opportunistic factors and state favoritism rather than consequences of systematic hard work. Furthermore, because the state had failed to levy any strong system of direct taxation on its citizens, the public was accustomed to viewing the state not as an institution it had to pay for but as one it should rely on (Beblawi and Luciani 1987, 2). In other words, the Iranian masses did not have a "welfare consciousness" because they did not perceive welfare benefits "as rights, but as gracious handouts from the Shah" (Najmabadi 1987, 223).

Therefore, in the mid-1970s the state, which until that time had not found itself accountable to the public for the expenditure of oil revenue, confronted a citizenry which was quick to realize that their ideals of a better life far exceeded reality. The public responded with a mixture of skepticism and outrage as the shah vaunted his goals of making Iran "the fifth greatest military power in the world" and entering the gates of the "Great Civilization." A crisis of expectations on the part of the citizenry had gradually materialized.

The state also failed on the ideological front. In an age of democracy and republicanism the regime accorded centrality to a royal ideology whose principal features were Persian chauvinism, loyalty to the person of the shah, depoliticization of the citizenry, and the glorification of pre-Islamic Iranian history. This hierarchically exclusionary ideology failed to fulfill either the ideological needs of the traditional masses or the recently expanded middle class. Because of its lofty nature, the royal ideology was fundamentally incapable of creating an ideological sense of political participation among the people or of subduing its political opponents. Throughout its rule the Pahlavi regime remained a dictatorship not predicated on real consensus. Inevitably, then, it relied increasingly on violence as the key to its security amid the rise of semiorganized countergroups, which were largely couched in Islamic discursive practices. By the mid-1970s the profound dubiety of state legitimacy took expression in military-economic manifestations. The state was stripped of whatever economic legitimacy it had previously accumulated. The crisis of economic legitimacy soon spilled over into the political sphere. An acute crisis of the state manifested itself when political and physical terror failed to spread fear as its ideological effect.

Although the shah and his lieutenants embarked on rapid modernization of the socioeconomic infrastructure of the country, there was no serious attempt to create a dynamic and open political system. It seemed as if the shah had borrowed the slogan of the turn-of-the-century Mexican leader Porfirio Díaz, "plenty of administration and no politics." Uneven economic development and the widening gulf between these two primary domains proved instrumental in the eventual downfall of the anachronistic monarchical regime. Following the advice of a number of his American-educated advisers, the shah founded his Rastakhiz (Resurgence) Party in 1975 as a "mass party" encompassing the entire Iranian population and encouraged everyone to join.[11] At a time when all the legal channels of participation were closed to the opposition—who were subjected to harassment, imprisonment, and torture—this call only proved to be a cruel joke.[12] The shah's formula for political stability was based on two main pillars: ruthless suppression of the opposition and encouragement of civil privatism. The state used the former to encourage the latter. It failed to realize that even among the nouveaux riche rapid modernization would foster a sense of deprivation in terms of political participation, rational decision making, and national independence. And, more importantly for the lower classes, such questions as wealth distribution, conspicuous consumption, and moral decadence would generate strong antistate emotions.

Hence, the rentier nature of Iran's economy and the actual policies of the regime caused the gradual erosion of the bonds linking the state and civil society. The state viewed itself as independent from civil society and failed to exercise any ideological hegemony over its constituents. The people, by contrast, having been accustomed to a rentier mentality, did not develop a *welfare consciousness*. Not having to pay for the state, they, nevertheless, came to rely on it. Against the backdrop of these conditions the crisis of legitimacy quickly engulfed the precarious state when it floundered on its many overambitious promises to different segments of the population. Political repression failed to stop the disenchanted masses once they realized it was possible to alter the status quo.

The opposition of secular Iranian intellectuals to the state was largely the result of political factors. Having come mainly from the ranks of the new middle class, they had benefited from the shah's economic programs. Yet the neopatriarchal and pro-Western nature of the regime left much to be desired. These intellectuals could not easily forgive the shah for ousting former Prime Minister Mohammad Mosaddeq. Their first experimentation after World War II with a democratic, nationalist government had been abruptly terminated. In addition to this bitter historical memory the state's conservative, pro-Western attitudes in foreign

11. By September 1976 the party reported that it had a membership of 5,191,312 and that 60 percent of these members came from rural areas (Echo of Iran 1977, 119).

12. Daryush Homayun, a leading pro-shah intellectual who served in such capacities as a journalist, founder of *Ayandegan* daily newspaper, secretary-general of the Rastakhiz Party, and finally minister of information (1977–78), provides an account of the artificial nature of the party (Homayun 1982).

policy, notorious repressive apparatuses, prohibition of political dissent, censorship, and internal corruption all contributed to the alienation of the intelligentsia from the state. As one contemporary Iranian social thinker points out, in countries such as Iran, Saudi Arabia, and other rentier states where wealth was accumulated through oil rather than through labor (as it was done in Japan, Korea, and the Soviet Union) a structure of economic and political discipline never took shape. In Iran, where political satire is a popular way of expressing opinions, government employees jokingly referred to their salaries as their *sahm-e naft* (share of the oil). The idleness of the state and the arbitrariness of the existing income and merit system are implicit in this sarcastic remark. The rentier mentality allowed routine bribes, kickbacks, favoritism, and corruption to develop as prevalent methods of conducting business (Ashuri 1989).

The shah's state and the Iranian intelligentsia each posed a problem for the other. The state relied heavily on technocrats and bureaucrats to manage its rapidly expanding industrial machinery. At the same time the technocrats' demand for an increasing voice in government matters was a source of worry for the state. Viewing himself as the leader of the campaign to modernize Iran, the shah could not do away with the army of intelligentsia who were supposed to spearhead this movement. Yet, as the embodiment of the neopatriarchal power configuration, he could not delegate authority to the intelligentsia whom, based on the experience of Mosaddeq, he could not trust. Thus, the dilemma confronting the state was how to use the technical skills of the intelligentsia while avoiding any concessions. To compensate for its deficit of legitimacy the state tried to "buy off" the intelligentsia with monetary incentives and employment.

The intelligentsia, however, lacking many options in a still relatively undeveloped private sector, had to rely on the state as their primary source of employment. Consequently, the intelligentsia were absorbed into such state institutions as the Plan and Budget Organization, the National Iranian Oil Company, Central Bank, Iranian National Radio and Television, the Center for the Intellectual Development of Children and Young Adults, and various universities. Despite their dependence on the state for their economic livelihood, these intellectuals did not perceive themselves as part of it. Quite to the contrary, having observed the corruption, inefficiency, waste, and mismanagement of the Iranian bureaucracy—in addition to the repressive nature of the political infrastructure—they became further alienated from the state. As one intellectual put it, having been employed as hired subordinates, "intellectuals developed a sense of guilt . . . about their cooperation with the state, so much so that opposition to the state became a value in itself" (Ashuri 1989).

The close affiliation of the Pahlavi regime with the West, although fruitful in economic terms, proved to be a political liability. The shah's generally obsequious demeanor toward the West (particularly toward the United States, as a way of reciprocating for his reinstatement to power) became an undiscussed national embarrassment. The presence of European and American advisers, technicians, military personnel, missionaries, educators, and administrators reached unjustifiable proportions. Furthermore, a goodly number of ruling elites were not only too closely associated with the West, they also came to view their own society through the eyes of the West. They were a class of "native colons" who although "of the same flesh and blood as the rest of the collectivity . . . developed a cultural autonomy vis-à-vis the rest of the populace" (Alavi 1985, 340). In light of the strong tradition of opposition to foreign domination embedded within Iranian political culture along with the still-lingering memory of the 1953 coup, this identification became a handicap in the eyes of Iranian intellectuals. The ruling elites apish imitation of the West, alas, was not just a matter of fondness for European philosophy texts. The programs and solutions promoted by Iran's Western-educated social engineers more often than not resembled a prefabricated foreign import without the necessary provisions for the country's indigenous conditions. How else is one to make sense of capital-intensive industrialization in a country with a massive reserve army of unemployed laborers?

As Crane Brinton points out in *The Anatomy of Revolution*, intellectuals' transfer of allegiance is generally regarded as one symptom of a prerevolutionary condition. Two events, one in the beginning of the 1950s and the other in the early years of the 1960s, proved instrumental in this process of intellectual desertion: the overthrow of Mosaddeq in 1953 and the June 1963 uprising in Qom. After the 1953 coup, all political parties were outlawed. In the absence of its charismatic leader *Jebheh-ye Melli* (National Front) gradually sank into anonymity. Khalil Maleki's Niruy-e Sevvom (Third Force), which had brought together some of Iran's leading intellectuals and literati, strove once more to stage a comeback when it reorganized itself under the name of Jame'eh-ye Sosiyalistha-ye Nehzat-e Melli-ye Iran (Socialist League of Iran's National Movement) in the early 1960s. This organization, however, did not last long and was reduced to a mere memory once many of its cadres abandoned the realm of organized political activity in pursuit of more individualistically oriented and often apolitical endeavors. The Tudeh Party suffered the most casualties in the execution and imprisonment of its members. Many of its leading cadres fled to the Soviet Union and Eastern Europe to seek political asylum. In short, it ceased to operate as an effective political party. Furthermore, the bloody suppression of the June 1963 uprising led by Ayatollah Ruhollah Khomeini reinforced the opinion of Iran's more radical intellectuals that it was no longer possible to challenge the state through legal and peaceful means. Thus, they went underground, turning to armed struggle as their only viable means of resistance. The more moderate elements, however, pursued their agenda not through guns but through literature, poetry, and the arts. The activities, goals, and impact of these two tendencies each represent ways of engaging with the state.

The Secular Militants

In the 1960s Iran's political culture underwent a radical turn. The defeated, disillusioned radical youths and rank-and-file cadres of the National Front and the Tudeh Party could not console themselves with the glory days of the past. They replaced the old leadership's intellectual pessimism with a rejuvenated optimism of will. Conservative realism was no solution for these romantic visionaries. Failing to follow the example of National Front leaders' retirement from political activism or the mild criticisms expressed by the Tudeh Party's leaders in exile, they turned toward radical political action. This radicalism manifested itself primarily in armed struggle waged by underground guerrilla organizations among which two main groups stand out: Sazman-e Cherikha-ye Feda'i-ye Khalq-e Iran (Organization of the Iranian People's Self-Sacrificing Guerrillas) and Sazman-e Mojahedin-e Khalq-e Iran (Organization of the Iranian People's Holy Warriors).[13]

The Feda'iyan organization was formed in March 1971. Its roots, however, can be traced to the mid-1960s when two independent underground groups (later to merge) began operations. The first group, formed in 1963, was led by Bizhan Jazani (a former member of the Tudeh Party); the second, formed in 1967, was headed by Mas'ud Ahmadzadeh and Amir-Parviz Puyan (former members of the National Front). On the one hand, having maintained much of the theoretical infrastructure of the Tudeh Party, Jazani's group emphasized political organization. Ahmadzadeh and Puyan, on the other hand, were influenced by the ideas of such revolutionary thinkers as Régis Debray, Ernesto Guevara, Mao Zedong, and Carlos Marighela. Modeling them-

13. Hereafter, the two organizations will respectively be referred to as the Feda'iyan and the Mojahedin. As a group of religious intellectuals, however, the Mojahedin will be discussed in chapter 5.

selves after these revolutionaries, they advocated guerrilla warfare as the only means available to shatter the all-powerful image of the state. Thus, the first group's more seasoned tradition of political reflection was complemented by the latter's sense of idealistic activism. Yet sharing a common belief in the idea of revolutionary agency, both groups promoted a voluntaristic strategy for change. After some deliberation, they approved Ahmadzadeh and Puyan's theory of armed struggle on the assumption that heroism and self-sacrifice were the only ways to awaken a "retired nation."[14] This decision was in tune both with the winds of radicalism sweeping the region in the aftermath of Nasserism, the 1967 Arab-Israeli War, the rise of the Palestine Liberation Organization (PLO), the Algerian war of liberation, Mu'ammar Qaddafi's rise to power in Libya, and with the general state of revolutionary intellectuals' isolation from the masses.

On 8 February 1971 thirteen Feda'i guerrillas, trying their new approach of rural guerrilla warfare, attacked a gendarmerie post in Siyahkal in the northern Gilan province. The government responded with a disproportionate show of force, sending a much larger army to smash the guerrillas. Two of the Feda'i guerrillas were killed in combat, and those captured were summarily executed (or died under torture). Although the Siyahkal attack was a total military failure for the Feda'i guerrillas, it proved to be an astonishing propaganda victory. A mere four months after the Siyahkal event, Ahmadzadeh summed up the Feda'iyan's goal as follows: "The goal of the armed struggle in the beginning was not to inflict a military blow on the enemy but rather a political blow. The aim is to show the path of struggle both to the revolutionaries and to the masses, make them aware of their power, show that the enemy is vulnerable, that the possibility of struggle exists, to expose the enemy and awaken the masses" (Ahmadzadeh 1974, 6–7). Siyahkal, thus, became a watershed event in contemporary Iranian history. It signified, first, the vulnerability of the state and, second, the inauguration of a new revolutionary approach to political struggle.

The Feda'iyan, however, generated the greatest enthusiasm, not among the rural peasantry whom they had originally aimed to mobilize but among the urban college students. The Iranian peasantry could not have been further away from what Fanon in *The Wretched of the Earth* referred to as "the revolutionary proletariat of our time." On the contrary, from their lack of any particular ideology or language of protest, the Iranian peasantry came more to resemble Eric Hobsbawm's (1959)

14. The two major theoretical texts promoting this view were Puyan 1973 and Ahmadzadeh 1974, respectively.

"pre-political people." Judging from the examples of peasant rebellions in Russia, Mexico, China, Vietnam, Algeria, and Cuba, Eric Wolf (1973) designated the twentieth century as the era of peasant wars. Yet, as two longtime observers of Iranian politics have pointed out, what is significant in the case of Iran is not the frequency but the conspicuous absence of a tradition of revolutionary peasant movements (Kazemi and Abrahamian 1978). The Iranian peasantry, who had participated neither in the Constitutional Revolution of 1905–09 nor in the oil nationalization movement or other political events of 1941–53, were not stimulated by this guerrilla operation either.

The place where the Feda'iyan's heroism had the greatest influence was in the urban areas, in general, and on university campuses, in particular. This was not surprising, given that the guerrillas carried out many of their attacks in the urban areas, targeting military posts, banks, and power plants. Moreover, the Feda'iyan themselves had come mainly from the ranks of the new professional middle class and had acquired their academic and political education in the universities.[15] In studying the history of the Feda'iyan organization one finds a positive correlation between the location of institutions of higher learning and the places were the Feda'iyan branches were most active. A former high-level cadre of the organization ranked the provinces where the Feda'iyan were most organized before 1976 as follows: Tehran and its suburbs, Gilan, Mazandaran, Azerbaijan, Khorasan, and Esfahan (Mahfuzi 1984). Tehran was the logical front-runner because five of the twelve universities operating by 1975 were clustered there. Gilan, Mazandaran, and Azerbaijan located in the north or northwestern regions shared such characteristics as geographical proximity to the Soviet Union, historical links with Russian revolutionaries, and a more progressive and secular political culture. Khorasan and Esfahan, respectively in the northeast and the central parts of the country, however, represented the more traditional and religious provinces. Yet even there, the infusion of oil wealth, the establishment of heavy industries (e.g., the Esfahan Steel Mill founded in 1965 with Soviet cooperation) and the new technocratic elites needed to run these businesses, plus the rapidly expanding centers of higher education, all made the appeal of the Feda'iyan's message more powerful.

Tehran, Tabriz (capital of Azerbaijan), and Mashhad (capital of

15. Abrahamian's (1982, 481) survey of 172 Feda'i guerrillas who lost their lives between 1971 and 1977 revealed the following occupational breakdown: college students (73); high school students (1); teachers (17); engineers (19); office workers (7); doctors (3); intellectuals (4); other professionals (11); housewives (8); conscripts (5); workers (12); not known (12).

37

Khorasan) are three examples of places where a fair number of Feda'i leaders became acquainted with one another on university campuses. At Tehran University, Bizhan Jazani, Abbas Surki, Ali-Akbar Safa'i-Farahani, Mohammad Saffari-Ashtiyani, and Hamid Ashraf came together.[16] Behruz Dehqani, Ashraf Dehqani, Ali-Reza Nabdel, Kazem Sa'adati, along with such literary figures as Samad Behrangi and Gholamhoseyn Sa'edi (who were working closely with the organization), all came from the city of Tabriz. In Mashhad, such figures as Mas'ud Ahmadzadeh, Amir-Parviz Puyan, Hamid Tavakkoli, Sa'id Aryan, and Bahman Azhang formed yet a different clique.[17] As the above brief biographical sketches demonstrate, the universities served as the prime recruitment centers for the Feda'iyan organization. Campus sports clubs for mountain climbing or even the broader literary clubs were secretly patronized by Feda'iyan sympathizers attempting to enlist new members. This practice was by no means limited to the Feda'iyan. The Mojahedin-e khalq as well as such smaller armed Marxist groups and circles as the Palestine Group,[18] Khosrow Golsorkhi's group,[19] Mostafa Sho'a'iyan's group,[20] the Tufan Organization,[21] and the Arman-e Khalq Organization[22] all followed a similar procedure.

16. Jazani, a student of political science who graduated first in his class, became the foremost theoretician of the organization. Safa'i-Farahani, an engineering student, served as the leader of the Siyahkal raid. Ashraf, another engineering major, later became the leader of the organization. Surki and Saffari-Ashtiyani, respectively, majored in political science and law (Abrahamian 1982, 483–84).

17. The academic disciplines of these guerrillas was as follows: Ahmadzadeh (mathematics); Puyan (literature); Tavakkoli (History); Aryan (English); and Azhang (English). The first two were, respectively, students at Tehran University and National University in Tehran, whereas the latter three were students at Mashhad University.

18. The Palestine Group was a small leftist organization whose eighteen members were arrested in the early 1970s. Three of its leaders Shokrollah Paknezhad, Mas'ud Batha'i, and Naser Khaksaz were condemned to life imprisonment. They were released in the midst of the revolutionary uprising in 1978.

19. Educated at Tehran University, Khosrow Golsorkhi, was a poet and art critic. His courageous defense of his Marxian beliefs in a televised trial in 1974 captivated thousands of viewers. His execution (along with fellow comrade Keramat Daneshiyan) following the trial became another rallying point for the militant intellectuals.

20. Sho'a'iyan was a welding engineer, a teacher, and a brilliant independent Marxist thinker who in a series of debates with Hamid Mo'meni, the leading theoretician of the Feda'iyan, criticized the organization's Leninist-Stalinist doctrines. In order not to be captured alive he took his own life during a gunbattle with the government's security police on 5 February 1976. For some of his writings see Sho'a'iyan 1975; 1976a; 1976b.

21. Tufan (storm) was a small pro-China Marxist-Leninist organization that was established in 1962.

22. This was yet another small communist underground organization that began armed struggle around the same time as the Feda'iyan and was active in Azerbaijan, Khuzestan, and Lorestan. Five of its leading cadres (Homayun Katira'i, Naser Karimi,

Several factors contributed to the turn toward universities. First, the 1953 coup, by putting an end to organized legal political opposition, inadvertently transferred the locus of opposition from factories and work sites to such places as high schools, universities, and even mosques. This development was only natural because the government could outlaw political parties and threaten striking workers with termination of employment. What the government could not do, however, was storm the mosques, outlaw prayers, or close the universities indefinitely because the state itself depended upon university graduates to staff its own bureaucratic machinery.[23] A classic case of what Samuel Huntington has called the "king's dilemma" was, thus, at hand. A second factor contributing to the turn toward universities had to do with demographic changes occurring in Iranian society at the time. Iran's population, which stood at almost sixteen million in 1946, rose to thirty-four million by 1976. In addition, thanks to the drastic reductions in the infant mortality rate brought by improving medical techniques, Iran's population was becoming younger. According to the Iranian government's Plan and Budget Organization, by 1976 two-thirds of the Iranian population was under the age of thirty, and the median age was close to 21.4 (Sazman-e Barnameh va Budjeh 1978, 32). Finally, this population was also becoming more urbanized. The expansion of the population along with its compositional transformation precipitated a large increase in the number of young men and women entering the universities. Despite the increase in the number of university admissions (from 5,781 in 1961/62 to 28,500 in 1978/79), the universities were still unable to accommodate the rapidly growing pool of college-bound high school graduates, which rose from 15,924 in 1961/62 to 235,000 in 1978/79. This meant that the percentage of high school graduates gaining university admission dropped from 36.3 percent in 1961/62 to a mere 12.1 percent in 1978/79 (Menashri 1992, 207).

Faced with the dim prospect of having their children rejected for admission to Iranian universities, the upper and middle classes started to send their sons and daughters abroad in the hope of providing them with the newly cherished commodity of higher education. The vast majority of these students chose to go to the United States and Europe for their higher education. According to a report by Iran's Ministry of Sci-

---

Naser Madani, Bahram Taherzadeh, and Hushang Targol) were executed on 9 October 1971.

23. This is not to say that the regime did not carry on these activities. Quite to the contrary, on more than one occasion it attacked the mosques and closed the universities. Yet each time it was under the pressure of public opinion to reopen these centers.

ence and Higher Education, in 1969 and 1970, respectively, 95 and 92 percent of Iranian students sent abroad went to North America and Western Europe (Vezarat-e Olum va Amuzesh-e Ali 1971, 4–5). Although dispatching students overseas lessened the pressure on the government to accommodate all prospective students, in the end it proved to be a liability. In light of the greater freedom found in Western democracies, these students were now able to voice their often critical political opinions more freely.

One organization instrumental in politicizing a great number of newly arriving Iranian students was the Confederation of Iranian Students (hereafter, the confederation). Formed as an umbrella organization, the confederation accommodated a number of competing groups (supporters of the National Front, the Tudeh Party, the Third Force, and various guerrilla organizations) all with their own separate agendas. Almost all of the early activists had left Iran immediately before or after the 1953 coup. The first Iranian student association was formed in Vienna, Austria, in 1957. Similar associations were gradually formed in France, Switzerland, Germany, and the United States.[24] Spread throughout many countries outside of Iran, the confederation did an apt job during the 1960s and 1970s of coordinating Iranian student opposition to the shah's regime.[25] Influenced by the success of revolutionary movements in Egypt, Cuba, Algeria, China, and Vietnam, those with more militant tendencies within the confederation established contacts with progressive and revolutionary organizations both within and outside Iran. They were often warmly received by the revolutionary leadership of Egypt, Algeria, Iraq, Libya, and the Palestine Liberation Organization (Shakeri 1983). Once armed resistance was underway inside Iran in 1971, the militant wing of the confederation provided it with monetary and logistical support. They facilitated contact between guerrilla organizations inside Iran and those in the region and went as far as to send some of their own members to the PLO camps to be trained in the techniques of armed struggle. Furthermore, the confederation smuggled people into and out of Iran, held rallies and conferences to mobilize Western public opinion against the shah, publicized the plight of Iranian

24. Mehdi Khanbaba-Tehrani (1989, 311–13), a founder of the confederation, identifies, among others, the following people as some of the leading activists of the organization in these countries: Firuz Towfiq; Mehrdad Bahar, Hamid Enayat, Homayun Katouzian, Manuchehr Hezarkhani, Hoseyn Malek, Homa Nateq, Naser Pakdaman, Amir Pishdad, Ahmad Ashraf, Sadeq Qotbzadeh, and Khosrow Shakeri.

25. Nikki Keddie (1995, 69) writes: "The Iranian student movement abroad was by far the largest and most oppositional of any such student movement, and this was due not only to its superior numbers, but also to its political commitment."

political prisoners, broadcasted radio messages to Iran, published a variety of newspapers, translated books and articles, and reprinted many of the books outlawed in Iran.[26] All in all, the confederation transformed many would-be students into full-time revolutionaries working to overthrow the regime from abroad.

Inside Iran, the situation was no better for the regime. The government and university administrations requested obedience from an increasingly restless student body. In line with its policy of promoting civil privatism the state proscribed student participation in any type of political activity. Nonetheless, as one of the most critically aware strata within Iranian society, the student body could not remain secluded from the impact of the occurrences around them. Within the university they requested freedom of expression and assembly, a greater role for students in decision making, and evacuation of police guards from the campuses. In the society at large they demanded that the government address some of the social ills besetting Iranian society.[27] Often ignored or given false promises, the students would subsequently turn more radical. They boycotted classes, held rallies, staged sit-ins, and organized hunger strikes.[28] These protests were almost exclusively secular and were often dominated by the leftist forces who have traditionally concentrated much of their energy in the cultural/educational realm. The emergence of underground guerrilla organizations strengthened this trend but also

26. According to a list prepared by the notorious secret police, Sazman-e Ettela'at va Amniyat-e Keshvar (better known by its acronym, SAVAK), disclosed by the confederation by 1971, the government had banned more than 200 books considered to be "harmful." By the late 1970s the list covered some 770 titles. See Tonokaboni 1978, 199–208; Farda-ye Iran 1981.

27. In a 1966 survey of Tehran University and Melli University students' attitudes toward the most important task confronting the government, 46 percent mentioned elimination of inequality and injustice followed by 30 percent who called for raising the general level of education and increasing educational opportunities (Bill 1972, 89).

28. The following is a partial list of their daring acts of resistance. In 1961 they waged demonstrations for such causes as supporting teachers rights (April), protesting the Central Treaty Organization (CENTO) Conference (June), expressing solidarity with the Algerian resistance (November), and objecting to the presence of American technicians (December). In May 1962 they went to Javadiyyeh, a poor section of Tehran damaged by a flood, to build a bridge. In June 1967 they demonstrated against Israel for its occupation of Arab lands after the Six-Day War. In January 1968 they took an active part in commemoration services for Gholamreza Takhti, an admired Olympic gold medalist wrestler who they suspected was killed on the orders of the shah's brother out of personal jealousy. In March 1970 they organized commemoration services for the Siyahkal martyrs and joined in a popular outcry against increasing bus fares. Finally, in May 1970 they attacked a number of American-owned institutions and centers. In short, for the students the 1970s began the same way the previous decade had begun, with a wave of unswerving protests.

lent legitimacy to antigovernment Muslim student groups active in the universities.

The government's response to student discontent was a mixture of intimidation and diversionary appeasement. Following its regular practice of buying off opponents, the government offered scholarships, living allowances, jobs, and other incentives to the students as unofficial bribes. When these attempts failed, the government resorted to the age-old practice of using threats and sanctions. The students were threatened with such prospects as failing grades, loss of scholarships or dormitory rooms, or even expulsion. The more militant students had to face SAVAK interrogations, tortures, and imprisonment. Judging from the continuation of demonstrations in the universities, it seems that these government tactics were not successful. After all, it is much more difficult to induce a young, single, unemployed, and idealistic generation than an aging, married, economically pressed generation of aspiring mid-level bureaucrats with the promise of monetary rewards and the threat of loss of privileges.

The government's university predicament was not limited to the students; the faculty were also a cause for concern. In an environment of political repression the socially minded faculty were prohibited from speaking on certain subjects. Faced with student informers, inquisitions by the administration, SAVAK, politically dictated high-level appointments, administrative corruption, expulsion or imprisonment of their students, besides a host of other difficulties, a sizable number of the faculty also harbored strong grievances against the government. This problem was most acute in young professors returning from abroad.

The case of Naser Pakdaman, a professor of economics at Tehran University and founder of the Organization of University Professors (1978), is illustrative of this group. Born in 1933 to a middle-class family in Tehran, Pakdaman graduated first in his field in 1954 from the Tehran University Faculty of Law and Political Science. In 1955 he went to France where he earned his doctorate in economics. Despite receiving a government scholarship Pakdaman took part in the formation of the confederation and later on initiated the League of Iranian Socialists in Europe with a group of like-minded intellectuals. In 1967 he returned to Iran and faced such harassment as the confiscation of books sent to him from abroad and direct and indirect SAVAK inquisitions, interferences, and warnings (Pakdaman 1994). Pakdaman compares the plight of a university professor in Iran at the time to a man imprisoned inside a steam pipe, living in a place for which he was not made but was condemned. The imprisoned man develops a language of symbolism, indulges in self-censorship, and becomes negative-minded and isolated

(Pakdaman 1984). His case represents those of a great many young professors with impeccable academic credentials who returned to Iran only to experience the impediments to true intellectual pursuits caused by authoritarian political machinery.[29]

The self-sacrificing militants, the nonconformist students, and the dissident faculty all counterbalanced their isolation from the ordinary masses with a populist approach to political struggle. They attempted to reflect the demands of "the masses" while not necessarily succumbing to the latter's worldview. Toward that end, they resorted to an imitation of the language and demeanor of the masses as a way of building ties with them. This, however, was a futile attempt from the very beginning. The underground, full-time, and perilous life of a guerrilla and the elite, urban nature of a university student or professor in a country with an illiteracy rate close to 60 percent were too much of an impediment for such a fanciful solidarity ever to materialize. At best, "the masses" could only remain bystanders, admirers of the guerrillas' heroic acts, or courteous listeners to discourses by university types on the malevolent nature of Iran's socioeconomic system. Hence, the relationship between the guerrillas and the students became a symbiosis in which the guerrillas recruited students while the students became the most enthusiastic supporters and promoters of the guerrillas.

The Literati

Besides underground safe-houses and university campuses, a third arena wherein the secular intelligentsia's other-ness to the state manifested itself was in the pages of literary and artistic journals. Having closed the doors to any meaningful social or political activity, the government viewed literature, arts, and sports as arenas where much of the attention and energies of the youth activists could be redirected without endangering its own existence. By retreating from these public spaces the state inadvertently provided an arena for the opposition to voice its subtle, yet still effective, criticism. The socially minded members of the literati community used the open forums of literary journals to articulate some of the same grievances raised earlier by the guerrillas and the students. Devoid of the means used by the former groups, they used

29. Other examples include Homa Nateq (a leading historian), Hamid Enayat (professor and chair of the Department of Political Science at Tehran University), Ahmad Ashraf (a leading sociologist), Reza Baraheni (a well-known literary critic), Ali Shari'ati (a foremost Islamic theoretician), Manuchehr Hezarkhani (a prominent translator of literary and political theory texts), and Simin Daneshvar (Iran's preeminent woman novelist).

the only weapon in their possession—the pen. For them literature became an instrument of change and a political medium to underscore censorship, corruption, repression, despotism, and the plight of the disenfranchised.

This new concept of literature led to a division in the ranks of the literary community between the engagé literati and the literary neutrals.[30] The engagé artists, poets, translators, and writers, on the one hand, were advocating Adabiyyat-e mota'ahhed (committed or engagé literature), one that would operate as the mouthpiece of the poor and the underprivileged. The literary neutrals, on the other hand, wanted to pursue "in letters a beauty or an understanding quite outside politics" (Brinton 1965, 44). The government's patronage of the literary neutrals only exacerbated the already developing rift between the two competing groups. The engagé literati described the neutrals with such adjectives as government puppets, alienated from the masses, superficial, absurdists, escapists, nihilist, decadent, imported, artificial, illegitimate, lifeless, and unethical. They perceived their own art as attentive, loyal, dutiful, ethical, and authentic.

The engagé literati's use of literature as a means to contest the regime and inculcate popular political consciousness led some to an adaptation of progressive realism via intellectuals such as Bertolt Brecht, Anton Chekhov, Nikolai Chernyshevsky, Maxime Gorky, Pablo Neruda, Romain Rolland, and Ivan Turgenev. Like the writers themselves, the Iranian proponents of these engagé writers and social poets came almost exclusively from the ranks of the Left. Such novelists, poets, and translators as Bozorg Alavi, Reza Baraheni, Mahmud E'temadzadeh (Behazin), Samad Behrangi, Ali-Ashraf Darvishian, Khosrow Golsorkhi, Gholamhoseyn Sa'edi, Sa'id Soltanpur, Ehsan Tabari, and Fereydun Tonokaboni were emissaries of this school of thought. A second group of engagé literati consisted of those writers who believed in partisan literature but were not adherents of radical realism. This group consisted mainly of disillusioned Marxists, religiously inspired poets, and liber-

30. A word of caution is due here about categorization such as "engagé," "literary neutrals," "modernist," and "traditionalist." Considering the fact that many of the literary and artistic figures mentioned here had only recently come of age and/or were experimenting with new styles of prose and poetry, classification as designed here may at times be misrepresenting. For example, some engagé intellectuals were often experimenting with modernist styles, whereas the themes explored by the literary neutrals were not always devoid of a subtle political message (either in favor of or against the regime.) Thus, the engagé compared to literary neutrals is only meant to differentiate in the broadest sense those who had made a premeditated and conscious decision about whether their artistic products were to serve a particular cause, ideology, or class from those more concerned with the purely aesthetic nature of their work.

al members of the Iranian literary community. Among its leading figures
were Jalal Al-e Ahmad, Mehdi Akhavan-Sales, Sadeq Chubak, Simin
Daneshvar, Forugh Farrokhzad, and Ahmad Shamlu. These writers, poets, and filmmakers were influenced by Western artists and thinkers
such as Albert Camus, Ernest Hemingway, Henry James, Bertrand
Russell, Jean-Paul Sartre and others. Bozorg Alavi, the doyen of Iran's
realism movement, summarized his commitment to partisan literature
by saying, "I know I cannot write about flowers and nightingales."
Shamlu, a protégé of Nima Yushij and Iran's preeminent poet since the
1960s, spoke of "poetry as mankind's weapon" and demonstrated his
cosmopolitanism by proclaiming:

> I, an Iranian poet, first learned about poetry from the Spaniard Lorca,
> the Frenchman Eluard, the German Rilke, the Russian Mayakovsky . . .
> and the American Langston Hughes; and only later, with this education,
> I turned to the poets of my mother tongue to see and to know, say, the
> grandeur of Hafiz from a fresh perspective.[31]

The group of literary neutrals also consisted of two major tendencies.
The modernist wing was led by figures such as Hushang Golshiri, Shah-
rokh Meskub, Nader Naderpur, Yadollah Ro'ya'i, and Sohrab Sepehri.
This group of literary writers was inspired by the works of Edgar Allan
Poe, Samuel Becket, William Faulkner, Eugène Ionesco, James Joyce,
Franz Kafka, and John Steinbeck. The traditionalist wing, consisting
mainly of aging Persian classicists, was represented by Sadeq Rezazadeh-
Shafaq, Badi'ozzaman Foruzanfar, Jalaloddin Homa'i, Mojtaba Minovi
Parviz Natel-Khanlari, Sa'id Nafisi, and Zabihollah Safa.

Whereas the modernist wing of the literary neutrals remained more
or less apolitical, the traditionalist wing became very much involved
with the officially sanctioned culture of the time. The government provided these traditionalist literati with numerous forums, extended its
financial patronage to their circles, and even allowed them to walk in
the corridors of power as university chancellors, court consultants, am-
bassadors, and senators. These traditionalists dominated such govern-
ment-supported foundations as Anjoman-e Qalam,[32] Bonyad-e Farhang-e
Iran (Iranian Culture Foundation),[33] Showra-ye Ali-ye Farhang (Supreme

31. Quoted in Karimi-Hakkak 1977, 202–3.
32. This was the Iranian branch of the International PEN Society, which was led by
such literary figures as Mohammad Hejazi, Ali Dashti, Parviz Natel-Khanlari, and
Ebrahim Sahba.
33. The foundation was established in 1964, under the auspices of Queen Farah's

Cultural Council),[34] Office of the Queen,[35] Bonyad-e Farah Pahlavi (Queen Farah Pahlavi Foundation),[36] Bonyad-e Farabi (Farabi Foundation), and numerous other organizations. As leading authorities of the Persian language and literature, they designed and supervised the academic curriculum of literature departments throughout Iranian universities. At a time when in nonestablishment intellectual circles the new poetry movement was flexing its muscles, students of literature at Iranian universities were only trained in the time-honored texts of the past. For example, in 1967 the master's program in Persian language and literature at Tehran University consisted of reading only such classics as the *Shahnameh* of Ferdowsi, the *Divan* of Onsor-i, the story of *Khosrow va Shirin* of Nezami Ganjavi, the *Masnavi* of Jalaloddin Rumi, the *Bustan* of Sa'di, the *Divan* of Hafez, *Tarikh-e Abolfazl Bayhaqi, Kalileh-o Demneh* of Ibn Moqaffa', and *Jahangosha-ye Joveyni* (Brodsky 1967, 178).

In the politically charged milieu of the time those intellectuals and artists active in the literary field decided to politicize literature as a way of countering both the aloofness of the modernists and the conformist posture of the traditionalists. These engagé literati criticized the modernist doctrine of "art for art's sake" as well as the traditionalists' subdued sense of literary aestheticism. Against the first group they advocated "committed art and literature" and against the second group, a strategy of antiestablishment political activism. The combined impact of this twin struggle was the development of a formidable adversarial counterculture.

---

office, to promote Iranian cultural heritage. It was run by Parviz Natel-Khanlari, the secretary-general of the foundation, with the assistance of Ali-Akbar Sa'idi-Sirjani. By the time of the revolution the foundation had published more than three hundred titles on the literature, culture, and history of Iran.

34. Following United Nations Educational, Scientific, and Cultural Organization (UNESCO) emphasis on the importance of cultural development in the Third World, this council was formed to coordinate cultural outreach activities around the country. The president of this council was Mehrdad Pahlbod, minister of culture and arts; Jamshid Behnam and Zabihollah Safa, respectively, served as the council's secretaries-general. Because of rivalries with the Ministry of Culture and Arts, however, the council was not successful in carrying out its mandate.

35. This office was responsible for maintaining Iran's museums and for sponsoring a host of other cultural events.

36. Formed in October 1976, this foundation defined its mandate as one of preserving Iranian culture and language through the support of creative arts and scholarly research. Overseen by the queen herself, this foundation was directed by Abdolmajid Majidi. Two of the major institutions under its umbrella were Anjoman-e Shahanshahi-ye Falsafeh-ye Iran (Imperial Iranian Academy of Philosophy) and Markaz-e Irani-ye Motale'eh-ye Farhangha (Iranian Center for the Study of Civilizations).

This counterculture is best represented in the works and life of Samad Behrangi (1939–1968), a young writer and social critic from the city of Tabriz. After earning a bachelor's degree in English from Tabriz University, Behrangi went on to became a primary school teacher. As a leftist and an arch antagonist of escapist literature, Behrangi set for himself the task of reclaiming an ignored domain of literary endeavor— children's literature. He was heavily influenced by a literary-political triangle: the Russian literary tradition of socialist realism, the guerrilla warfare of Latin American revolutionaries, and the cultural revolution that was occurring in China at the time. Behrangi picked the field of children's literature, which was unpolluted, uncontested, and symbol-ically oriented. His most famous work, *Mahi-ye siyah-e kuchulu* (The Little Black Fish), published in 1968, depicts the account of an adventurous, self-sacrificing young fish who leaves his little stream to explore the larger world of a sea (Behrangi 1976). On his way he encounters all sorts of savage acts committed against fishes by larger creatures such as the crab, the pelican, and the shark. It becomes his responsibility to fight these injustices. Finally, while attempting to free a comrade, the little black fish dies at the hands of an oppressing heron. In short, the story produced a living legacy of a courageous nobody who took on the powers that be.

Like Antoine de Saint-Exupéry's *The Little Prince* and Lewis Carroll's *Alice in Wonderland,* Behrangi's *The Little Black Fish* was a folktale meant to be read by adults as well. The literary rearticulation of Mao's theory of how a guerrilla must be like a fish swimming in the ocean of the people was not lost on the receptive adult audience. Behrangi's imagina-tive use of allegory and metaphor proved successful as the book be-came the most popular "children's book" of the 1970s. Behrangi's "accidental" drowning in a river the same year the book was published baptized him both as a best-selling writer and a martyr. Furthermore, his close affiliation with the Tabriz branch of the Feda'iyan and, in particular, with his close friend, confidant, and coauthor, Behruz Dehq-ani (who was later tortured to death by the SAVAK for being a leading member of the Feda'iyan), helped to strengthen the bond between the underground activists and the legally functioning literati.

The significance of Behrangi's stories stems not so much from their aesthetic nature (they followed straightforward plots and employed a simple language) but lies in the folk style and rich symbolism with which they were narrated. Behrangi represented the best of what can be regarded as populist and partisan literature. He is to be credited with having turned the committed teacher into an antiestablishment activist. Behrangi set an example for many young and idealistic conscripts who went into the Sepah-e Danesh (Literacy Corps) hoping to improve the living conditions of the peasantry.[37]

Besides his children's stories, Behrangi wrote a number of critical monographs on the dismal state of education both in his native Azerbaijan and in the rest of Iran. He criticized the bureaucracy's increasing emphasis on academic pedigree as a type of "credentialism" or "diploma disease." Labeling many of Iran's educational policies as *Amrikazadeh* (imitative of the United States), Behrangi brought a tempestuous indictment against the government policymakers sitting in Tehran for implementing programs totally out of touch with the needs of rural Iran (Behrangi 1969). He even invented a fictitious character, Aqa-ye Chukh Bakhtiyar, (Mr. Prosperous) as the prototype of the middle-class government bureaucrat (Behrangi 1978, 290–94). Behrangi made a mockery of this character for his apolitical, submissive, and selfish behavior. His unrelenting satirical berating of Aqa-ye Chukh Bakhtiyar was a symbolic indictment of the value systems governing the new Iranian middle class. By using this fictitious character Behrangi once again proved the inherent wisdom of a Persian proverb that says epigrams succeed where epics fail.

Gholamhoseyn Saʿedi, a psychiatrist and Iran's foremost playwright, characterized the decade of the 1960s as the era when Iranian literature and literati blossomed (Saʿedi 1984). Echoing Saʿedi's sentiments, Mohammad-Ali Sepanlu, a leading literary critic, summarized the accomplishments of this era as follows: the consolidation of Persian new poetry; drastic improvements in the quantity and quality of novels and literary criticisms; the advent of a serious filmmaking industry; profound improvements in the composition and distribution of children's literature; publication of numerous short stories and poems; publication of a variety of original research on Iranian history, philosophy, and literature; and the appearance of Iran's most important plays by such talented dramatists as Bahram Beyzaʾi, Akbar Radi, Ali Nasiriyan, Mohsen Yalfani, and Saʿedi himself (Sepanlu 1988, 11). The plays were often

37. Formed in the early 1960s, Sepah-e Danesh was an imitation of the Cuban Literacy Corps entrusted with the task of eradicating illiteracy in the rural areas. It was made up of recent high school and, later, university graduates (men and women) who, instead of serving in the regular army, were sent to the countryside. They were assigned such responsibilities as educating rural children and adults and helping with welfare enterprises such as building roads, public baths, infirmaries, and a host of other sanitary projects. Thus, for the young antiestablishment Iranian intellectuals who historically were urban based and without access to mass media such as radio and television, becoming a teacher or serving in the Sepah-e Danesh became a suitable vehicle for reaching out to the peasantry. It is estimated that more than 150,000 people served in the literacy corps.

adapted by equally talented New Wave film directors such as Mas'ud Kimiya'i, Daryush Mehrju'i, Sohrab Shahid-Sales, and Naser Taqva'i. Considering the great popular potential of film, this joint venture between the writers and the directors proved most beneficial to both parties. Writers' works were now reaching an unprecedented number of people while the caliber of film scripts was dramatically improving.[38] Similarly, great strides were being made in painting, translation, and publishing.

While benefiting from these strides, however, the engagé literati had ample cause for discontent. Despite the infusion of oil wealth, these artists and poets, like the rest of the dissident intellectuals, viewed themselves as politically defeated. In the aftermath of the 1953 coup d'état, many poets affiliated with the National Front or the left translated this defeat into poetry. Akhavan-Sales's poem entitled *Zemestan* (Winter) epitomized the literary community's dejected mood.

> They don't want to answer your greetings.
> The weather, depressing; doors, closed;
> heads, in collars; hands, hidden;
> breaths, clouds; hearts, tired and sad;
> trees, crystal-embroidered skeletons;
> the earth, lifeless; the roof of the sky, low;
> dusty the sun; dusty the moon;
> it is winter. (Akhavan-Sales 1976, 133–34)

Yet at the same time the poets experimented with a new style and a new semiology. Implicit within the masterpieces of the new poetry genre was an allegorical style fully supported by the fertile mythological symbolism of Persian language and literature. Fredric Jameson has asserted: "'Third-world' texts, even those which are seemingly private and invested with a properly libidinal dynamic—necessarily project a political dimension in the form of national allegory: the story of the private individual destiny is always an allegory of the embattled situation of the public third-world culture and society" (Jameson 1986, 69). Despite his unjustified generalization about the nature of Third World literature as a whole, Jameson's point about the allegorical nature of many of these texts is well taken. Much of this can be attributed to political censorship and strangulation and to the illiteracy of a general public in need of mythical-symbolic characters to whom they could relate. Studying the fiction, poetry, and other works of many Iranian literati in the 1960s and 1970s, one is struck by the amount of symbolism, allegory, meta-

38. For an analysis of some of these films see Fischer 1984.

phors, and allusions used to avoid the institution of censorship.[39] One Iranian literary critic summarizes the censorship/symbolism mechanism:

A life of concealment develops progressively in the misty atmosphere where all channels of communication are rigidly held in control. Ingenious forms of protection and secrecy are devised as substitutes for ordinary privileges of privacy. Walls surround houses. Veils cover women. Religious *taqiyeh* [deliberate dissimulation] protects faith. *Ta'arof* [ritualistic modes of discourse] disguise real thoughts and emotions. Houses become compartmentalized with their *daruni* [inner] and *biruni* [outer] areas. Feelings become disjointed in *zaheri* [external] and *bateni* [internal] spheres. Abstractions imprison concreteness. Slogans suffocate dialogues. Overworked generalities replace the specific. (Milani 1985, 327)

The most recurring themes and symbols in the literature of this era deal with subjects such as corruption, darkness, fear, hypocrisy, loneliness, nothingness, solitude, and walls. The terms expressed the haughtiness of the upper class, the superficiality of the middle class, the hopelessness of village life, and the alienation of the urban poor. It was in such an atmosphere that Kanun-e Nevisandegan-e Iran (Writers' Association of Iran) was founded in April 1968. The association was formed in response to a Congress of Iranian Writers and Poets that the government was planning to organize in February 1968. Faced with the objection of the engagé writers, the government abandoned the idea of the congress. Celebrating their small victory, the writers decided to form a writers' association to represent their cause and to take on the government collectively. Discussions among members of the association centered around such themes as the meaning of freedom, the social stance of the writer, and the necessity of a committed literature. As a result, however, of the untimely death of Jalal Al-e Ahmad (the major figure behind the association) and internal factionalism and disagreements among its members, the association disintegrated after March 1970. Despite this brief period of activity the Writers' Association served to sharpen criticism voiced against the government.

Almost one year later the rise of armed struggle waged by the Feda'iyan threw its shadow over Iranian intellectual and literary communities. The Siyahkal episode helped implant a whole new set of themes

39. Two principal censorship agencies were SAVAK and the Composition Bureau of the Ministry of Culture and Art. The magnitude of censorship could be gauged by the frequency with which such literary periodicals as *Ferdowsi, Jahan-e Now, Negin, Omid-e Iran, Sepid va Siyah,* and *Towfiq* were censored or closed. At the same time, however, such periodicals as *Sokhan* and *Yaghma,* representing the literary establishment, were left free to operate.

into the literature of this era. Renunciation, resistance, revolution, sacrifice, prison, and heroism entered the depository of subjects from which artists, poets, and writers could draw. Guns, forests, and roses dominated the symbolism of the new spirit.[40] The populist themes championed by the guerrillas soon spilled over into the literary community as more and more poets and writers rushed to support the new activist visionaries.[41] To counter the guerrilla attack, however, the government responded to this literary campaign of "sabotage" with an equally heavy hand. During the period between 1971 and 1975 writers witnessed the peak of censorship, horror, and intellectual suffocation when many engagé literati were imprisoned,[42] blacklisted, or denied permission to write or publish.[43]

Faced with various factors such as the stalemate reached with the urban guerrillas, President Jimmy Carter's arrival at the White House in 1976, the launching of his ambitious human rights campaign, and the greater success of Iranian student organizations abroad in exerting public pressure against the government for its treatment of political prisoners, the government relaxed some of its rules of engagement. The Iranian writers and poets took advantage of this gesture by once again reviving the Writers' Association. Their first plan of action was to organize ten nights of public poetry reading by well-known writers and poets. These readings were held in the Irano-German Cultural Society (also known as the Goethe Institute) in Tehran 10–19 October 1977 (see Mo'azzen 1978). For the first time almost sixty prominent poets and writers recited their poetry and other works to thousands of enthusiastic listeners composed mainly of urban and university-educated youths. Emerging from years of censorship, the speakers used the occasion effectively to voice their opposition to the regime from different ideological positions. Some, such as Sa'id Soltanpur, who had just recently been released from prison, exalted his Feda'i comrades while

---

40. Guns and forests denoted the means and the place, respectively, where armed resistance was first inaugurated; the red rose symbolized blood and the memory of Khosrow Golsorkhi, whose last name meant "the red rose."

41. Examples of this group include Yadollah (Maftun) Amini, Reza Baraheni, Esma'il Kho'i, Ne'mat Mirzazadeh, Mohammad-Ali Sepanlu, Ahmad Shamlu, Sa'id Soltanpur, and Gholamhoseyn Sa'edi.

42. These included Mahmud E'temadzadeh (Behazin), Manuchehr Hezarkhani, Ne'mat Mirzazadeh, Mohammad-Ali Sepanlu, Sa'id Soltanpur, and Fereydun Tonokaboni. E'temadzadeh provides a firsthand account of his imprisonment by the security forces in his sarcastically entitled book (1970).

43. Karimi-Hakkak (1985, 204) charges that "according to official statistics, the number of volumes published and marketed annually in Iran dropped from over 4,000 in 1969 to about 700 in 1976."

others invoked more religious terminology and metaphors.[44] The poetry reading nights also indicated the extent to which government and the opposition were able to restrain themselves in a charged atmosphere.

These ten nights are crucial in modern Iranian intellectual history. They provided closer relations between the artists and their audiences, and they helped raise the political consciousness of the young university and high school students. In addition, the writers attending these events were able to maintain a sense of political pluralism among themselves, irrespective of their contrasting ideological convictions. The poetry nights also made it possible for the opposition to experiment with a more peaceful mode of resistance to the government. Because of these factors, the poetry reading nights are considered a prelude to the waves of protest that engulfed Iranian cities only a few months later. The militants and the literati had contributed their share to undermining the rentier state.

44. For two firsthand accounts of the delicate behind-the-scenes politics leading to these poetry reading nights see Parham 1989; Pakdaman 1995.

3

The Other-ing of the West

The Monster—in innocent womanhood—
Standing upon a hill of dollars
                    . . .
In her hand, a torch burning bright
The Monster—in holy aura—
Carrying high the awesome torch
Laying bare
The depths of the "Bolivian" jungle
While
With other hand unfurled
Plunges a dagger into "Che Guevara"'s heart
And, in the darkness of "Congo" forests
Crushes the spirit of "Lumumba."
Standing upon a hill of dollars
Carrying high the awesome torch
With which to stoke the war in "Vietnam"
                    . . .
O Monster! O Holy Gangster!
O Torch!
                    O Lighthouse for pirates!
With the East Wind
                    I shall
                        At last
                            Overtake you-!
—Neʿmat Mirzazadeh, "Statue of Liberty"

ANALOGOUS TO THEIR SENSE of other-ness vis-à-vis the state, the secular Iranian intellectuals of the 1950s, 1960s, and 1970s faced a second type of other-ness vis-à-vis the West. Whereas the first other-ing act was more immediate, concrete, dangerous, and well defined, the second was more distant, abstract, safe, and vague. The adversary was not an armed, repressive, limited entity called the state but a more remote and undefined totality designated as the "West" or the "Occident."[1] These two types of other-ness in relation to the state and the West became inextricably bound as secular intellectuals came to perceive the Iranian regime as an extension of a larger entity called the West.

One discussion that came to the forefront of Iranian intellectual life in this time span made the most significant contribution to the social construction of the West as an "other." The first discussion, which began soon after the end of World War II, was rekindled in 1962 with the publication of a polemical monograph by Jalal Al-e Ahmad entitled *Gharbzadegi* (Westoxication)(Al-e Ahmad 1962). This work gave birth to a discourse of the same name which in my view was the modern Iranian articulation of nativism.[2] To trace the epistemological, historical, and political genesis of *gharbzadegi,* in this chapter, I concentrate on the works of three leading post–World War II Iranian intellectuals: Seyyed Fakhroddin Shadman, Ahmad Fardid, and Jalal Al-e Ahmad. The selection of these intellectuals, as explained in the prologue, was not based on their popularity but on the following criteria: they articulated some of the most philosophically consequential ideas on the discourses of gharbzadegi, orientalism, and occidentalism; they represented different views and political affiliations; and they exemplified the predominant response of Iranian intellectuals during the 1950s, 1960s, and 1970s to the problem of encounter with the West. Seyyed Fakhroddin Shadman was one of the earliest Iranian statesmen and thinkers to detect the rise of an intellectual enigma with respect to the West. Ahmad Fardid was a philosopher who had considerable influence on many Iranian intellectuals from the 1950s onward. Jalal Al-e Ahmad was Iran's most eminent antiestablishment intellectual and social critic of the 1950s and 1960s.

1. Throughout this book I use the two dichotomies of East/West and Orient/Occident interchangeably to remain loyal to the literal translations and the tone of the works cited. The East/West dichotomy refers not to the cold war political division of the world but to a geographical division of the globe. The East, or Orient, encompasses all of the Middle and Near East, Asia, Far East, and North Africa, whereas the West, or Occident, refers mainly to Western Europe and North America. As noted later, however, the term *West* was misused by a number of Iranian intellectuals. Although it represents a geographical entity for some, others hold a more symbolic or mystical view of it, regarding it as a way of life or as a set of ontological doctrines.

2. Throughout this book, to differentiate the two concepts, I have used the upper case *Gharbzadegi* to refer to the title of Al-e Ahmad's monograph and the lower case *gharbzadegi* to refer to the broader discourse under investigation.

Seyyed Fakhroddin Shadman: The Forgotten Historian

The trajectory of the gharbzadegi metadiscourse in the post–World War II era was guided considerably by Seyyed Fakhroddin Shadman (1907–1967). He was born into a clerical family in Tehran. As was customary, he was trained in the traditional curriculum where he learned the principles of Arabic and Persian language and literature, jurisprudence, and logic. He then attended a number of modern schools, including Darolfonun, Darolmoʿallemin-e Markazi, and Madreseh-ye Ali-ye Hoquq from which he earned his Bachelor of Arts in 1927.[3] During 1927–28, while teaching at Darolmoʿallemin-e Markazi, he also served as the editor of the weekly literary journal *Tufan-e Haftegi,* which was set up by the socialist-minded poet Mohammad Farrokhi-Yazdi.[4]

Shadman was recruited by Reza Shah's minister of justice, Ali-Akbar Davar, into the newly formed Ministry of Justice. Davar, who can be rightfully considered the founder of the modern Iranian judicial system, appointed Shadman as Tehran's deputy public prosecutor. One of Shadman's early accomplishments in this post was his successful prosecution of a German adviser to the Iranian National Bank who was charged with financial fraud. Meanwhile, he translated parts of Albert Malet and Jules Isaac, *Siècle histoire moderne,* from French into Persian. With his enhanced reputation Shadman was dispatched to London as an oil commissioner to represent Iranian interests in the Anglo-Iranian Oil Company. This assignment lasted fourteen years, the last five years of which coincided with World War II. During this time Shadman obtained a doctorate in law from the Sorbonne (1935) and a second doctorate in history from the London School of Economics and Political Science (1939). After spending some time at Harvard and teaching at the University of London for a while, Shadman returned to Iran where he held

3. Darolfonun, a polytechnic institute, was built in 1851 in Tehran under the initiative of Mirza Taqi Khan Amir-Kabir, a capable, reform-minded prime minister of the Qajar era. Staffed by European and, later, Iranian teachers, this high school was considered to be the best of its kind in Iran; students were taught in such disciplines as natural sciences, engineering, medicine, mathematics, foreign languages, music, and military techniques (artillery, infantry, and cavalry). Darolmoʿallemin-e Markazi (Central Teachers' Training College) was established in Tehran in 1919 to train elementary and secondary school teachers. In 1928 it merged with Darolmoʿallemin-e Ali and formed a single school, which in 1934 was renamed as Daneshsara-ye Ali-ye Tehran (Tehran's Higher Teachers' Training College). Madreseh-ye Ali-ye Hoquq (Faculty of Law) was a free-standing school within the Ministry of Justice that was established in Tehran in 1920–21.

4. Two other notable contributors to this journal were the poet laureate Mohammad-Taqi Bahar and Ahmad Kasravi.

a variety of important appointments. His portfolio included positions as director of the Iran Insurance Company, vice-delegate of the Iranian government to the Anglo-Iranian Oil Company, minister of agriculture, head of the Plan and Budget Organization's Supreme Council, minister of finance, minister of justice, and the vice-gerent of Imam Reza Shrine Properties in Khorasan. Shadman also served as a member of the Farhangestan (Iranian Academy), Showra-ye Farhangi-ye Saltanati (Cultural Council of the Imperial Court of Iran), Showra-ye Ali-ye Farhang, a trustee of the Pahlavi Library, and director of the United States Point Four aid program in Iran (1954). He was instrumental in the envisioning and founding of Abadan's Oil College, which provided Iran with the corps of professional technicians and managers needed to operate its oil industry. Finally, Shadman also held an appointment as a professor of history at Tehran University from 1950 to 1967 where he taught such courses as methodology in history, philosophy of history, and the evolution of Islamic civilization.

In 1948, equipped with both his traditional and modern training, Shadman published his most important work entitled *Taskhir-e tamaddon-e farangi* (The conquest of Western civilization). Reflecting on the nature of the challenges facing Iranian society, Shadman put forward the following argument. In order for Iran not to be taken over by Western civilization and made into a powerless captive, it should attempt to appropriate that civilization willingly and thoughtfully. The only means to do that, however, is through the use of the Persian language, which he regarded as the common denominator of all Iranians and the embodiment of the ageless wisdom of the ancestors.

Shadman was convinced that "the victory of the Western civilization in Iran would be our last defeat" (Shadman 1948, 23). As an historian, he was well aware that the Western intrusion into Iran during the Qajar era (1785–1925) had been most detrimental. He believed that the two devastating defeats at the hands of Russia in 1813 and 1828 put an end to Iranians' independence of thought and self-esteem (Shadman 1964, 704). Earlier, in his doctoral dissertation, he had written:

But never before had Iran found herself so much in connection with Europeans as at the beginning of the nineteenth century. Within a few years the Iranians were obliged to learn new methods in dealing with Europeans, to speak the same political language which was entirely new to them and master to the best of their ability the intricacies of a novel life that their relations with foreigners had forced upon them. Within a short time they had to contend with the overtures, the presents, the bribes, the friendliness and the threats of the British, the fears and the promises of the French and the overwhelming force of the Russians. They paid dearly for their ignorance, weakness and for relying at times almost too sincerely upon foreign support and counsel. (Shadman 1939b, 9–10)[5]

Shadman viewed Russia and Japan as two countries that were deliberately able to appropriate Western civilization and succeeded in that task while countries such as Algeria, which were "taken over" at the time by Western civilization, became destitute. He maintained that, in the face of the Western intrusions into Iranian culture, Iran was going to experience a fate similar to Algeria's unless it absorbed Western civilization confidently and reflectively. In a metaphorical language in tune with the militaristic spirit of the 1940s he wrote: "We can compare Western civilization to an army made up of one hundred million soldiers. Every valuable book that we bring to Iran, every accurate translation that we give to our countrymen, and every blueprint of a factory, a building, a machine . . . that we gather in Iran is as if we have captured one soldier of this huge army and made him into our own servant" (Shadman 1948, 75).

In *Taskhir-e tamaddon-e farangi* Shadman criticized the views of two groups of his compatriots in the face of the political and ideological permeation of the West. By depicting two fictitious characters, Sheykh Vahab Ruf'ay and Hushang Hanavid, respectively representing the traditionalist clerics and the Western-educated pseudomodernist intellectuals infatuated with the West, Shadman attempted to indict both groups. In choosing these names Shadman engaged in a bit of word play. Reading it in reverse order, Hanavid becomes *divanah,* or insane. Similarly, Sheykh Ruf'ay becomes Sheykh "Ya'fur," a term used by theology students to refer to a blockhead. He criticized Ruf'ay and his lot for their ignorance of the modern world, their opposition to the accomplishments of Western countries, and their nostalgia for the tranquillity of a bygone era. Shadman, however, saved his most severe criticism for the members of the second group and their prototype, Hushang Hanavid.

5. Shadman was not the only Iranian intellectual in the 1930s who had shown an interest in investigating his country's relations with the outside world in a scholarly fashion. At least four other intellectuals of his generation wrote their doctoral dissertations on similar subjects. See Ahmad Matin-Daftari, "La suppression des capitulations en Perse: L'Ancien Régime et le statut des étrangers dans l'empire du 'Lion et Soleil'" (1930); Ali-Akbar Siassi [Siyasi], "La Perse au contact de l'Occident (étude historique et sociale)" (1931); Khanbaba Bayani, "Les Relations de l'Iran avec l'Europe Occidentale a l'epoque Safavide (Portugal, Espagne, Angleterre, Hollande et France)" (1937); and Mohsen Azizi, "La domination arabe et l'épanouissement du sentiment national en Iran, étude politique et sociale sur l'Iran musulman, 650–900" (1938).

He labeled these individuals with the pejorative term *fokoli*.[6] Shadman's enmity toward the *fokoli*, whom he regarded as Iran's most treacherous enemies, emanated from their advocation of full or partial imitation of the *farangi* ways of life.[7] The fokoli nemesis of Shadman fell into three clusters: the group of literati figures working with *Farhangestan*,[8] pseudointellectuals who had recently returned from abroad, and advocates of the new style of Persian poetry.

His criticism of the first group concerned their flirtation with the idea, originating in next-door Turkey, of conversion to the Latin alphabet and their spurious coining of supposedly "pure" Persian terms. Speaking of this group, he wrote: "*Fokoli* is an ignorant or an ill-intentioned Iranian who thinks that if the Persian alphabet is replaced by a Latin one, all Iranians will suddenly be able to read and write." The second group was castigated for their Faustian bargain, which involved sacrificing their national religious roots and customs to become superficially Westernized. As a nationalist with a religious upbringing, Shadman declared that a "fokoli is an unaware Iranian who does not understand that the Western missionaries' castigation of Islam as the root cause of Iran's misfortune stems from their malevolence, egocentrism, and prejudice emanating from their Christian belief in belittling the religions of others. They are the enemies of our religion and not the

6. *Fokoli*, which comes from the French term *faux-col*, meaning one who wears a necktie or a bow tie, was often used in a pejorative sense by the clergy and the common people to describe Western-educated Iranians wearing European dress. Other terms synonymous to "*fokoli*" that were used were *farangi ma'ab*, (one who imitates the demeanor of Westerners), *qerti* (effete), and *zhigol* (gigolo).

7. The term *Farang* is not clearly defined in Persian parlance. Originally, it referred to the French people, but it soon acquired a more generic definition, referring to Western Europe or the West (Occident) in general. Accordingly, *farangi* has come to delineate a Westerner or things Western. More often than not, speakers or writers do not bother to define what they mean by these terms. Recognizing this issue, Shadman addresses himself to this definitional problem. He uses the term *Farang* to designate all countries that have an entirely or majority Christian population that are descendants of a European race, speak one of the European languages, and have reached the highest stages of civilization. As such, Shadman considers Europe, Australia, and North America as part of *Farang* but not Haiti whose population is Christian and speaks French (Shadman 1967, 167).

8. Inspired by the L'Institute de France (French Academy), the Farhangestan (Iranian Academy) was founded in 1935 on the orders of Reza Shah. Composed of some forty literary figures, its task was to standardize and enrich the Persian language by coining words and by encouraging the literary community to be productive. It soon, however, developed a mandate to combat the contamination of Persian language by "purifying" it from "foreign" (primarily Arabic) influence. The Allies' occupation of Iran and Reza Shah's abdication in 1941 put a temporary end to the academy's existence. A second Farhangestan was established in 1970.

friends of our country" (Shadman 1948, 14). Shadman reminds his readers that a country such as Portugal, which is European, Christian, and has a Latin alphabet, has not made much progress and is a few centuries behind a country such as Sweden. As such, he forcefully opposed those who saw the causes of Iranian's backwardness to be in their religious beliefs by declaring that "Islam cannot be contradictory to science. The heyday of Islamic civilization, and the thousands of scientists, writers and philosophers who have dealt with the most subtle questions while under the inspiration of Islam, prove that this religion can live with science" (Shadman 1939a, 72). Finally, the advocates of the new style of poetry were reprimanded for abandoning the rhythmic and intricate classical poetry of Persia for a nonconventional, enigmatic poetry imitative of Western styles. Shadman considered classical Persian poetry to be "the best of its kind in the world" and as such did not have much appreciation for the new "shallow" poetry (with its broken rhyme and free verse style) that was becoming fashionable.

Shadman was convinced that the superiority of the West resided in its scientific outlook and not necessarily in the force of its moral convictions. Hence, he contended that although Iran needed to send students to the West to acquire the latter's technical knowledge and to translate scientific textbooks, they did not necessarily have to embrace its ethical standards or ways of thinking. In his lengthy novel, *Tariki va rowshanai* (Darkness and light), Shadman further elaborated on what he had previously put forward in *Taskhir-e tamaddon-e farangi*. This metaphorically named ("darkness" signifying ignorance and "light" signifying knowledge) and moralistically written novel revolves around a certain Mahmud Sirvand, a young, well-educated Iranian patriot, who in many ways resembles Shadman himself. Mahmud, who has an inquisitive mind, studies philosophy in France and England, travels throughout Europe, and with the help of a number of like-minded intellectuals becomes Iran's leading expert in *farangshenasi*, or occidentalism.

> The vastness of the precise science of farangshenasi was revealed to me in England when I first realized how difficult a task it was. But inquiry into the conditions of other nations, particularly farangi ones, is so beneficial that it is worth the trouble. I believe this subject is so important that it must be taught in all Iranian schools. . . . The task of a *farangshenas* has at least ten times more importance, variety, and hardship than that of an Orientalist. It is a pity that in all of Iran there are not even ten farangshenas [while] for us to get acquainted with farangi civilization, we need thousands of enlightened, Persian speaking Iranians who are [both] *Iranshenas* and farangshenas. (Shadman 1965, 620–21)

Only a few individuals met Shadman's qualifications. He himself names such scholars as Mohammad-Ali Forughi, Qasem Ghani, Ali-Asghar Hekmat, and Isa Sadiq (Shadman 1937, 172–73; Shadman 1948, 9). His choice of these intellectuals is revealing. Forughi, an erudite, intellectual statesman, served as Iran's prime minister on a number of occasions, wrote a book entitled *Sayr-e hekmat dar Orupa* (A history of European philosophy), which in the Iran of the 1930s, 1940s, and 1950s was considered to be the most authoritative account of its subject matter. Ghani, a medical doctor, Majles deputy, minister, and ambassador translated three of Anatole France's books into Persian.[9] Hekmat, a French-educated scholar, ambassador, and university chancellor, who also served in such capacities as minister of culture, interior, health, justice, and foreign affairs, symbolized a most learned politician. Finally, Shadman mentions Isa Sadiq, Iran's foremost expert in educational policy who was trained in Iran, France, England, and the United States and later served as a professor, university chancellor, senator, and minister.[10] These four men of letters and politics were a far cry from the fokoli-type "returnees" from Europe whom Shadman had lambasted for their obliviousness and frivolousness: "*Fokoli* is an indecent and narrow-minded Iranian who thinks Western civilization amounts merely to dancing cheek to cheek, gambling, and going to smoke-filled pubs, yet is oblivious to the fact that the foundation of Western civilization is actually based on reading, deliberation, and argumentation" (Shadman 1948, 18).

Shadman further expanded on the theme of farangshenasi in a multipart article that was published posthumously. He argued that the Iranian intelligentsia needed to undertake a massive effort to explore the character, culture, and psychological mind-set of other nations. This was to be carried out in an interdisciplinary manner by relying on the scientific findings of anthropology, ethnography, ecology, geopolitics, demography, linguistics, and literature. Shadman considered this "new science" to be of utmost importance for Iranians because by examining other nations they would come to know themselves better (Shadman 1968).

Shadman, who had stayed in England throughout World War II, considered this most devastating war in human history to be the last chapter of Europe's glorious history. His high esteem for Europe, manifested in the following quotation, had now given way to skepticism:

Oh Europe, what meanings are embedded within your name! Europe as the incarnation of ancient Greece and its wisdom, ancient Rome and its

9. For more on Forughi and Ghani, see Varedi 1992, and Ghani 1983.
10. Absent from his list are Ali-Akbar Dehkhoda and Hoseyn Kazemzadeh-Iranshahr.

magnificence, France and its intellectual stocks, Italy and its innovative art, Switzerland and its government. Hearing the name Europe, one is reminded of Greek philosophy, British poetry, German music. . . . Europe equals the accumulating and self-correcting science from Aristotle to Planck, splendid poetry from Homer to Hugo, and rationalist philosophy from Plato to Russell. Its discoveries and inventions are beyond measurement. . . . The vast Americas is one of its discoveries and powerful electricity its other accomplishment. The telescope is one of its inventions and an airplane traveling faster than the speed of sound its other. (Shadman 1967, 112)

He considered democracy to be Europe's most significant discovery and regarded the mechanisms designed to guarantee its protection to be Europe's greatest invention. Nonetheless, as a conscientious Third World intellectual familiar with the agonies of colonialism, Shadman continued to object to European hypocrisy and dishonesty.[11] He saw Europe's greatest vice, alas, to be its denial of freedom to non-Europeans at the same time that it was continuously boasting about the virtues of freedom and democracy (Shadman 1967, 113). Shadman was not impressed by the rising prestige of the United States of America either.

America is a huge country, it is affluent and powerful. Yet it is young and inexperienced. Who is their greatest poet? Who is their grand philosopher? What is the name of its most famous artist? America has still not passed the most difficult examination which every nation has to face. Throughout its history there is not a single defeat and as such one should be cautious and hesitant before speaking of its spiritual grandeur. Is not defeat the touchstone of the greatness of nations? How else besides disaster and defeat can the world test individuals and nations? (Shadman 1965, 340)

Shadman vociferously reprimanded his own compatriots for constantly looking up to the deceptive West while remaining totally ignorant of the geography, history, science, literature, and arts of such Eastern countries as India, Russia, and China. Furthermore, he criticized the Western-inspired political and intellectual elites of Iran for their total neglect of the religious seminaries, which he regarded as the forerunners of Iran's oldest universities. Shadman reminded his secularist colleagues of the scholastic merits of such theological centers as Qom, Esfahan, Qazvin, Mashhad, Shiraz, Kashan, and Yazd from which many lyricists, physicians, astronomers, teachers, translators, and

11. In a short novel set in the time of the Safavid Empire, Shadman provides an account of the British deceitful policies in Persia and India. See Shadman 1956.

scientists had emerged. He concluded by saying that the gap between the universities and the religious centers should be bridged (Shadman 1967, 71–76). Once again making a mockery of the fokoli, the ╷ ╷udo-intellectual by-products of this new educational system, he sarcastically declared:

> Since becoming a *fokoli* does not require much [intellectual] capital, who-ever reads a few chapters of an economics book by Charles Gide or [Alfred] Marshall becomes an economic expert; whoever tightens up the screws on his aunt's sewing machine becomes an engineer; whoever writes the account of his cousin's wedding in poor Persian becomes a creative writer; whoever writes or talks about politics, party, Metternich, Lord Curzon, and Bolsheviks and Mensheviks becomes an expert on politics. So much so, that compared to our overall population we have more economists than the United States, and more political experts and commentators than England. (Shadman 1948, 41)

In retrospect one can see that Shadman was an intellectual heir to a movement that began around the turn of the twentieth century and considered language the wellhead of national identity. For Shadman and for numerous other members of his generation language was the com-mon denominator of all Iranians and the embodiment of the ageless wisdom of the ancestors. As such, they considered its preservation as their quintessential task. A number of objections, however, can be raised against Shadman's axiomatic suggestion that safeguarding the Per-sian language is the most effective weapon possessed by Iranians against the encroaching civilization of the West. It goes without saying that language is vital in the sense that it forms the most important non-material link among members of a community. Language, after all, is the medium in which cultural symbols are created and articulated, and it contains the elements of a concept of the world and of a culture. Al-though it is justified to claim that language expedites communication, it is neither warranted to claim that language necessarily facilitates social homogenization nor is it justified to assert that a versatile language is a sign of "proper" thinking on the part of the linguistic community that shares it. Languages are far too contested symbolically, discursively, and competence-wise (in the abilities of speakers and listeners) to allow for the interminable reign of metanarratives, master codes, and homoge-nous worldviews. Language is a crucial but certainly not the only means to shape a nation. Furthermore, language cannot be considered as the vehicle or foundation of a nation's thoughts insofar as it does not take into consideration such factors as acculturation, relations of power, lim-inality, and exclusion of certain traditions and narratives. Here one does well to remember Thomas Hobbes's dictum that whereas "mathematics unites men, politics divides them."

Shadman's fixation on language suggests that he had not discerned the multidimensional and fundamental nature of the challenge of modernity. He was at a loss to explain the case of all those nations that vehemently safeguarded their languages yet fell prey to the onslaught of Westernization and modernity (the Japanese, the Arabs). Shadman's preoccupation with rebuffing the ideas of those of his radical contemporaries who were calling for the purification of the Persian language and those who were advocating a change of script seems to have prevented him from paying any attention to the culture of modernity as a whole.[12] Shadman did not adopt a holistic view of language, one that would have allowed him to look at language as an object and to look at its questions as problematics. Finally, Shadman's employment of a wide range of military metaphors such as *weapon, capture, escape route, surrender, resistance, cultural invasion, collaborating with the enemy,* and *the fifth column* to depict the process of cultural encounter between different civilizations was rather simplistic. His bookish view of culture, militaristic imagery, crusading righteousness, and polemical discourse seem rather inadequate if not outright erroneous.

Despite these shortcomings Shadman must be remembered as perhaps the first Iranian intellectual to propose a systematic study of the West under the rubric of farangshenasi. This proposition had its root in his deep conviction regarding the exigency of cultural independence. He was a man quite familiar with Western intellectual traditions, yet more at home with his own cultural heritage. Shadman stood in the center of the labyrinth that lies between two generations of Iranian intellectuals who held different views regarding the West. He provides the missing link between the earlier staunch supporters of the West and its later arch-critics. His views on the West were both devoid of the overall enchantment of earlier generations and the antagonistic radicalism that beset their successors. Shadman's criticism of the West, the Western-oriented pseudomodernists, and the traditional sectors of his own society represented an important turn by Iranian intellectuals toward a more homegrown version of modernity. It is fair to say that this moralist statesman was the harbinger of the discourse of gharbzadegi. The nearly unanimous omission of Shadman from any evaluation of the historical evolution of this discourse is attributable to his high-profile positions in various government posts before and after the 1953 coup, which com-

---

12. For a rather upbeat assessment of Shadman's contribution see Milani 1995.

pelled antiestablishment intellectuals to overlook his contributions.[13] To grow out of its infancy, however, this discourse needed to obtain a philosophical foundation. It was to be provided by one of Shadman's contemporaries, Ahmad Fardid.

Ahmad Fardid: The Oral Philosopher

Leon Trotsky's famous dictum, "publish or perish," always popular among academics, does not seem to apply to Ahmad Fardid, one of Iran's least known yet most influential contemporary philosophers. Fardid (1912–1994) was born into a relatively well-to-do agriculturist family in Yazd. Like Shadman, he first went through the traditional Iranian educational curriculum and then the modern academic training of Germany and France.[14] After graduating from the Daneshsara-ye Ali-ye Tehran, he taught at that school as well as at various local high schools. In the 1940s and 1950s Fardid was a member of the intellectual circle formed around Sadeq Hedayat and was active in the research branch of the Iran Teachers' Association. In the late 1960s he was appointed professor of philosophy at Tehran University where he taught such courses as history of modern philosophy (from Bacon to Kant), history of modern and contemporary philosophy (from Kant to the present), philosophical anthropology, and philosophies of existence. Fardid gradually formed a scholarly circle made up of some of the country's leading intellectuals, philosophers, translators, and social thinkers. Among these were Daryush Ashuri, Najaf Daryabandari, Reza Davari, Amir-Hoseyn Jahanbeglu, Abolhasan Jalili, Shahrokh Meskub, and Daryush Shayegan. This group, which became known as the Fardid Circle, used to deliberate on oriental and occidental philosophical questions.

Fardid is generally regarded as a brilliant yet unsystematic thinker who introduced Iranian intellectuals to German philosophy.[15] Since the 1950s he served as Iran's leading authority on the philosophy of Martin Heidegger. Influenced by Heidegger and the German historicist tradition, Fardid gave the Orient/Occident dichotomy a philosophical twist.

13. Interestingly enough, however, Shadman was introduced to the European audience as early as 1956 by Basile Nikitine (1956).

14. Fardid was, for a while, a disciple of the Shiʿite modernist cleric, Mirza Reza-Qoli Shariʿat-Sangalaji, who is mentioned in chapters 4 and 5.

15. His published works are extremely sparse. He helped to translate Henry Corbin's essay, *Les Motifs Zoroastriens dans la philosophie de Sohrawardi* (1946), contributed to Yahya Mahdavi's translation of Albert Felice's *Cours de metaphysique,* which appeared as *Falsafeh-ye Omumi va Mabaʾdottabiʿeh* in 1968, and helped Ehsan Naraqi with his book on the genesis of the social sciences (1969).

Rejecting the political, economic, and geographical definitions of this binarism, he used a philosophical language rooted in strong symbolism to designate the two competing *Weltanschauungen*. Employing Heidegger's premise that during each historical era a truth arises that obscures competing truths, Fardid maintained that the historical destiny of the contemporary world is the destiny of the Occident. He declared,

> In my view, the present age throughout the world is the age of civilizational traditions and not cultural memoirs. All Islamic countries and indeed all oriental nations, without exception, are situated in a phase of history in which, contrary to their Western counterparts, they can no longer be in possession of their own historical trust. This is due to the fact that since the eighteenth century, Western culture has metamorphosed into *the* [my emphasis] historical tradition or civilization. (Fardid 1974, 19)

Fardid contends that with the advent of Greek philosophy the moon of reality has risen while the sun of truth has gone into an eclipse (Fardid 1971, 33). Since then, he maintains, the Orient, representing the essence of the holy books and divine revelation, has been concealed under a variety of occidental mantles. Conceiving of history of philosophy as a centrifugal motion away from the essential Truth, Fardid envisions the ontological circuits of oriental and occidental philosophy in such a way that the authentic ecclesiastical thought of the Orient has engendered Greek cosmologism and cosmocentrism, which later brought the theologism and theocentrism of the Middle Ages, and finally led to the anthropologism and anthropocentrism of the Modern Age. Fardid charges that during each of these eras the primary subject of contemplation went through a metamorphosis. While the Orient was contemplating the "true and spiritual essence," Greek philosophy was preoccupied with the "world," the Middle Ages with the metaphysical "God," and finally, modern humanity with the individual "self" (Fardid 1974, 34). Fardid's criticism of the Middle Ages concerns the fact that, although the subject of contemplation changed once again from the world to God, this "God" is still understood based on Greek cosmological and metaphysical thought and not on "true" religious thought. For Fardid, then, the West's inception occurs with Greek philosophy and its growth with Renaissance humanism. He viewed this humanism as the historical destiny of the Modern Age. By treating human nature or dignity as its central subject, Renaissance humanism managed to make the *Homo sapiens* the focus of ethics and politics, to say nothing of the arts and historiography. This evolution, Fardid claims, has given rise to a technological, all-encompassing ethos that has deprived modern humans of morality. Thus, according to his ontological couplet, the Orient is the kingdom of benevolence and compassion while the Occident is the terrain of domination. Persuaded by Heidegger's views on the spirit of historical eras, the philosophy of being, and the imprisoning nature of modern technology, Fardid speaks of gharbzadegi as the interlude between the self and the being. According to him, such humanistically oriented philosophical schools of thought as existentialism or nihilism do not provide a means of escape from the present crisis that is besieging humanity.

Fardid advocates a type of *Geisteswissenschaften,* or a moral philosophy not bereft of theosophical introspection. He argues that humans have three dimensions: scientific, philosophical, and ethical. Although the first two have been prominent in the Western tradition of thought, the last has been conspicuously absent.[16] As such, Fardid reaches the conclusion that *Gharb* (the West) has to be abandoned both as an ontology and as a way of life. He believes that gharbzadegi is, thus, a transitional phase that one has to leave behind to reach to the essence of the West. To undertake this intellectual odyssey, however, one has to become Westernized, not in the sense of becoming alienated from one's own self but in the more subtle sense of becoming cognizant about the adversary. To confront the West, Fardid asserts, one needs to get to the very core of its philosophy and ontology. Getting to know the other became, in Fardid's analysis, a prerequisite for knowing the self.

Fardid's concept of the West was warmly received by an important segment of the community of Iranian intellectuals eager to reassert their own identity during a time of change both in the East and in the West. Although this oral philosopher should rightfully be acknowledged as the progenitor of the term *gharbzadegi,* the person who did the most to popularize this concept was a Bohemian belletrist.

Jalal Al-e Ahmad: The Bohemian Belletrist

Jalal Al-e Ahmad (1923–1969) was born into a religious family from northern Iran. At the age of twenty he was sent by his father to the holy city of Najaf in Iraq to become a *talabeh* (theology student), but Al-e Ahmad stayed there for no more than a few months. Upon his return to Iran he enrolled in the Tehran Teachers' College from which he graduated in 1946. Al-e Ahmad then enrolled at Tehran University to pursue a doctorate in Persian literature but quit in 1951 before he had defended his dissertation (Shams Al-e Ahmad 1990, 466). During this

16. For more on Fardid's views on this subject see Parham 1968.

time he broke with religion and joined the ranks of the Marxist Tudeh Party where he soon rose to a high position within the party's publicity department. In 1947, however, he and a number of other intellectuals, led by Khalil Maleki, seceded from the Tudeh Party initially over some internal matters while still remaining faithful to the Soviet Union. After they were denounced as traitors by Radio Moscow, Al-e Ahmad retired from the political arena for a few years. Yet he became involved with politics once again in 1950 when he introduced Maleki to Mozaffar Baqa'i-Kermani and later joined the two as they formed Hezb-e Zahmatkeshan-e Melat-e Iran (Iran's Toilers' Party). Despite playing an influential role during the oil nationalization campaign led by Prime Minister Mosaddeq, Al-e Ahmad and a group of dissident intellectuals left the ranks of this party in 1952 to form an independently oriented Third Worldist party called Niruy-e Sevvom (Third Force). In the aftermath of the 1953 coup Al-e Ahmad severed all his party ties and concentrated more on his literary interests as a teacher, belletrist, translator, and ethnographer while remaining an independent political activist.

The 1940s and the 1950s were, thus, the formative decades of Al-e Ahmad's intellectual life. During this period he became acquainted with the ideas of Ahmad Kasravi and those of such prominent intellectuals as Sadeq Hedayat, Nima Yushij, and Khalil Maleki. From the ideas and life of each of these men Al-e Ahmad learned a different lesson: deism from Kasravi, short-story writing from Hedayat, the new style of poetry from Yushij, and political activism from Maleki. Al-e Ahmad was particularly attracted to Nima Yushij and Khalil Maleki who, like himself, were independent-minded pioneers in their respective roles as poet and intellectual politician. He considered Yushij as a humble literary marvel and applauded Khalil Maleki as the most unique example of intellectualism in modern Iran. The cumulative result of these exposures was that during this time period Al-e Ahmad abandoned religion, experimented with Marxism, and gradually moved toward a more nationalistically oriented ideology. These experiences would leave their mark upon him for years to come.

In the fall of 1962 Al-e Ahmad published a monograph entitled *Gharbzadegi,* which was essentially a report he had prepared for the Commission on the Aim of Iranian Education within the Ministry of Education.[17] The commission was a brainchild of Mohammad De-

---

17. There is no general consensus about the exact translation of the title of this monograph. *Gharbzadegi* has been rendered into various English translations as "West-struckness," "Occidentosis," "Plagued by the West," "Western-mania," "Euromania," "Xenomenia," "Westitis," "Westamination," and, finally, "Westoxication." In all instances the term *gharbzadegi* was generally meant to convey Iranian society's and its

rakhshesh, leader of Jame'eh-ye Mo'alleman-e Iran (Iran Teachers' Association), who had recently been appointed minister of education in Ali Amini's cabinet. The ten-member commission (which included Ahmad Fardid) discussed Al-e Ahmad's report in its entirety in November 1961 and January 1962 and decided that it was not able to publish this essay because of its overtly critical view of the regime (Derakhshesh 1990). The commission's apprehension about the monograph proved to be rather justified. As soon as Al-e Ahmad managed to publish it in a different venue, the monograph was hailed as an intellectual bombshell. With its blunt style *Gharbzadegi* compensated for nativism's tardy and torpid entry into the universe of Iranian intellectual discourse. As the antithesis of a tongue-tied critic, Al-e Ahmad questioned the basic foundations of Iranian social and intellectual history at a time when the country was undergoing rapid socioeconomic transformations. This quality transformed *Gharbzadegi* into the holy book for several generations of Iranian intellectuals and earned Al-e Ahmad a reputation as the most dauntless and effective rabble-rouser of his time. One prominent writer and literary critic, Reza Baraheni, described the significance of the book as follows:

> Al-e Ahmad's *Gharbzadegi* . . . has the same significance in determining the duty of colonized nations vis-à-vis colonialist nations that the *Manifesto* of Marx and Engels had in defining the responsibility of the proletariat vis-à-vis capitalism and the bourgeoisie, and that Franz Fanon's *The Wretched of the Earth* had in defining the role of African nations vis-à-vis foreign colonialists. Al-e Ahmad's *Gharbzadegi* is the first Eastern essay to make clear the situation of the East vis-à-vis the West—the colonialist West—and it may be the first Iranian essay to have social value on a world level.[18]

Although Baraheni's praise may have been hyperbolic, it is true that *Gharbzadegi* performed a variety of important functions for the Iranian intellectual community. First, it depicted the dilemma of a changing society by providing a critical chronicle of a century of Iranian enlightenment. Second, by putting the question of national and ethnic identity once again on the agenda *Gharbzadegi* enunciated a nativistic alternative to the universalism of the Iranian Left that had been so popular in the

---

intellectuals' indiscriminate borrowing from the West. I prefer "Westoxication" because it most closely resembles Al-e Ahmad's usage of gharbzadegi as a medical metaphor denoting a social illness. Throughout this book, however, I continue to use the original Persian term *gharbzadegi* because its use somewhat differs from one author to another.

18. Reza Baraheni, *Qessehnevisi,* 2d ed. (Tehran: Ashrafi, 1969), 465, quoted in Hillmann 1987, 73–74.

previous decade. Third, by providing a passionate eulogy for a passing era and its customs *Gharbzadegi* articulated a Third-Worldist discourse very much skeptical of what the West had to offer. Fourth, it exhorted Iranian intellectuals to reassess their passive and servile embrace of Western ideas and culture and called for an awakening and resistance to the hegemony of an alien culture that increasingly dominated the intellectual, social, political, and economic landscape of Iranian society.

Al-e Ahmad began his defiant monograph with a definition of *gharbzadegi* as "the aggregate of events in the life, culture, civilization, and mode of thought of a people having no supporting tradition, no historical continuity, no gradient of transformation." His clear intention was to sensitize the Iranian public to the problem of growing "rootlessness" in their country. "I am speaking of a disease: an accident from without, spreading in an environment rendered susceptible to it. Let us seek a diagnosis for this complaint and its cause—and, if possible, its cure" (Al-e Ahmad 1984, 34, 27). Al-e Ahmad's concept of gharbzadegi as a contaminating social malady was approached from two angles. The "accident from without" and the "environment rendered susceptible to it" represented, respectively, the foreign and domestic dimensions of the sense of other-ness that Al-e Ahmad addressed. Influenced by Heidegger's views on science and technology (which were somehow conveyed to him through Ahmad Fardid), Al-e Ahmad regarded these instruments of human mastery as the essence of Western civilization. Viewing machinery and technology as a "talisman" to the "Westoxicated," he formulated his basic concern in the following terms:

> We have been unable to preserve our own historico-cultural character in the face of the machine and its fateful onslaught. Rather, we have been routed. We have been unable to take a considered stand in the face of this contemporary monster. So long as we do not comprehend the real essence, basis, and philosophy of Western civilization, only aping the West outwardly and formally (by consuming its machines), we shall be like the ass going about in a lion's skin (Al-e Ahmad 1984, 31).

Al-e Ahmad believed that this pandemic could result in the eradication of Iran's cultural authenticity, political sovereignty, and economic well-being. His usage of a medical analogy to symbolize a cultural, political, and economic ailment deliberately emphasized intellectual vigilance. Grounding his discussion in the familiar dichotomy of "us" versus "them" or "East" versus "West," Al-e Ahmad depicts himself as "an Easterner with his feet planted firmly in tradition, eager to make a two- or three-hundred year leap and obliged to make up for so much anxiety and straggling." Later, continuing his comparative reasoning, he writes:

"As the West stood, we sat down. As the West awoke in an industrial resurrection, we passed into the slumber of the Seven Sleepers." In criticizing the *we*, however, Al-e Ahmad first and foremost incriminated those Iranian intellectuals who were looking to the West as an alternative. He viewed these intellectuals as the agents most responsible for creating an environment susceptible to Western ingress and domination. He denounced all notable thinkers of the Constitutional era as follows:

> So far as I can see, all these homegrown Montesquieus of ours fell off the same side of the roof. . . . They all had an instinctive feeling that our ancient society and tradition could not withstand the onslaught of Western technology. They all went astray in opting for "adoption of European civilization without Iranian adaptation," but in addition to this vague and unproven remedy, each sought a different cure. One thumped the tub for foreign embassies; another believed one must, in imitation of the West, revive ancient tradition through a religious "reform" like Luther's; a third called for Islamic unity in an age when the Ottomans' ignominy was being trumpeted about the world with the slaughter of the Armenians and the Kurds. (Al-e Ahmad 1984, 58).

Akin to the manner in which the fokolis were depicted by Shadman (who is acknowledged in two of the notes of *Gharbzadegi*), Al-e Ahmad used a style of prose based on repetitive rhetorical tropes to incite his readers against the "Westoxicated person." He characterized the latter as one who is effete, devious, comfort seeking, with no specialty, character, belief, or convictions, and who hangs on the words and handouts of the West (Al-e Ahmad 1984, 92–97).

It will be a grave mistake, however, to conclude from the above polemical tropes that Al-e Ahmad himself was immune from Western influences. To the contrary, he was inspired by many Western (primarily European) thinkers and writers. For example, Al-e Ahmad was a great admirer of Jean-Paul Sartre, whom he considered a political and literary "pressure gauge" who stood up to every form of domination (Al-e Ahmad 1966, 91). From Sartre he borrowed the idea of social commitment as a fundamental component of a writer's task. Mohammad-Taqi Ghiyasi, an Iranian literary critic, recalls an encounter he had with Al-e Ahmad upon Ghiyasi's return to Iran from France in 1964. Asked by Al-e Ahmad about Sartre, Ghiyasi responded, "Sartre is now [intellectually] dead; nowadays everyone is talking about Michel Foucault." Upon hearing this, Al-e Ahmad retorted irately "But for us he [Sartre] has just been born" (Ghiyasi 1988, 41). Al-e Ahmad's attraction to Sartre, the iconoclastic philosopher who turned down the Noble Prize, embraced the Cuban revolution, and passed out revolutionary newspapers on the streets of Paris as late as 1968, was not just a matter of personal taste. His preference for Sartre over Foucault was also an unequivocal vote for modernism over postmodernism.

Notwithstanding the fact that Fardid did not think too highly of the Existentialism of Sartre and Camus, Al-e Ahmad viewed it as the first genuine postwar movement bent on calling into question the very foundations of Western thought.[19] It is also true, however, that Fardid's intellectual influence led Al-e Ahmad to develop an affinity for the works of Martin Heidegger as well. In particular, he was attracted to Heidegger's ideas on the nature of technology and materialism in the West.[20] Following his lead, Al-e Ahmad purported that the West was not just an imperialist entity but also the heart of technological development, which was to be viewed not as a mere instrument but as a mode of thought. Al-e Ahmad maintained that technology did not allow for an equal exchange among nations because some were exporters of it while others were its importers; some were producers of machinery while others were mere consumers of it. As the first eloquent critic of machinism in Iran, Al-e Ahmad lamented the crumbling of his traditional society at the hands of machines: "As the machine entrenches itself in the towns and villages, be it in the form of a mechanized mill or a textile plant, it puts the worker in local craft industries out of work. It closes the village mill. It renders the spinning wheel useless. Production of pile carpets, flat carpets, felt carpets is at an end" (Al-e Ahmad 1984, 68).[21] Al-e Ahmad, however, was willingly oblivious to the reality that these "alien" machines also curtailed workers' hardships by reducing their work hours and increasing their productivity. He wanted to put the machine, a monstrous giant, back in the genie bottle and turn it into an obedient servant ready to obey its master at any time. Al-e Ahmad did not discuss

19. It does not seem to me, however, that Al-e Ahmad was bothered too much with inconsistencies. He liked both Camus and Sartre irrespective of the fact that the former had distanced himself from the "northern" existentialism of the latter.

20. One should bear in mind here that Al-e Ahmad's knowledge of Sartre, Heidegger, and other Western philosophers was quite fragmentary. Al-e Ahmad was not a man of philosophy, nor did he have a thorough grasp of French or German. His rudimentary acquaintance with Western philosophy was mainly acquired through conversations with his friends and colleagues who had studied in the West.

21. For further elaboration on Al-e Ahmad's views on technology, one should consult the series of ethnographic essays he wrote between 1954 and 1960. These anthropological studies deal with how modernization along Western lines is upsetting the natural social relationships in Iranian villages. Like the Russian Slavophile writers of the nineteenth century, Al-e Ahmad maintained that Iran's model for development and modernization should correspond to the country's unique history, character, values, and institutions.

how this could be accomplished, however. In the entire *Gharbzadegi* essay no mention is made of the positive results of technology. His criticism of machinism was later picked up by such other critics as Ali Shari'ati, Daryush Shayegan, Ehsan Naraqi, Reza Davari, Morteza Motahhari, and Reza Baraheni, among others.[22] What is most troubling about Al-e Ahmad's criticism of machines is his parroting of Heidegger. Whereas Heidegger's criticism of machines was pertinent to post-World War I Europe (with the unbelievable carnage and destruction left behind), one wonders how appropriate it was to criticize "machinism" in the Iran of the 1960s. Al-e Ahmad's preoccupation with the role of machines prevented him from appreciating the complexity of technology and advanced capitalism. Although he did not comment on such 1950s and 1960s debates as the dependency theory, or the North-South controversy, Al-e Ahmad was clearly influenced by the amalgamation of these debates. His theory of gharbzadegi could be viewed as a less-systematic version of dependency theory.[23] Sure enough, Al-e Ahmad was not alone in promulgating this type of discourse in Iran.[24]

The imprint of Western scholars is also present on Al-e Ahmad's two-volume book pointedly entitled *Dar khedmat va khiyanat-e rowshanfekran* (On the service and treason of the intellectuals), where he delves further into the history of the Iranian intellectual movement.[25] He identified nobility, clerics, landlord/tribal leaders, and the urban middle class

22. It should, however, be pointed out that a number of Iranian intellectuals did criticize Al-e Ahmad's negative view of machines and technology. Referring to Al-e Ahmad, one critic writes: "There are some who are trying to convert opposition to Western bourgeoisie to opposition to a lifeless machine. . . . No! [A] machine, which in the hand of the Western bourgeoisie has caused the subjugation of the Orient, is surely a means of defense in the hand of the Orientals (granted that they make and use it themselves). You cannot fight [a] jet fighter with bows and arrows" (Rahimi 1968, 39). For two more examples of critical responses to Al-e Ahamd see Ashuri 1967 and Mo'meni 1985.

23. For a treatment of the dependency theory as it was articulated by Iranian intellectuals see Mashayekhi 1987.

24. A number of other books that were published more or less at the same time as Al-e Ahmad's *Gharbzadegi* and conveyed the same type of message included Abdolrahim Ahmadi, *Nahamahangi-ye Roshd-e Eqtesadi va Ejtema'i dar Donya-ye Mo'aser* (The disharmony of economic and social development in the contemporary world); Majid Rahnama, *Masa'el-e Keshvarha-ye Asiya'i va Afriqa'i* (Problems of Asian and African countries); and Mehdi Bahar, *Miraskhar-e Este'mar* (The heir to colonialism). In addition, the overtly critical works of Aimé Césaire, Frantz Fanon, Tibor Mende, and Albert Memmi on colonialism were published in translated forms.

25. It is highly probable that in choosing the title of this book Al-e Ahmad was inspired by Julien Benda (1867–1956), who in his classic book *La Trahison des clercs* (1927) brought an indictment against Western intellectuals.

as the four fountains of Iranian intellectuality. Al-e Ahmad designated
the last group as the most logical birthplace of intellectuality and described its members as the "hopes" of Iran's future intellectual movement. At the same time, however, he was also very critical of this group.
Al-e Ahmad criticized secular Iranian intellectuals for their isolation
from the masses, their superficiality, their rejection or ignorance of the
majority's traditional beliefs, and the ease with which they were often co-
opted by the ruling classes. To rectify this condition he concluded that
intellectuals must form an alliance with the clerics who historically have
been the second major pillar of intellectuality and dissent in Iran. His
encounter with Western thought and the process of modernization
compelled Al-e Ahmad to turn toward nativism. Judging from the progression of his ideas as they were explicated in *Gharbzadegi* and *Dar khedmat va khiyanat-e rowshanfekran,* one realizes that Al-e Ahmad came more
and more to believe that the preservation of indigenous customs would
be possible through a turn toward Shi'ism. Although the above works
manifest an eclecticism on the part of their author, who alternatively
drew from Iranian nationalism, Marxian economic analysis, and European existentialism, one can discern a strong subterranean religious ambiance in Al-e Ahmad's discourse (Mir Ahmadi 1978). He believed that
ever since the advent in the sixteenth century of the Safavid dynasty—
who upheld Iran's sovereignty against the Ottomans in the name of
religion—Shi'ism had acquired a special position within the core of the
Iranian social psyche. Thus, for Al-e Ahmad Shi'a Islam had become an
indispensable component of Iranian identity. As such, he prescribed the
revival of Shi'a Islam as Iran's most effective "vaccine" against the pandemic of gharbzadegi and came to consider the clergy as the most
qualified "doctors" able to provide this identity-saving vaccine. His high
esteem for the clergy stemmed from his regard for the ulema as the
only consequential social group in Iran that did not succumb to Western
domination. Al-e Ahmad maintained that the clerics have four particular
advantages which make them valuable allies to secular intellectuals: they
tend to be men of learning by the very nature of their profession; they
tend to be radically minded, coming mainly from lower class backgrounds; they tend to be trusted by the masses as guardians of the faith;
and, finally, they can be agents for social or political uprising as a result of
their ability to speak the language of the masses. Here Al-e Ahmad was
referring to the historical role the clergy had performed in such events as
the Tobacco Rebellion (1891–92), the Constitutional Revolution of
1905–11, oil nationalization of the early 1950s, and the June 1963 protest
led by Ayatollah Khomeini. Al-e Ahmad was so appalled by the indif-
ference shown toward this last event by the secular intelligentsia that he

began to write *Dar khedmat va khiyanat-e rowshanfekran* shortly after it. Al-e Ahmad's major thesis was that in the previous one hundred years of Iranian history whenever the intellectuals and the clergy have cooperated with one another, they have been able to achieve victory and progress. By the same token, however, their disunity has resulted in defeat and decadence (Al-e Ahmad 1978, 2:52). To facilitate this cooperation he insisted that the intellectuals must reach out to the clergy and the masses and the clerics must abandon their conservative stances.

Al-e Ahmad's charitable attitude toward the ulema was also extended to the intellectual heritage of the East as well. He believed the Western orientation of Iranian intellectuals must be balanced with a more Eastern outlook. Al-e Ahmad looked in particular to India as an example from which Iranian intellectuals could draw inspiration. This proposition was rooted in several premises. India had both well-endowed religious traditions and strong historical ties with Iran. In addition, India had just fomented a strong anticolonial movement and produced a world-class statesman and thinker, Mohandas Gandhi (1869–1948). Al-e Ahmad was impressed by the populist, "man of the people" image of Gandhi and viewed him as a model intellectual who was more committed to his utopian ideals than to any class interests. Al-e Ahmad further praised Gandhi as one who had the most accurate views on Third World independence (Al-e Ahmad 1978, 1:169). Indeed, he went as far as to say that India was the mother of Iran and even suggested that instead of sending students to the West, Iran should start dispatching students to India and Japan. As such, Al-e Ahmad encouraged many Iranian intellectuals and translators to start writing about and translating from oriental languages.[26]

This suggestion was a legitimate one because most educated Iranians were quite unaware (and still remain so) about intellectual developments in their neighboring countries to the East. Richard N. Frye, an emeritus professor of Near Eastern languages at Harvard University who had been the director of the Asia Institute of Pahlavi University in Shiraz from 1969 to 1974, maintained that "Iranian universities did not teach their students anything about the Far East or even neighboring India, but they were offering courses in the history of Europe and even American history" (Frye 1984). This situation began to be rectified toward the later part of the Pahlavi reign when a handful of professors were recruited to teach courses on Indology and oriental philosophy. For the

26. Daryush Shayegan recalls that on one of the few occasions he saw Al-e Ahmad the latter congratulated him for his two-volume work on Indian religions and philosophical schools of thought (Shayegan 1967), which he liked very much (Shayegan 1989a).

most part, however, secular Iranian intellectuals were quite up to date on European, North American, and even Latin American intellectual and literary trends but remained largely ignorant of what was happening closer to them in such neighboring states as India, Pakistan, Afghanistan, Turkey, and the Arab world.

Al-e Ahmad deserves credit for making sure that nativism did not remain an excessively scholastic discussion. He managed to make nativism a de rigueur component of modern political discourse in Iran. After him, it has been almost impossible for Iranian intellectuals to speak of their cultural conflict with contemporary Western civilization without paying homage in some way to his theory of gharbzadegi. Al-e Ahmad's criticism of the role of intellectuals, however, leaves much to be desired. He viewed intellectuals as the promoters of gharbzadegi but was not willing to accept that as a social group they were only a reflection of the internal contradictions and incoherence of their own society. He criticized intellectuals while he ignored the fact that in a society such as Iran, which was rapidly becoming urbanized, industrialized, and incorporated into the world capitalist system, new social classes were emerging that demanded a new definition of self. Inappropriately, Al-e Ahmad held Iranian intellectuals solely accountable for all the anguish and misery of their society. It is as if there were no relationship between these intellectuals and their place of upbringing—as if they were weeds that grew at will. Al-e Ahmad's chiding critique puts the intellectuals, rather than social relations, on trial. Perhaps it was in an imaginary debate with Al-e Ahmad that Jean-Paul Sartre declared: "As products of torn societies, the intellectual can be the spokesperson of these societies because (s)he has internalized their fissures. The intellectual is a historical phenomenon. Therefore, no society can blame its intellectuals without accusing itself, insofar as they are the products of these very societies" (Sartre 1972, 41).

Al-e Ahmad's indignation toward the intellectuals should be understood in the context of the puzzling state of mind that besieged this community in the post-World War II era. This was a generation tormented by the nuclear attacks on Hiroshima and Nagasaki, the cold war, de-Stalinization, the Vietnam War, student rebellions, and endemic dictatorships, economic dependency, and nationalist uprisings as well. Al-e Ahmad belonged to a generation that was at once inspired by the West yet politically opposed to it; a generation xenophobic toward the West, yet drawing inspirations from the thoughts of its leading thinkers; a generation dodging religion and traditionalism, yet pulled toward them; a generation aspiring for such modernist goals as democracy, freedom, and social justice, yet skeptical of their historical precedents and contemporary problems. As Iran's leading intellectual of the 1960s, Al-e Ahmad epitomized this state of mental torment. He was representative of a generation of Iranian intellectuals who became disillusioned with both liberalism and socialism as political alternatives. Al-e Ahmad's disillusionment with liberalism was caused by the fact that despite its vow to safeguard democracy all that the West provided for Iran was (neo)colonialism and support of autocratic rulers. One should bear in mind that Al-e Ahmad flourished as a social critic at the same time that some of the most sensitive minds of the Western intellectual world, men such as Albert Camus (1913–1960), Erich Fromm (1900–1980), Herbert Marcuse (1898–1979), Jean-Paul Sartre (1905–1980), George Bernard Shaw (1856–1950), and Arnold Toynbee (1889–1975) and before them Oswald Spengler (1880–1936) and Henri Bergson (1859–1941) were expressing doubts about the merits and the future direction of Western civilization. Similarly, his disillusionment with socialism was the result of Soviet expansionism, the failure of existing socialism to live up to its many promises, and the submissive attitude of the Tudeh Party leadership toward Soviet demands and policies.[27]

Al-e Ahmad's turn toward religion was equally representative of a broader ideological reversal on the part of many in the Iranian intellectual community. The agnostic, atheistic, and deist ideas of Mirza Fath-Ali Akhundzadeh, Mirza Aqa Khan Kermani, Ahmad Kasravi, Ali Dashti, Taqi Arani, and Sadeq Hedayat were now being abandoned in favor of a more socially minded and activist Islam. Al-e Ahmad adopted an instrumentalist view of Shi'ism as a mobilizing political ideology.[28] He was further encouraged by the course of events in India, Algeria, and Vietnam, and in the 1960s European rebellious movements in which the left-wing clerics played a progressive role. One of Al-e Ahmad's major accomplishments was to bridge the gap between mod-

27. In this regard, a comparison of Al-e Ahmad's *Safar-e Rus* (The Russian journey), written in 1964 after a trip to the Soviet Union, bore striking resemblance to Andre Gide, *Retour de l'U.R.S.S.* (1936) and Arthur Koestler, *The Invisible Writing; an autobiography* (1954). In addition to translating Gide, *Retour de l'U.R.S.S.* and *Les Nourritures terrestres*, Al-e Ahmad also managed to translate Fyodor Dostoyevski, *Igork;* Albert Camus, *L'Etranger* and *Le Malentendu;* Jean-Paul Sartre, *Les Mains sales;* Eugne Ionesco's *Le Rhinoceros;* and Ernest Jünger, *Über die Linie* into Persian.

28. Manuchehr Hezarkhani, an Iranian leftist writer, translator, and close friend of Al-e Ahmad, professed that the scenario Al-e Ahmad saw for the future of Iran was modeled after the Algerian revolution. He recalls a conversation with Al-e Ahmad in which the latter told him: "How come you [leftists] do not understand that the cells of the Communist Party must be formed within the mosques? The Algerians, who were neither Muslims nor as committed Communists as you are, realized this and won" (Hezarkhani 1984).

ern intellectuals and the clergy. On the one hand, he tried to lower the anticlerical tone of the modern intelligentsia by convincing them that the clergy were the only stratum in Iran that did not succumb to Western domination. On the other hand, he tried to convince the ulema that a clergy-intellectual alliance was the only effective way to challenge the tyrannical rule of the shah. It is, thus, not a surprise that Al-e Ahmad's works were read seriously and discussed both on the university campuses and in the theological seminaries. People on both sides of the historical divide were beginning to show an interest in a rapprochement. It was soon to emerge.

4

The Clerical Subculture

Thus they display a paradoxical modernity; the ideas are today's; the attitudes yesterday's.
—Octavio Paz, *One Earth, Four or Five Worlds*

THE CIRCUMSTANCES THAT CULMINATED in the 1979 Iranian revolution have been designated by a variety of labels, such as the rise of "Islamic revivalism," "Islamic fundamentalism," and "Islamic resurgence," labels that are grounded in Western history or rooted in its cultural antipathy toward the Muslim world or both. The process leading to and following the revolution has mainly been described as a counterresponse by the traditional segments of the Iranian polity to rapid modernization and the idea of progress.

In chapters 4 and 5, however, I contend that what transpired in Iran was much more complicated than the facile speculations that modernization theorists have led people to believe. Examining the ideas, actions, and political platforms of the clerical forces and the religious intellectuals, I argue that what took place was the development of a "religious subculture," which was more innovative, enduring, and popular than its secular counterpart. This religious subculture involved a "politicization of Islam," transforming the latter into the primary agency of political socialization and contestation. In other words, Islam became an ideology par excellence, capable of such functions as granting identity and legitimacy upon and integrating and mobilizing the masses. Politicized Islam, in turn, promulgated the other-ness of the state, the West, and the secularists. These acts of other-ing are to be understood against the background of a declining base of power vis-à-vis the monarchical state, an ideological challenge offered by their secular counterparts, and a response to the received Western philosophical doctrines and political actions.

Finally, I suggest that, as the organic intellectuals of religious classes, the ascendancy of clerics to political power in 1979 can be attributed to the following comparative advantages: financial independence from the state; strong communication networks; capable orators and liturgists; legal centers of mobilization (mosques, seminaries, Islamic associations, religious foundations); numerous religious occasions; historical/mythical figures; populist slogans; bazaar support; a centralized leadership with a well-defined hierarchical structure; a ready blueprint for action; and the help given to them by the state to counter the Left.

Historical Ambiance

Since the advent of Shiʿism as the official state religion in 1501, the political culture of Iran has hinged on the two pillars of religion and state to sustain itself. The union of clergy and the royal court as the two main backbones of Iranian political life has been at times cordial and at times antagonistic. Despite the proliferation of revisionist historiographies that have claimed an interminable and pervasive oppositional role for Iranian Shiʿa ulema because of the state's misdeeds, the relationship between the two has been more nuanced.[1] The congenial relation during the Safavid era (1501–1722), the lukewarm/antagonistic association of the Qajar period (1785–1925), and the courteous/confrontational encounter of the Pahlavi era (1925–79) all defy the naïve categorizations presented by the apologetic of both the clergy and the state. The clergy historically has had much common interest with the court. Maintenance of the status quo, preservation of private property, shrewd political alliances to sustain social privileges, and common opposition to unsettling heretical, radical, and secularist movements have constituted some of the common grounds between the two. On the contrary, as the two chief institutional adversaries, they have challenged one another over greater supremacy, popular allegiance, prestige, the pool of disciples, and economic rewards as well.

With the coronation of Reza Shah as the first Pahlavi ruler in 1925 the balance of power turned decidedly against the clergy. Secularization of the vital domains of education, mass media, justice, and politics, along with such controversial acts as the change of civil codes and dress, women's enfranchisement, the purification of language by removing Arabic words, and a host of other events signaled this turn of tide. The reign of Mohammad-Reza Shah exacerbated this already drifting alliance. The diminishing political clout of the ulema, reflected in their declining presence in the Majles and other governmental institutions,

---

1. For an example of this revisionist line of historical inquiry see Algar 1972. For a critique of this same view see Floor 1983.

was one cause of concern. More consequentially, the regime had decided to transfer the Iranians' source of allegiance and identity from one based on religion to one grounded in pre-Islamic monarchical legacy. The extravagant commemoration ceremonies marking the celebration of 2,500 years of monarchical rule in 1971, along with a decree in March 1976 to change the calendar from one based on the date of migration of the Prophet Mohammad from Mecca to Medina (A.D. 621–22) to an imperial one dating back to the coronation of Cyrus the Great, founder of the Achaemenid Empire, were only two visible examples of this contestation of Islamic legitimacy by the shah's regime. In addition to all these, the open identification of the government with a secular, powerful, and technologically superior West was quite disheartening to the conservative clergy.

Economically, the clergy became deprived of independent sources of revenues as the state began to carry on its land reform program and decided to set up its own Sazman-e Owqaf (Endowments Organization) in 1964 to bring under its control all lands donated for religious uses. Furthermore, the government presumed that through the Endowments Organization it could help to institutionalize the proper collection and distribution of revenues and bridge the emerging gap between itself and the clergy by using the mechanism of patronage (through contributing funds to apolitical or progovernment clergy).[2] Finally, a rapidly expanding new middle class meant that the ranks of the traditional petty bourgeoisie, which had served as a recruitment ground for the religious establishment, was shrinking. As a result of the mushrooming of nonreligious kindergartens, primary and secondary schools and universities, the number of pupils and theology students was also dwindling.

The above trends provided more than ample reasons for the clergy to conceive of the state as its antagonistic other. This perceived otherness brought along an era of self-questioning, reorganization, innovative thought, and, finally, victory for the clerical establishment. Bryan S. Turner has criticized a central thesis of Western sociology that claims that the economic character of capitalism has been accountable for the dwindling significance of the church. Turner maintains, quite to the contrary, that the power of Christianity in the modern world is positively linked to its crucial association with the growth of the European nation-state. In other words, as the state institutional apparatus ex-

2. To accomplish these goals, the prime minister appointed Nasir Assar, the son of the eminent theologian and university professor Seyyed Mohammad-Kazem Assar, as the head of the Endowments Organization (1964–72). The organization, however, was not able to carry out its designated tasks because it was besieged from the outset by allegations of favoritism and corruption. See Assar 1982, 60–65.

panded, so did the church thrive as a national institution (Turner 1988).
A similar analogy can be drawn for the clergy-state relations in the
Pahlavi era. The increasing state bureaucratization of power under the
two Pahlavi kings had paradoxical results. On the one hand, it reduced
the previous authority enjoyed by the ulema; yet, on the other hand, it
recognized the clerical establishment as the quintessential alternative to
state power. In effect, state monopoly of power forced the clergy to
turn more and more toward the masses. Populism replaced elitism as
the predominant discursive repertoire of the clerical class.

The clergy faced the herculean task of reforming their institution if
they were to meet the challenge of the state. Internally, they had to put
their house in order while externally they regained its lost stature. The
clerics also stood bewildered in front of a wave of Western philosophical doctrines embodied in the ideas of Marx, Nietzsche, Darwin, and
Auguste Comte, which had found their way into Iranian philosophical
discourse. These doctrines, which had previously contributed to the decline of religion in the West, were now constituting a challenge with
which the clergy had to grapple. "Closure of discourse," to borrow
Herbert Marcuse's term, was no longer a viable formula for combating
the skeptics and the unbelievers.

The clerical response to this challenge conformed to the contours of
what Max Weber has identified as the rationalization of life. Rationalization of financial revenues and economic affairs, advancement of systematic theology, standardization of the academic curriculum of religious
centers, cultivation of extensive communication networks throughout
the country, and establishment of religiously inclined publishing houses
and journals were only some of the "rationalizing" reform moves undertaken by the Iranian clergy in the aftermath of World War II.

The reform movement can be said to have begun during the tenure
of the Grand Ayatollah Hoseyn Borujerdi, who was regarded as the sole
marja´-e taqlid (source of emulation) of the Shi´ite world from the
mid-1940s until his death in 1961. While maintaining a conservative
outlook that promoted aloofness from political involvement, Borujerdi
did much to inaugurate a reform movement within the ranks of the
clergy. A prominent student of his summarized his accomplishments as
follows: centralization of the financial distribution process to religious
leaders and seminaries; development of accounting procedures to re-
cord all such transactions; dispatching Muslim missionaries to Western
countries (such as West Germany and the United States) to promote
Islam; establishing closer ties between Shi´ite and Sunni theologians in
Iran and the Arab world with the goal of attaining Islamic unity; founding religious primary and secondary schools; contributing to the construc-

tion of mosques and seminaries throughout Iran; and encouragement of theology students to contemplate concrete logical problems instead of abstract and obscure theological hair-splitting (Motahhari 1963a).

Borujerdi's departure from the scene created an "uncertainty over the matter of the succession and a fear that government intervention might present the community with a fait accompli." These concerns led the younger generation of theologians to "consider the functions and choice of the marjaʿ-e taqlid" (Lambton 1964, 119). Shortly after Borujerdi's death, a group of social reformers, who two decades later would become the leading personalities of the 1979 revolution, came together to map an appropriate strategy.[3] In January 1963 the proceedings of their discussions were published in a book entitled *Bahsi dar bareh-ye marjaʿiyyat va ruhaniyyat* (A discussion on the principle of emulation and the religious establishment). This book earned such praise as the "most important work to have been published in Iran in the last fifty years" (Akhavi 1980, 119). The publisher's introduction to the second edition of the book highlights its significance by saying: "This book, which is written by a number of informed religious leaders and enlightened writers of the Islamic world, as expected, caused a massive wave [of debates] and can be considered as representing the prospect of a deep and reform-minded movement within the ambient of religious institutions. This book shows that the clergy has reached such a degree of cerebral maturity that it can criticize itself, based on precise scientific and social standards, as well as seek a remedy."

Akhavi (1980, 119–20) summarized the group's major resolutions as presented in the book.

(1) The need for an independent financial organization for the clergy; (2) the necessity of a *shura-yi fatva*—i.e., a permanent committee of *mujtahids*, the members of which were to be drawn from the country at large, to issue collective authoritative opinions in matters of law; (3) the idea that no Shiʿi society is possible without the delegation of the *Imam*'s authority; (4) an interpretation of Islam as a total way of life, therefore incorporating social, economic and political issues into the religious ones; (5) the need to replace the central importance of *fiq* in the *madrasah* [traditional

3. These individuals included Mehdi Bazargan, first prime minister of the Islamic Republic; Ayatollah Seyyed Mohammad Beheshti, generally regarded as the leading political strategist of the revolution after Ayatollah Ruhollah Khomeini: Seyyed Morteza Jazayeri, a pro-Mosaddeq cleric; Morteza Motahhari, a leading ideologue of the Islamic Republic; Allameh Mohammad-Hoseyn Tabatabaʾi, a most learned Shiʿite theologian; Ayatollah Mahmud Taleqani, the most popular religious leader of postrevolutionary Iran after Khomeini; and Haj Seyyed Abolfazl Zanjani, a liberal-minded and politically active cleric.

theological seminary] curricula with *akhlaq* (ethics), *aqaʾid* (ideology) and *falsafah* (philosophy); (6) the need for a new concept of leadership of youth based on a correct understanding of responsibility; (7) the development of *ijtihad* as a powerful instrument for the adaptation of Islam to changing circumstances; (8) a revival of the nearly-defunct principle of *al-amr bi-maʿruf wa al-nahy ʿan al-munkar* [injunction to enjoin the good and prohibit the evil] as a means of expressing a collective and public will; (9) specialization among mujtahids and making *taqlid* (emulation of a mujtahid) contingent upon it; (10) the need for mutuality and communal spirit to overcome the individuality and mistrust that pervades Iranian culture.

These resolutions signified two notable developments within the clerical establishment. The first concerns the launching of a systematic "war of position" by the clergy to politicize Islam (resolutions 1, 4, 6, 8, and 10). Motahhari, Beheshti, Bazargan and other politically minded clerics and laymen argued that the clerical institution was neither capable of challenging the state nor its secular opponents if the clergy persisted in maintaining their presently ossified ideas and conventions. According to them, the clergy had no political literature or organization; was too preoccupied with apolitical, nonsocial, and noncontemporary issues; abused their positions or became accomplices of the government or both; had nothing to offer Iranian youth; and maintained very lax rules of behavior among themselves. Motahhari went even further and accused his colleagues of having committed yet a bigger offense, that of succumbing to *avamzadegi* (catering to superstitious longings and fallacious beliefs of the masses).[4] He alleged that "because of their dependence upon the people for their sustenance they [the clergy] have lost their intellectual freedom and become subservient to the wishes of the common people, who are, for the most part, ignorant and opposed to reform" (Lambton 1964, 133). According to Motahhari, the dilemma confronting the religious classes was as follows: "If they rely upon popular support they acquire political power but lose their intellectual freedom; whereas if they rely upon the government, they surrender their political power but retain their intellectual freedom" (133)." The remedy, according to him, was to create a financial institution in which the clergy would no longer be directly dependent upon contributions. In

4. Reminiscent of Al-e Ahmad's underscoring of gharbzadegi, Motahhari accentuates the predicament of *avamzadegi* by writing "what has paralyzed and weakened our religious establishment is this affliction of avamzadegi, which is worse than the distress caused by floods, earthquakes, snakes and scorpions" (Motahhari 1963b, 184).

this way they could sustain their independence against both the government and the masses.

The second development resulting from the publication of *Bahsi dar-bare-ye marja'iyyat va ruhaniyyat* concerned the emerging prominence of a new school of jurisprudential interpretation, which later acquired the title of *feqh-e puya* (resolutions 2, 3, 5, 7, and 9). While maintaining their belief in the necessity of upholding the principles of *taqlid, ejtehad,* and *marja'iyyat,* the reform-minded clerics also called for their modification. They argued that because of the constantly evolving nature of scientific and social issues that faces the community, jurisprudence needs to adapt itself to remain a viable alternative in today's world. Motahhari argued that the clergy needs to follow the example of the scientific community by seeking specialization in their particular fields of expertise. Bazargan contended that while time, space, life, and humans undergo transformation, so too should jurisprudence and jurisconsults. Taleqani and Jazayeri both called for a showra-ye fatva as a more democratic, logical, and authoritative alternative to one-man lawmaking. In short, the contributors to this book advocated a set of new-fangled ideas to ensure the durability and further prosperity of the clerical establishment.

Nonetheless, history had a different course of action in store. On 5 June 1963, a mere five months after the publication of this book, Ayatollah Khomeini, a clergyman who survived Borujerdi, delivered an inflammatory sermon against the regime for its domestic and foreign policies. In the subsequent confrontation between the government and theology students at the Feyziyyeh Seminary in Qom, many protesters lost their lives. Khomeini was sent into exile, first to Turkey and then to Iraq. The June revolt had two important ramifications: it inaugurated a phase of open confrontation in clergy-state relations, and it helped to polarize the clerical class into those who were advocating confrontational political activism and those in favor of quietist, apolitical, and theologically bound pursuits.

Khomeini's "war of movement" in 1963 had mixed repercussions for the two central goals of the social reformers: politicization of Islam and the development of a new theological hermeneutics. Although not adhering to the thoughtfully crafted and gradual strategy of the latter, it nevertheless produced some of the intended results. The activist clerics established their personal and communication networks throughout the country; propagated explicitly political literature; suffered imprisonments and martyrdom for the cause of political struggle; and, finally, formed or joined already existing political organizations such as Hezb-e

Melal-e Eslami (Islamic Nations Party) and Nehzat-e Azadi (Liberation Movement).[5]

The clergy's political comeback begot a great deal of goodwill for them in the eyes of the more discontented sectors of the population. The more the shah tried to bask in pre-Islamic monarchical glory, the more powerful the appeal of Islamic symbolism, myths, and jargon grew. The youth adored the bold pronouncements of Khomeini and his lieutenants, whereas the traditional propertied middle class and bazaar merchants took to heart the clergy's call for maintaining the immutable values of traditional culture and for opposing the large capitalists and their Western backers. Considering the fact that the polarization of the clerical class undercut the formation of a centralized financial organization (as promoted by the social reformers), the financial support provided by the bazaar merchants and brokers to the radical clerics proved instrumental. Their financing of clergy politics helped to shape the latter's discourse of dissent and accommodation.

Likewise, the 1963 events also had major repercussions for the development of feqh-e puya. In light of the polarization that engulfed the ranks of the clerical class, the progressive-minded idea of a showra-ye fatva never materialized. While in exile in Iraq, Khomeini published a book on Islamic government in which he intentionally remained ambiguous about whether *velayat-e faqih* should reside in one person or a collective body (Khomeini 1971, 66–67). The book, which consisted of a series of lectures, further argued that sovereignty emanates and resides in God; a fundamental opposition exists between Islam and monarchy; an Islamic government based on the *shari'ah* must be created; and the *faqih* or *foqaha* should serve as the "custodian" of the people until the advent of the hidden Imam. In broad terms Khomeini's idea of an Islamic government can also be analyzed within the confines of feqh-e puya. He agreed with such ideas as delegation of authority, development of ejtehad to fit changing circumstances, and the neces-

5. Hezb-e Melal-e Eslami (Islamic Nations Party), an armed underground organization made up mainly of the defunct Feda'iyan-e Eslam (Devotees of Islam), was formed shortly after the June 1963 revolt. It was responsible for the 1965 attempted assassination of Prime Minister Hasan-Ali Mansur. Some of its leaders were Musavi-Bojnordi, Haj Mehdi Eraqi, Jannati-Kermani, and Abolqasem Sarhaddizadeh. Nehzat-e Azadi (The Liberation Movement of Iran) was formed in 1961 by Mehdi Bazargan (a French-educated engineer and university professor) and Ayatollah Seyyed Mahmud Taleqani. Other leading members of the organization included Ahmad Alibaba'i, Abolfazl Hakimi, Ezzatollah Sahabi, Yadollah Sahabi, and Abbas Sheybani. This organization attempted to bridge the gap between the lay middle class and the clergy (Alibaba'i 1991).

sity of supplementing jurisprudence with lessons on ethics, ideology, and philosophy.[6]

More importantly, however, Khomeini's book signified a drastic politicization of a sizable segment of the clerical class, which was estimated by the 1976 census to be more than 23,000. Khomeini had learned from his 1963 setback and was not again willing to endure the agony of defeat. His political stand stabilized; Khomeini no longer criticized this or that wrongful or despotic policy of the government but instead attacked its mandate to rule. He no longer hinted about a possible accord with the court but called for its overthrow. In short, Khomeini had turned Islam into a powerful alternative ideology capable of challenging its rich adversary. This metamorphosis nonetheless must be understood against the background of a formidable religious subculture that had painstakingly been developed in the decades preceding the publication of Khomeini's book.

Ideological Vigilance

The activities of the clerical class were by no means limited to those of Ayatollah Khomeini. Indeed, in the 1960s and the 1970s the greater clerical community and their lay collaborators had launched an inconspicuous campaign aimed at the educated as well as the disenfranchised. The result was the development of a religious subculture that proved quite a challenge for the monarchical establishment. In the aftermath of the 1953 coup certain members of the clerical class had come to realize that resignation and grumbling were not going to repudiate the sense of other-ness that was thrust upon them. As moralists they could not simply be preoccupied with the past because it was in the present that the challenge was most noticeable. For them the geography of discourse changed from yesterday, there and them, to today, here and us. True, the present was still evaluated with an adoring eye for the past, but this was far different from falling into the oblivion of antiquity. What was taking place was not so much the traditionalization of modernity but the modernization of tradition.

The French philosopher Henry Corbin has argued that tradition, by its very essence, is a rebirth, and every birth is the renewal of tradition

6. Khomeini, who had studied philosophy under the learned Ayatollah Seyyed Abolhasan Rafi'i-Qazvini, was one of the very few clerics who used to teach that subject in religious seminaries. He came under heavy criticism from the more conservative clerics for having tutored his students in Greek and Islamic philosophy as well as mysticism. For more on Khomeini's philosophical predilections see Knysh 1992.

in the present; it is, hence, that the verb signifying tradition (transmission) is generally used in the present tense. The American sociologist Craig J. Calhoun has argued similarly, contending that tradition is "grounded less in the historical past than in everyday social practice." He maintains "tradition is the medium in which interactions take place. Like language, it is at once passed from individual to individual through use and given much of its substantive meaning by the particular instances of its use" (Calhoun 1983, 896). Viewing traditionality as a mode of organizing social action, Calhoun argues that "the validity of traditional ideas or practices comes not just from their antiquity but from the element of consensus and universality of their use" (895). In what follows I argue that the clerical subculture is best represented by this concept of tradition. This interpretation explains why religion gained momentum in Iran while the process of modernization was in full swing.

While the process of secularization was initiated in Iran in the early parts of the twentieth century, the Iranian state actually never followed a full-fledged ideology of secularism. Neither the Iranian Constitution nor the Iranian government ever proclaimed itself to be secular. The two Pahlavi administrations followed the precedent set by the Safavid kings in the sixteenth century of maintaining Shi'a Islam as the official religion of the country. Furthermore, the Constitution had allowed for the formation of a supervisory body composed of the ulema to oversee the compliance of civil laws passed by the Parliament with the basic doctrines of Islam.

One should bear in mind that despite the presently fashionable interpretation of Twelver Shi'ism as an incessantly politicized doctrine, the Shi'a position on the separation of religion and state is rather controversial. Whereas radical jurists, such as Ayatollah Khomeini, insist that the sacred cannot be separated from the temporal, more conservative jurists point to the fact that a de facto break took place at the time of the sixth Imam, Ja'far al-Sadeq (700–765). This Imam separated the Imamate from political rule and impressed upon his followers that any notions of conflating the purely soteriological concerns of the faith with the political ones should be rejected. His aloof and quietist politics were necessitated by the insistence of Umayyad and later Abbasid caliphs that the legitimacy of their rule be blessed by the descendants of the Prophet's family. It is Imam Ja'far al-Sadeq's tradition of keeping theology separate from politics that enabled such grand ayatollahs as Borujerdi, Kho'i, Golpayegani, and Mar'ashi-Najafi to insist that clerics remain apolitical.

The clergy and the monarchy were also bound together by common enemies and mandates. The Allied occupation of Iran during World War

II, the threat of a rising communist movement, and the half-hearted support for the oil nationalization campaign constituted some of the commonalties between the two camps. Furthermore, the elitist disposition of both institutions led them fervently to oppose the idea of democracy and popular rule. To begin with, monarchy as a hereditary institution had no place in its system for mass representation. Contrary to their popular rhetoric, the ulema were also not too disposed toward democratic rule. Allameh Tabataba'i had clearly stated this position by writing

> Islam is not just another democratic system as some [have] claimed. Nor is it a communist system. It is a different order: The decrees of the Islamic community (as distinct from the immutable laws of Islam), although they are the results of consultation, are based fundamentally, not on the wishes of the majority, but on the truth, and depend for their stability, not on the desires and inclinations of the people, but on a realization of what is true. (Lambton 1964, 128)

The understanding between the two institutions, however, did not survive subsequent political vicissitudes. The land reform program, the granting of "capitulation rights" to American military personnel in Iran, women's enfranchisement, the 1963 Qom revolt, the state patronage of such rival organizations as the Religious Corps and the Endowments Organization and the overall depreciating magnitude of the clerical power base all contributed to the sense of rancor that came to mark the later stages of the clergy-state association.

By the 1960s the clergy had recognized that in the marketplace of ideas the only way to reclaim Islam from the dominance of competing schools of thought was through an ideological struggle. The method of assassination of political and ideological adversaries as carried out by the Feda'iyan-e Eslam in the 1940s was no longer judged appropriate.[7] The nonintellectual orientation of the Feda'iyan-e Eslam had to be abandoned if the clergy was to proselytize from among the more moderate and intellectually minded sectors of the Iranian polity. Hence, the clergy embarked upon a course of ideological struggle, challenging their contestants.

One way to wage this battle was through the publication of scholarly books. In 1944 Ayatollah Khomeini published his first major work entitled *Kashf al-asrar* (Unveiling of secrets). This 428-page book was a si-

7. This religio-political organization, which was formed in 1946 by Seyyed Mojtaba Navvab-Safavi, was responsible for the assassination of the famous historian and political thinker Ahmad Kasravi in 1946 as well as Prime Ministers Abdolhoseyn Hazhir in 1949 and Ali Razmara in 1951.

multaneous rebuttal to both Ali-Akbar Hakamizadeh and Mirza Reza-Qoli Shari'at-Sangalaji. Hakamizadeh, who had deserted the ranks of the clergy and had became a disciple of Ahmad Kasravi, had previously published a 38-page essay entitled *Asrar-e hezar-saleh* (Thousand-year-old secrets), which posed some challenging questions to the clergy.[8] Shari'at-Sangalaji was a modernist theologian who had questioned the Shi'ite eschatological doctrine of *raj'at* (return) by the vengeful Hidden Imam to salvage the world. This unorthodox idea was considered to have called into question the whole messianic beliefs of Shi'ism (see Richard 1988). In another response to the secularists Allameh Tabataba'i drafted *Osul-e falsafeh va ravesh-e re'alism* (1953–71), which became the clergy's most sophisticated rebuttal to materialist philosophy.[9]

Furthermore, in another lengthy book entitled *Khadamat-e motaqabel-e Eslam va Iran,* Ayatollah Motahhari responded to those Iranian national-ists who were renouncing the contributions of Islam to Iranian culture (Motahhari 1987). Ayatollah Naser Makarem-Shirazi published an in-triguingly titled book, *Asrar-e aqabmandegi-ye Sharq* (Secrets of the Ori-ent's backwardness) in 1969, assailing Western civilization, culture, science, and politics while promoting an Islamic/oriental alternative. Ayatollah Taleqani authored *Eslam va malekiyyat* (Islam and ownership), which addressed Islam's views on such crucial economic issues as own-ership, private and public property, banking, and interest rates. Finally, the lay thinker Mehdi Bazargan helped the clerical discourse by writing a series of works allegedly demonstrating the compatibility of many Islamic canons with modern scientific doctrines and findings. As if to preempt any criticism from those who may have objected to his ap-proach, Bazargan also translated a number of works by the Frankfurt School psychoanalyst and social psychologist Erich Fromm that de-picted the alienating conditions of life in the West.

These books, which discussed secularism, Marxism, Western civiliza-tion, Orient/Occident dichotomy, Iranian nationalism, and Islamic views on economics and politics as well, are only a sampling of the enormous body of literature produced by the clerical class. What is arresting in the choice of these topics is their modern form and their pertinence of content. Islam was becoming politicized or, more impor-tantly, was turning into an ideology.

The clerics' intellectual presence also extended to popular journals. In

8. For more on Khomeini's exchange with Hakamizadeh see Haj-Bushehri 1989 and Hakamizadeh 1991.

9. This five-volume work was Ayatollah Motahhari's reconstruction of the dis-courses delivered by Allameh Tabataba'i in the 1950s, with Motahhari's own extensive commentary.

1958 the first issue of the monthly periodical *Darsha'i az Maktab-e Eslam* was published in Qom by a publishing house (Daroltabliq-e Eslami) supervised by Ayatollah Mohammad-Kazem Shari'atmadari. The statement of purpose in the first issue of the journal spoke of the need to present an alternative to the ethical corruption, irreligiosity, and the spirit of materialism falling over Muslim society, especially its youth (Maktab-e Eslam 1958). This journal soon found its appropriate place in the Iranian intellectual scene, so much so that, according to one study, by the late 1970s it was sold at a rate of fifty thousand copies per month compared to a mere circulation of three thousand for *Sokhan*, Iran's best-known literary magazine since World War II (Tehranian 1980, 21).[10] *Darsha'i az Maktab-e Eslam* was followed by a second Islamic journal published in Qom entitled *Maktab-e Tashayyo'*. Pursuing goals similar to its counterpart's, yet in a more politically engaging manner, the new journal began with a sizable circulation of ten thousand copies in May 1959 and underwent a second reprint one month later, whereby an additional five thousand copies were printed.

These statistics were not an aberration. According to a bibliography of philosophical works published in Iran in 1975–76, more than 154 works (83 books and 71 articles) were written on Islamic topics compared to 48 works (30 books and 18 articles) dealing with modern philosophers' views on social and literary subjects (Eftekharzadeh 1977, 11–49, 103–13).[11] The religious works, which can mainly be divided into ideological, social, and theological categories, dealt with the following pertinent topics:

1. Ideological issues: critique of materialism, economic doctrines, world peace, political conditions in the world, concepts of ideal life, and the relationship between Iran and Islam.

2. Social issues: the youth, women, children, marriage, education, gambling, drinking, music, poetry, and social consciousness.

3. Theological issues: proving the existence of God, virtues of religious leadership, resurrection and afterlife, responding to Christian criticisms of Islam, and the relationship between science and faith.

In the early 1970s the three best-selling books, bought in hundreds of thousands of copies, were all religious in nature: *Qur'an* (700,000 copies), *Mafatih al-Jenan* [Keys to the Paradise] (490,000 copies), and *Rasa'il al-Amaliyya* [Dissertations on the practice of religious laws]

10. The editors of the *Maktab-e Eslam,* however, were claiming a circulation of two hundred thousand.

11. A note of caution should be mentioned here because, according to the compiler, the above bibliography does not represent an exhaustive list of all the philosophical works that were published in Iran during this time.

(400,000 copies). Furthermore, religious books as a percentage of all published books increased from 10.1 percent in 1963–64 to 33.5 percent in 1974–75 (Amir-Arjomand 1984, 214, 216).

The clergy and their allies also became involved in setting up publishing houses to disseminate their views. According to a 1976 survey cited by Amir Arjomand, there were "forty-eight publishers of religious literature in Tehran alone, of whom twenty-six had begun their activities with publication of religious books during the decade 1965–75" (Amir-Arjomand 1984, 213). These publishing houses were mainly concentrated in Tehran and Qom where the abundance of resources and a positive ambiance worked to their advantage. Hence, one can conclude that the ideological war had compelled the clergy to supplement oral discourse with the printed word as the primary means and mode of communication.

Educational Edification

Much of the intellectual and scientific heritage of Iran has developed within the Islamic intellectual life of religious schools and seminaries. The administrations of the Pahlavi shahs broke the clergy's monopolistic hold over the instructional domains by setting up modern, secularized, and state-supported counterparts. This secularization of the educational system deprived the clergy of one of their traditional sources of power. After a period of bafflement, the clergy realized that they were left with no other option but to pursue a two-tier policy of holding to their traditional institutions and abandoning their long-standing opposition to their modern educational counterparts.

The traditional clergy at first reacted negatively to the founding of institutions of higher education in the mid- and the late-1930s, referring to them as *ateshkadeh* (house of fire). The equation of a college (*daneshkadeh*) with an ateshkadeh was based on the belief that both were alien institutions belonging to an other: the first belonging to the non-Muslims, whereas the latter was the Zoroastrians' place of worship. Eventually, however, a number of their former students and sons deserted the ranks of the old guard and entered the universities. These defectors were employed mainly in *Daneshkadeh-ye ma'qul va manqul* (Faculty of Traditional and Contemplative Sciences) at various universities where they would cover such topics as jurisprudence, philosophy, history, Arabic, and comparative literature. Because of their previous background in the seminaries, these scholars were well equipped to teach their broadly defined subjects. Such learned scholars as Seyyed Mohammad-Kazem Assar, Nasrollah Falsafi, Badi'ozzaman Foruzanfar, Mohyeddin-Mehdi Elahi-Qomsheh'i, Seyyed Mohammad Meshkat, and

Mahmud Shahabi, all graduates of seminaries, were teaching at Tehran University in the late 1930s and the 1940s (Baheri 1983–84, 17–18).

From 1944 to 1961 when Ayatollah Hoseyn Borujerdi was at the helm of the Qom Seminary, the gap between the seminaries and the universities was further reduced.[12] Borujerdi was quite cognizant of the importance of propaganda both domestically and internationally (Algar 1990, 377). He sent emissaries to Egypt, Kuwait, Pakistan, Sudan, and Lebanon (the famous Ayatollah Musa Sadr) and set up the Islamic Center in Hamburg, Germany. In addition, he sanctioned many howzeh graduates to enter the universities to acquire knowledge of modern sciences and to promulgate Islam as well. His suggestion actually materialized as such traditionally trained scholars as Seyyed Jalaloddin Ashtiyani, Mohammad-Taqi Daneshpazhuh, Mehdi Ha'eri-Yazdi, Hojjatoleslam Mohammad-Javad Hojjati-Kermani, Ahmad Mahdavi-Damghani, Yahya Mahdavi, Ayatollah Mohammad Mofatteh, Mehdi Mohaqqeq, Javad Mosleh, Ayatollah Morteza Motahhari, Ayatollah Musa Sadr, and Seyyed Ja'far Shahidi, among others, entered the academic life of universities (Nasr 1972, 6–8). These scholars, many of them prolific writers, contributed much to the changing atmosphere of Iranian universities. Their authorship, editing, and commentary on various Islamic texts resulted in the efflorescence of such works. Furthermore, they organized centenary celebrations and commemorations of Islamic sages and saints, formed private discussion and study groups, led prayer services, engaged in theological or political debates and polemics with their opponents and, finally, trained a whole new generation of students and pedagogues.

These pioneers opened the way for many other theology students who followed them into the theology schools of modern Iranian universities. The provincial clerical elite had also consented to sending their sons into this new environment, allowing for a new lifestyle. Upon graduation, many of these individuals were recruited by such ministries as education, finance, and justice, which would send them back to their provincial towns as elementary or high school teachers, preachers, notary publics, and judges. Accordingly, the clergy secured an influential position for itself in the rapidly changing cultural life of Iran. Hence, an inadvertent consequence of the modernization process was to force a relocation of the terrain of contestation between the clergy and the

12. Binder (1965, 138) rightfully explains that this trend was also the result of the fact that the younger ulema and *tollab* realized that they were no longer on a par with the Westernized intelligentsia. Their learning was belittled, their behavior ridiculed, their clothing mocked, and all the best government jobs were closed to them.

state as the former attempted to undermine the latter's omnipotence from within its own structures.

The clergy's educational crusade went far beyond the universities. Another prime target of this drive was the primary and secondary schools. As early as the 1950s such activist clerics as Ayatollah Mohammad-Javad Bahonar, Ayatollah Mohammad Beheshti, Ayatollah Mohammad Mofatteh, and Ayatollah Motahhari had joined the mostly secular Iran Teachers' Association to advance their common cause against the state and the communist Left (Derakhshesh 1990). Mohammad Derakhshesh, the leader of the Teacher's Association who in 1961 became minister of education, contends that in the 1950s these clerics (in particular Beheshti and Bahonar) were able to set up a series of private boys' and girls' schools known as *Alavi* schools. Having been unable to dismantle the new secular school system, the clergy had decided to form their own alternative to it. The philosophy behind the establishment of these schools was rooted in the belief that the graduates of traditional religious seminaries were only capable of influencing the illiterate rural masses and not the educated strata of metropolitan Iran. Furthermore, the clerics and their lay colleagues expressed their irritation at the limited number of hours allocated for the teaching of theological subjects in modern Iranian high schools. Having conveyed these concerns, they were able to attract the support of the mostly traditional bazaar merchants and brokers who were more than willing to provide financial support.

With the financial backing of the bazaar the clergy were able to build modern schools; provide such benefits as a private bus service; and, most important, offer higher salaries to lure better teachers. In return they made sure that in addition to the regular curriculum designed by the Ministry of Education the students would get an adequate dosage of religious instruction, and the girls would be allowed to wear the veil in school. As a result of the more rigorous method of pedagogy that these students went through, many of them would succeed in the college entrance exams and make their way into highly competitive Iranian universities.[13] Although no precise statistics are available on these schools, it is safe to argue that they numbered in the hundreds and enrolled thousands of students.[14]

The clergy also infiltrated the regular secondary schools where they

13. After the 1979 revolution, many of the former Alavi school graduates, who were the equivalents of Mao's Red Guards, came to occupy influential positions within the new revolutionary administration.

14. Al-e Ahmad cites a figure of close to two hundred such primary and secondary schools with forty to fifty thousand pupils (Al-e Ahmad 1978, 2:31, 71).

were often hired as instructors of theology, composition, Arabic, and Persian literature. They would encourage their students to form Islamic student associations to carry a whole range of activities from offering classes on interpreting the Qur'an to forming study and discussion groups on philosophical and ethical issues, engaging in extracurricular activities, and organizing libraries. These activities proved attractive to many students.[15]

Besides university and high school students, the clergy also appealed to another group that was spawned by the country's overly rapid modernization—the urban poor. The clergy had historically been influential in the rural villages where they performed such diverse functions as being spiritual guides, literate clerks/teachers, family troubleshooters, trusted confidants, and guardians of the folk religion. The rural migration to the urban centers, however, brought along a transformation of their constituency. A changing locale demanded a modified strategy on the part of the clerical class to accommodate the new circumstances. The government inadvertently contributed much to this strategy by failing to fulfill many of its ambitious promises, which it was either unwilling or unable to deliver. The clergy responded by picking up where the government left off. Through their charitable enterprises, which were subsidized by the financial contributions of bazaar merchants and practicing Muslims at large, they managed to provide housing, education, health care, employment, and job-training services for numerous members of the urban poor. This was an ingenious way in which the clergy and their bazaari allies challenged the policy of civil privatism promoted by the state. In addition, the numerous *Mehdiyyeh, Hoseyniyyeh, rowzeh khani, dasteh* and *hey'ats, ta'ziyeh, anjomanha-ye tafsir-e Qur'an, Alavi* schools, Muslim student associations, Islamic libraries, and Islamic lending associations, which were developing at the time, strengthened the religious subculture.

The sheer size of the clerical class along with their extensive network of mosques (varying in estimates from 9,015 to 20,000), supported the rise of the clerical counterculture. This numerically significant size allowed the clergy to maintain a strong presence in their traditional stronghold of rural villages and in the metropolitan urban centers as well. Furthermore, the clergy's use of modern means of mass communication such as radio and television, cassettes, leaflets, books, and newspapers provided them with a broader audience with whom to interact.

15. Ali-Reza Mahfuzi, who later became a leading member of the Marxist-Leninist Feda'iyan-e Khalq organization, recounts how in high school he was pulled toward these Islamic libraries in which he studied books with the sole purpose of refuting the doctrines of Marx, Freud, and Darwin (Mahfuzi 1984).

This presence particularly increased during the three religiously marked months of Muharram, Safar, and Ramadan when they would deliver sermons and homilies, lead prayer services, and appear in radio and television interviews and discussions.

The popular religion was also reinforced by the general cultural inclinations and religious convictions of the greater masses. The social conservatism, male chauvinism, conspiratorial mindset, and patriarchal orientation of the society at large served as a fertile ground for the clerical summons. By emphasizing such provocative issues as the regime's numerous socioeconomic shortcomings, corruption, elitist orientation, disintegration of traditional family bonds, rampant irreligiosity among youth and their disrespect for elders, materialism, and consumerism, the clergy were able gradually to turn the tide of public opinion (especially among the urban lower classes) to their favor.[16] Henceforth, their calls about the prevalent moral decay, cultural malaise, economic hardships, political repression, and Western encroachment besetting Iranian society at the time fell on receptive ears. This orientational metamorphosis was further aided by the power of popular mythology.[17]

Transmutation of Theology

The formation of a viable subculture capable of ideological belligerency had another prerequisite—a theological coming-to-terms with the age of modernity. Since the beginning of the twentieth century, the Iranian ulema had been under mounting pressure to recognize that a rapidly evolving world requires a changing theology to ensure its durability. The age of modernity had drastically altered the terms of reference. Anthropomorphization of God was no longer a caveat, but a reality. Sovereignty had changed from one residing with the Holy Being to one emanating from the voice of the citizens. For the greatest majority of people secularism was no longer the incipient doctrine it once was, but a reality of everyday life. Scientific discoveries had subverted most, if not all, dogmas and superstitions.

16. It is important to remember that the bulk of religious activism does not take place in the countryside but in such urban centers as Esfahan, Kashan, Mashhad, Qom, Shiraz, Tabriz, and Tehran.

17. Eslam Kazemiyyeh cites as one example a case in which an oil well around the city of Qom allegedly was turned into salt water; people began to attribute this incident to the fact that the shah had offended the clergy in a public speech a few days beforehand (Kazemiyyeh 1983–84).

For the Iranian Shiʿite ulema this realization is said to have begun with the 1909 publication of Ayatollah Mohammad-Hoseyn Naʾini, *Tanbih al-umma va tanzih al-milla* (The admonition and refinement of the people). In this treatise the eminent theologian provided a critique of absolutism and supported the idea of constitutionalism.[18] As the precursor of a new way of political thinking, Naʾini faced a barrage of fierce criticism from his more conservative colleagues.[19] The second step toward a rapprochement with the modern era was taken by Naʾini's contemporary, Ayatollah Abdolkarim Haʾeri-Yazdi, who founded the Feyziyyeh Seminary in Qom, which became Iran's largest and most important theological center. Haʾeri-Yazdi's stewardship was significant in the sense that it introduced organizational coherence to the scattered and factionally ridden ranks of the clergy and allowed the development of systematic theology.

The clerical citadel of dogmatism experienced its third important act of imaginative challenge in the early 1940s when Mirza Reza-Qoli Shariʿat-Sangalaji questioned the Shiʿite belief in the return of the Hidden Imam (discussed earlier). During the 1940s and 1950s there rose such politically consequential leaders as Ayatollah Seyyed Ali-Akbar Borqehʿi, and Seyyed Mojtaba Navvab-Safavi, and most importantly Ayatollah Seyyed Abolqasem Kashani, who, despite their contrasting political standpoints, all engaged in politically mobilizing their supporters. In addition, the emergence of such clerics or clerical-born individuals as Mohammad-Kazem Assar and Mehdi Haʾeri-Yazdi, who had studied in the West and were competent in at least one European language, provided the clergy with a more reliable view of the modern world.

More consequentially, however, since the 1950s a number of Shiʿite ulema and scholars such as Hasan Hasanzadeh-Amoli, Seyyed Jalaloddin Ashtiyani, Mohammad-Kazem Assar, Mehdi Haʾeri-Yazdi, Ayatollah Mohsen Hakim, Ayatollah Khomeini, Ayatollah Motahhari, Seyyed Hoseyn Nasr, Ayatollah Mohyeddin Mehdi Elahi-Qomshehʾi, Ayatollah Seyyed Abolhasan Rafiʾi-Qazvini, Allameh Tabatabaʾi, and Ayatollah Mahmud Taleqani had overcome the traditional clerics' opposition to teaching courses in philosophy. They tutored students in the areas of gnosis and theosophy where the peripatetic and illuminationist philosophies of Avicenna (980–1037), Shahaboddin Sohravardi (1153–1191),

18. For a discussion of the treatment Naʾini's book has received in Iran see Parham 1988.

19. Naʾini's chief opponent was the anticonstitutionalist cleric, Sheykh Fazlollah Nuri, who was executed by the constitutionalists in 1909, the same year that Naʾini's book was published.

and Molla Sadra (1571–1640) were taught side by side with the works of Socrates, Plato, and Aristotle.

The late 1960s and the early 1970s also had their own share of theologically significant events as Ne'matollah Salehi-Najafabadi, a student of Khomeini, reinterpreted the Karbala episode as a mere political rebellion and called into question the Shi'a theological dogma on Imam Hoseyn's prescience about his impending martyrdom. Published in 1968, Salehi-Najafabadi's semischolarly *Shahid-e javid* (Eternal martyr) provoked heated debates in Iranian religious centers by its insistence on subjecting every orthodox source and conventional narrative to a rigorous historical-factual scrutiny. More importantly, however, in 1971 Ayatollah Khomeini published his treatise on velayat-e faqih, which altered the traditional Shi'ite doctrine of authority by advocating the establishment of an Islamic government (Khomeini 1971). This book laid the theoretical foundation for a revolutionary government that was to materialize only eight years later.

Despite the maturation process the politics of the clergy was not all homogeneous or progressive-minded. In fact, the majority of the leading ulema remained apolitical or quite conservative in their political outlook. Such leading figures as Ayatollah Hoseyn Borujerdi, Ayatollah Mohammad-Reza Golpayegani, Ayatollah Abolqasem Kho'i, Ayatollah Shahaboddin Mar'ashi-Najafi, Ayatollah Mohammad-Hadi Milani, and Ayatollah Mohammad-Kazem Shari'atmadari represented the voices of the conservative clerical establishment. After the ouster of Mosaddeq in 1953, the conservative clergy turned their attention inward and launched a campaign against Baha'is whom they considered to be the archenemies of Islam. At the forefront of this campaign was Sheykh Mahmud Halabi, an ultra-conservative cleric from Mashhad, who founded the Anti-Baha'i Society, which was the forerunner of Anjoman-e Hojjatiyyeh.[20]

The majority of clerics remained philosophically ignorant and narrow-minded. Their opportunistic demeanor, preoccupation with trivial concerns, intellectual rigidity, scientific ignorance, and authoritarian manner account for the overall low esteem in which they were viewed by most educated Iranians. For the most part the Iranian clerics' acquaintance with Western schools of thought remained frivolous. Even when they undertook such an inquiry, it was done not with the intention of understanding or appreciating these texts or thinkers but for refuting them. Whereas for the secular Iranian intellectuals Westerniza-

20. For more on Sheykh Halabi and the Anjoman-e Hojjatiyyeh see Vali and Zubaida 1985.

tion implied a positive attitude toward human beings and the world, a scientific spirit, and the creation of a tangible heaven in this transient world, the clergy would too readily indulge in emphasizing such negative traits of the Western life style as its consumerism, excessive individualism, and anthropomorphism of God.

Nowhere was the clerics' narrow-mindedness more evident than in issues regarding women's rights and equality. A dogmatic belief in the inequality of sexes underscored much of their social thinking. The clergy used to object vociferously to women's rights to education, employment, enfranchisement, birth control, becoming judges, or even wearing Western attire. The marginal status of women was further reinforced by the patriarchal canons of Islam, which had codified male polygamy, justified unequal inheritance laws between males and females, and even sanctified modes of appropriate punishment for women at the hands of men.[21]

The conservatism of the Iranian clergy was not limited to viewing women as second-class citizens. Additionally, they were opposed to land reform, investment in national banks, infringement of private property, socioeconomic prominence of such minorities as the Jews and the Baha'is, rise of Marxist or lay religious intellectuals, formation of new schools based on a secular educational curriculum, children's school uniforms, learning Western languages, listening to or watching radio and television, and a variety of other progressive causes and platforms. The intensity of their objections varied according to their class backgrounds, levels of education, and bonds to various social groups.

Notwithstanding these antediluvian ideas, the clergy's enjoyment of important comparative advantages made them the most organized sociopolitical force at the outbreak of the 1979 revolution. The emotional force generated on religious occasions, impressive popular support, well-rehearsed agitators, and an imposing agenda for political propaganda proved too much both for the state and for the secular contenders. Ali-Asghar Haj-Seyyed-Javadi, a leading secular opponent of the shah's regime, recounted the following event, which elucidates the way in which the secular opposition was subdued by the clerics:

On the day of Ashura or Tasuʿa [two consecutive days of mourning for the martyrdom of Imam Hoseyn in the battle of Karbala in 680] I and a group of well-dressed intellectuals, who were all technocrat types, started to march from a northern part of Tehran toward the 24 of Esfand

21. For two competent analyses of the lives of Iranian women see Tabari and Yeganeh 1982 and Sanasarian 1983.

Square. Suddenly, a massive wave of demonstrators marching from southern parts [of Tehran] approached us. At the head of every two hundred meters of demonstrators stood an *akhund* [religious preacher] shouting slogans. They were chanting an entirely religious slogan about Imam Hoseyn, which was suddenly reverberated by [our outnumbered group of] intellectuals. (Haj-Seyyed-Javadi 1984)

5

Lay Religious Intellectuals

The past is a foreign country; they do things differently there.

—L. P. Hartley, *The Go-Between*

IDEOLOGICAL STRUGGLES MORE OFTEN than not turn into a zero-sum game. The matrix of Iranian intellectual life in the post–World War II era reflected an ideological contest as modern/traditional, left-wing/right-wing, and state/clerical rivalries waged concurrently. The synthesis of these dichotomous struggles was the birth of a new breed of intellectuals who stood at the intersection of these three major divides. The emergence of this new class of religious intellectuals was, undoubtedly, one of the most important developments within Iranian political culture in the post–World War II era. Although sharing certain commonalties, the members of this class differed from both the laicized intellectuals and the clerical strata in a number of respects. Consisting of a diverse array of scholars, activists, and thinkers, they managed to articulate a formidable alternative to the state, the laicized intellectuals, and the clerical caste. These intellectuals were capable of taking radical or conservative, avant-garde or conventional, and revolutionary or statist positions. Nevertheless, they all proclaimed an allegiance to Shiʿa Islam as their principal source of inspiration and loyalty. Their combined influence, which was exhibited in the magnitude of their popular support and in the degree of their intellectual stamina, proclaimed the indisputable arrival of a new contender on the Iranian intellectual scene.

Iran's lay religious intellectuals waged several simultaneous ideological battles. First, they saw themselves in competition with an increasingly vibrant secular movement and a powerful state machinery that was becoming increasingly skeptical of its citizens' religious predilections. Second, their attempt to demystify and to reformulate their religion's history and heritage brought them into friction with the clerical class, which wanted to maintain its privileged monopoly as the guardians of faith, orthodoxy, and tradition. Finally, the religious intellectuals' desire to answer and challenge the West and its multiplicity of ideologies compelled them to spend much of their cerebral talent on these perceived contenders. This tripartite struggle is lucidly illustrated in the intellectual ambiance of the northeastern city of Mashhad, the capital of Khorasan Province and a celebrated hometown for many of Iran's leading religious intellectuals.

Mashhad: A Microcosm of Iranian Religious Life

Khorasan Province, located in northeastern Iran, has historically played an important role in Iranian cultural and intellectual life. Geographically, it has provided Iran with its window into India, Russia (Soviet Union), and the rest of Asia; it has been Iran's front-line province against invasions from the east (Uzbeks, Mongols, and Afghans) and a sanctuary from the more frequent attacks by Arabs from the west. Culturally, it has been Iran's most fertile intellectual territory, a place where philosophy, arts, and literature have historically flourished. As the birthplace or the favorite habitat of numerous well-known philosophers, artists, and poets (such as Avicenna, Ferdowsi, Omar Khayyam, and Jalaloddin Rumi [also known as Mowlana]), Khorasan's harvest of intellectuals and thinkers somewhat rivals that of the rest of Iran combined. Mashhad (which literally means the place of martyrdom) sprang up from the pilgrim traffic generated by Imam Reza's tomb, a revered Shi'ite Imam who was allegedly poisoned to death. It is the leading sacred pilgrimage site for Iranian Shi'ites as well as the country's second most populated city.[1] Mashhad's economy is dominated by the service sector, which caters to the needs of millions of pilgrims who visit it every year.[2] Given that Mashhad was the locus of Imam Reza's tomb, literature and religion became an integral way of life for the people of Khorasan. These qualities make Khorasan, in general, and its capital city Mashhad, in particular, an appropriate case study for deliberations on contemporary Iranian intellectual life.

The strength of Mashhad's religious mood was first tested in July 1935 when Reza Shah's decree prohibiting the wearing of veils in public places was met with strong opposition. A sermon delivered in the Gowharshad Mosque by a radical cleric denouncing this diktat ignited a

1. Mashhad's population increased from slightly more than one million in 1976 to more than two million in 1986 (Nazari 1989, 201).

2. The construction of the Tehran-Mashhad railroad in 1957 helped to boost the number of pilgrims going to Mashhad.

demonstration that was put down violently by the government. Facing police punishment for veiling, many of Mashhad's conservative families who viewed the law as contrary to their Islamic beliefs prohibited their wives or daughters from walking outside the house for many years. It was only after the abdication of Reza Shah and the Allied occupation of Iran in August 1941 that this situation began to change. Barely two weeks after the abdication of Reza Shah, the Tudeh Party declared its formation and began gradually to set up branches in the provinces. Needless to say, the religious forces in Mashhad considered the opening of the local Tudeh branch as yet another challenge that needed to be dealt with.

A local religious scholar, Mohammad-Taqi Shariʿati, decided to form an Islamic center to educate Mashhad's modern-educated youth about the erroneous beliefs of deists and the advantages of Islam over Marxism. His hope was that he could thereby discourage the youth from joining the ranks of the movement formed around Ahmad Kasravi or worse yet that of the Tudeh Party. Mohammad-Taqi Shariʿati was uniquely qualified for this task. Born into a clerical family in the village of Mazinan (near Sabzevar), he came to Mashhad in 1928 to continue his religious studies at the city's theological seminary. In the early 1930s this erudite cleric began his thirty-year career as a local high school teacher and assistant superintendent. He gradually abandoned his clerical garb to devote himself more freely to his lifelong interest in interpreting Qurʾanic exegesis. Banking on his reputation as a prolific exegete and popular teacher, Mohammad-Taqi Shariʿati founded Kanun-e Nashr-e Haqayeq-e Eslami (Center for the Propagation of Islamic Truths) in 1944.[3] For the next two decades Shariʿati and his colleagues advocated a brand of Islam that enabled them to attract many of Mashhad's high school and university students and a number of its progressive-minded clerics and bazaar merchants as well. Among the more prominent associates were such figures as Taher Ahmadzadeh (first postrevolutionary governor of Khorasan and father of the leftist Fedaʾiyan-e Khalq leaders Masʿud and Mastureh Ahmadzadeh); Abolfazl and Mahmud Hakimi (two of the leadership cadres of Nehzat-e Azadi); Seyyed Ali Khamenei (former president and present spiritual leader of the Islamic Republic); Amir-Parviz Puyan (ideologue of the Fedaʾiyan-e Khalq); Reza Puyan (engineer); Kazem Rajavi (professor of law and older brother of the Mojahedin-e Khalq leader Masʿud Rajavi); Neʿmat Mirzazadeh (well-known poet); Mohammad Shanehchi (influential

3. For more information on Mohammad-Taqi Shariʿati and his center see Rokni 1987 and Pazhum 1991.

broker in the bazaar with close ties to leading clergy, who lost four of his children in the fight against the shah's and Khomeini's government); and Mohammad-Taqi Shari'ati's own son, Ali. Such a distinguished group of associates propelled Kanun-e Nashr-e Haqayeq-e Eslami (hereafter referred to as "the center") into the forefront of Iranian intellectual life, making its presence known well beyond the city limits of Mashhad.

In the absence of organized political parties the center also performed a political task. The presence of such seasoned political individuals as Taher Ahmadzadeh and Mohammad Shanehchi ensured the center's political involvement as was the case during Mosaddeq's oil nationalization campaign of the early 1950s. After the downfall of Mosaddeq, the center continued its ties with the religiously oriented nationalists who had gathered around Nehzat-e Azadi through such individuals as Mehdi Bazargan and Ezzatollah Sahabi (Mirzazadeh 1984). Furthermore, the center maintained its contacts with the more secularly-oriented intellectuals. Ne'mat Mirzazadeh, a long-time patron of the center, remembers a meeting in 1969 in which Jalal Al-e Ahmad presented his thesis on the necessity of a clergy-intellectual alliance at one of the center's discussion groups. Al-e Ahmad's proposal met with the approval of all participants, including Mohammad-Taqi and Ali Shari'ati, and Seyyed Ali Khamenei (Mirzazadeh 1984).

The center's emphasis on an Islam that was militant, modern, and dynamic brought it into conflict not only with the government and the leftist forces it was trying to unseat but also with the city's conservative seminarians.[4] Mashhad's howzeh, which had been severely weakened as a result of the Gowharshad Mosque incident and the death of some of its leading theologians, staged a comeback after the abdication of Reza Shah in 1941. Under the supervision of Ayatollah Ahmad Kafa'i, who had a cordial relationship with the royal court, Mashhad's howzeh gradually developed a solid administrative and financial structure. The presence of such reputable theologians as Aqa Mirza Mehdi Esfahani, Ayatollah Ahmad Kafa'i, Ayatollah Mohammad-Hadi Milani, Ayatollah Hasan Qomi, Haj Mehdi Kadkani, Ayatollah Mohsen Hakim, Ayatollah Mahmud Halabi, and Hoseyn-Ali Rashed, at one time or another, helped to restore the intellectual stature of Mashhad's howzeh as a bastion of theological conservatism. These clerics, who were not too keen on philosophy or mysticism, could neither stand Mohammad-Taqi and Ali Shari'ati's unorthodox pedagogical approaches toward Islamic teachings nor support their political beliefs and unconventional modes of

4. The center was closed under pressure from the authorities in June 1963.

behavior. Ali Shariʿati recalls a time when he and his father were criticized for their views on the necessity of women's literacy, the importance of undergoing modern education, the possibility of interpreting
the Qurʾan differently, seeking nontheological reasons for such natural
disasters as earthquakes and tornadoes, and not believing strongly in
polygamy. He adds that they even had to endure disparagement for
such rudimentary practices as shaving the face, wearing a hat or a tie,
lecturing through loudspeakers, or even walking in a street designated as
"Pahlavi" (Shariʿati 1977, 20). This war of words and ideas escalated
later as the prominent Ayatollah Milani became a frequent subject of Ali
Shariʿati's indirect criticisms while the latter himself was severely criticized by the clerical establishment.[5]

The clergy were aided in their opposition to Shariʿati's center by the
conservative bazaar merchants who regarded the center as the congre-
gation site for the more reformist-minded and religiously lax individuals.
One such bazaar merchant was Haj Ali-Asghar Abedzadeh. A wood-
carver and glass merchant by profession and son-in-law of a local cleric
by kinship, Abedzadeh would attend the sermons of a semilearned
cleric and would then convey the same materials to his guild fellows in
more lay terms. Beginning in the mid-1940s, Abedzadeh's popularity
started to rise as he launched a philanthropic campaign by establishing a
number of charitable organizations (Mehdiyyeh, Askariyyeh, Naqaviy-
yeh, Javadiyyeh, etc.) named after the infallible Shiʿa Imams. Anyone
wishing to learn the Arabic language or the Qurʾan could attend one of
these endowments, which served both as free religious reading and lecture halls and affordable medical clinics.[6] These endowments mainly
catered to the needs of the urban poor and the lower classes, bazaaris,
school teachers, and students whose fold was rapidly swelling in a developing city such as Mashhad. Needless to say, the popularity of Abedzadeh's grass-roots foundations, which continued until the 1979
revolution, also translated into political clout. By the time of Mosaddeq's administration he had already become a local powerbroker to be
reckoned with. Abedzadeh also played a leading role in the founding of
such societies as Jamʿiyyat-e Peyrovan-e Qurʾan and Heyʾat-e Ali-Ak-
bariha. These societies along with Sheykh Mahmud Halabi's supercon-
servative Anjoman-e Hojjatiyyeh left their traditionalist imprint on
Mashhad's cultural life (Shanehchi 1983).

5. Both the senior and the junior Shariʿati were often accused of being under the
influence of Ismaili, Bahaʾi, or Sunni teachings.

6. Two of the most prominent alumni of these endowments were the literary researcher and translator Hoseyn Khadivjam and Iran's foremost classical singer, Mohammad-Reza [Siyavash] Shajariyan.

Until the 1950s Mashhad's intellectual milieu was confined to activities associated with the center, the shrine of Imam Reza, a few high schools, and a number of strong religious establishments. With the foundation of Mashhad University, however, things began to change.[7] The presence of a strong state-sponsored institution of higher learning and mushrooming commercial enterprises increased the rate of defections from the seminaries.[8] The clergy were most critical of Mashhad and other universities' Faculties of Traditional and Contemplative Sciences (later renamed Faculties of Theology), which, because they offered courses on Islam and Arabic language and literature, were considered to be a potential threat to their own base of power. More importantly, the Faculty of Theology was taking students away from the seminary schools. In the late 1960s while the total number of Mashhad's *tollab* stood at 1,400, a total of 260 students (all male) were enrolled in the Mashhad University Faculty of Theology (Khamenei 1986, 86; Mashhad University 1972, v). As these graduates, however, began to occupy such innocuous positions as government employees, notaries, judges, army chaplains, high school teachers, and university professors, the clergy softened its critical tone.

Furthermore, literary writing by authors in Mashhad underwent a transformation both in agency and in style and composition. The older generation, such men as Mahmud Farrokh, Badiʾozzaman Foruzanfar, and Mohammad Parvin-Gonabadi, who were advocates of purely scholastic and/or apolitical literature, observed the emergence of a younger generation the likes of Mehdi Akhavan-Sales, Mahmud Dowlatabadi, Esmaʾil Khoʾi, Neʿmat Mirzazadeh, and Mohammad-Reza Shafiʿi-Kadkani, who were calling for a committed literature.[9] The Mashhad Uni-

7. The university was first founded as the High Institute of Health in 1939. With the addition of the Faculty of Medicine in 1949, however, the Faculty of Literature and the Faculty of Dentistry in 1955, the Faculty of Traditional and Contemplative Sciences in 1958, and the Faculty of Sciences in 1962–63, it was transformed into a full-fledged university. In 1973 the university was renamed Ferdowsi University in honor of the great eleventh-century Persian poet.

8. Ahmad Mahdavi-Damghani, a former professor of theology and literature at Tehran University who presently teaches at Harvard University, is typical of this earlier generation. Born into a clerical family in 1926, he was the first graduate of Mashhad's seminary to enter a university. Interestingly enough, Mahdavi-Damghani recalls how his father, who used to teach at Mashhad's seminary, had to be persuaded by other high-ranking clerics to allow his son to attend Tehran University in 1944 (Mahdavi-Damghani 1990).

9. A notable exception among the older generation of literati was the poet laureate Mohammad-Taqi Bahar, who was one of the most loyal champions of the Constitutional Revolution. Although a poet of the modern age, Bahar insisted on composing

versity Faculty of Letters reflected this changing milieu as leftist and militant lay students contested the literary and theoretical explications offered by their traditionalist or apolitical professors.

The religious intellectuals' intrusion into the fortress of traditional Islam was fittingly personified in the life of one of Mashhad's prominent sons—Ali Shari'ati. As Iran's most celebrated religious intellectual of the 1960s and the 1970s, Shari'ati's life illustrates the process through which lay religious intelligentsia were able to contest the conservative and tradition-bound interpretations of Islam offered by the ulema.

Ali Shari'ati: The Aspiring Luther

A man ignored by the secularists, admonished by the clerics, and punished by the shah's regime is nowadays widely regarded as the "Voltaire" and "the main ideologue" of the 1979 revolution (Farhang 1979, 31; Richard 1981, 215). The first camp considered him peripheral, the second treated him as an enfant terrible, and the third viewed him as a troublesome Islamic-Marxist who needed to be silenced. For these reasons Shari'ati's popularity in Iran has come to exceed that of all other secular and religious intellectuals considered in this book. These characteristics qualify him for an in-depth scrutiny.

Shari'ati was born on 3 December 1933 into a religious family in the village of Mazinan in Khorasan. He attended secondary school in Mashhad and studied under the tutelage of his learned father, Mohammad-Taqi Shari'ati. His higher education included a Bachelor of Arts in Persian language and literature from Mashhad University (1958) and a doctorate in hagiology from the University of Paris (1963) where he submitted a partial annotated translation of a medieval Persian manuscript entitled *Faza'el-e Balkh* (Les Mérites de Balkh) (The meritorious of Balkh) as his dissertation (Association Internationale des Docteurs de l'Université de Paris, 1967). Upon returning to Iran in 1964 he was imprisoned for six months for his involvement in antigovernment activities in Paris. Beginning in 1966, he taught intermittently at Mashhad University as an assistant professor of Islamic history and was arrested a number of times by SAVAK because of his political activities. After spending a couple of years under house arrest, Shari'ati left Iran for England where he died unexpectedly of a heart attack on 6 June 1977. The circumstances surrounding his death led his supporters to claim probable foul play by SAVAK.

---

poems in the classical style. He is considered to have succeeded in this endeavor like no one else.

If the Iranian intellectual panorama of the 1960s was dominated by Jalal Al-e Ahmad, that of the 1970s undoubtedly belonged to Ali Shari-ʿati. Al-e Ahmad had masterfully articulated the dilemma confronting Iranian intellectuals but fell short of offering a solution. Shariʿati, however, preoccupied himself with theoretical propositions and practical remedies for altering this predicament. His major notion of *bazgasht beh khishtan* (return to the self) complemented Al-e Ahmad's discourse of gharbzadegi, of whom he had written: "Al-e Ahmad was an intellectual, but he did not yet know himself. He did not know how he should operate and only in the last few years did he begin to practice returning to his self" (Shariʿati 1985, 415).

Shariʿati thus decided to go beyond Al-e Ahmad's mere condemnation of the intelligentsia by articulating a more concrete definition of their commitment and mode of praxis. As such, gharbzadegi and bazgasht beh khishtan came to constitute the two interrelated and ever-popular discourses of the Iranian intellectual polity in the 1960s and the 1970s. To better comprehend the second discourse, one needs to first examine Shariʿati's ontological and epistemological predispositions, his view of the Orient/Occident divide, and his perception of intellectuals.

Shariʿati can, perhaps, best be described as a sociologist of religion. This assigned label can be rationalized in view of two important facts: first, much of what he wrote about did not digress from the framework of religion and religious thought; second, his approach to religion was informed by certain schools of thought within contemporary sociology. Shariʿati primarily spoke the language of Franco-German social philosophy. As a student in France in the 1960s, he was influenced by the ideas of Raymond Aron (1905–1984), Jacques Berque (1910–1995), Henry Corbin (1903–1978), Frantz Fanon, Roger Garaudy (1913–   ), Georges Gurvitch (1894–1965), Louis Massignon (1883–1962), and Jean-Paul Sartre. Furthermore, as demonstrated through his sporadic references to Hegel, Marx, Husserl, Jaspers, Heidegger, and Marcuse, one can surmise that Shariʿati was also exposed to the ideas of these German philosophers.

Shariʿati borrowed from both traditions. His social thought does conform to the tenets of nineteenth-century sociological tradition as represented by Hegel and Marx. He saw merits in Hegel's idealistic and historicist school of thought, which posed a counterweight to the mechanistic materialism of the Enlightenment. Yet he borrowed Marx's idea of praxis as the basis of human epistemology and came to appreciate such indispensable principles of his philosophy as base and superstructure, class conflict, alienation, and ideology. To a lesser extent he was inspired by Heidegger's idea of the "prison of self," which Shariʿati included along with naturalism, "sociologism" (materialism), and historicism as constituting the four major "prisons of humanity" (Shariʿati 1983b, 117–84). Finally, Shariʿati was influenced by the Husserlian phenomenology, which he summarized as follows:

> Phenomenon and phenomenology are based on the principle that absolute truth, core of reality, and the essential essence of the world, nature, and matter can never be known. What is and can be known, experienced, and subjected to our scientific analysis is the appearance and not the being. . . . Physics, chemistry, and psychology can only analyze, interpret, and, finally, know the recognizable signs and symbols of the world and the spirit. Hence, science [can] only speak of the signs and symbols of being. (Shariʿati 1983b, 38–39)

Shariʿati's attempt to incorporate the insights of Hegel and Marx within his broader Shiʿite worldview led him toward phenomenology as an alternative. He found himself in agreement with the phenomenologists' heuristic contention that all one perceives as concrete objects and subjects are only appearances of the primary reality. Shariʿati interpreted this view according to his Shiʿite beliefs, maintaining that the primary reality is hidden, unknown, and beyond one's grasp.[10]

Despite these Germanic influences Shariʿati's methodological and epistemological tone is closer to that of contemporary French thinkers. This was partly because he was a product of social and human sciences as opposed to the discipline of philosophy. Shariʿati's epistemology centered around his repeated invoking of principles and theories from such disciplines as sociology, economics, history, anthropology, and mythology to bolster his arguments. Speaking of his approach, Shariʿati wrote:

> The greatest lesson that I as a teacher can give to my students . . . is that in order to know religion we should follow the same road as that taken by nonreligious or even antireligious scientists. I travel along this road and I speak with the same language, which in the name of science, sociology, economics, philosophy of history, and anthropology, renounces religion or negates its metaphysical roots. I find this to be the best language for examination of scientific and human issues, and I employ the same methods that Europe used after the eighteenth and the nineteenth centuries in its examination of human issues. (Shariʿati 1983d, 52–53)

This approach was markedly different from one taken by another faction of religious intellectuals, represented by Mehdi Bazargan, who were trying to prove the accuracy of Qur'anic teachings based on the

10. For more on Shariʿati's epistemology see Akhavi 1983.

modern scientific findings in nuclear physics, biochemistry, and thermo-
dynamics. Clearly, Shariʿati was not a positivist social scientist. Indeed,
he criticized "scientism" as the doctrine most responsible for substitut-
ing reality for truth. He approached anthropology not from its scientific
entrance but through its philosophical back door and acknowledged
that he preferred mythology over history because the former represents
history as it should have happened, whereas the latter embodies realities
that were made up by others. Shariʿati's pull toward the metaphysical
should be understood against the backdrop of his larger desire to help
bridge the gap between two abstract views of humans: the *Homo econom-*
icus of occidental philosophy and the *Homo symbolicus* of oriental
philosophy.

Finally, Shariʿati was strongly attracted to the neo-Marxist dialectical
sociology of Georges Gurvitch, the existentialism of Jean-Paul Sartre,
Louis Massignon's reading of medieval Islamic mysticism, and Frantz
Fanon's psychoanalytical approach to Third World revolutionary movements. He translated either parts or full texts of Alexis Carel's *La Prière,*
Fanon's *The Wretched of the Earth* and *Five Years of the Algerian War;* Sartre's *What is Poetry?* and parts of *Being and Nothingness;* Che Guevara's
Guerrilla Warfare; Louis Massignon's *Salman Pak et les premices spirituelles de*
l'Islam Iranien and *Etude sûr une courbe personnelle de vie: Le Cas de Hallaj*
martyr mystique de l'Islam. Shariaʿati was convinced that all these approaches could contribute to the reconstruction of the "authentic existence" of the Oriental, a goal he eagerly pursued to the very end of his
life.

Shariʿati considered Orient and Occident to be different from one
another in a number of respects. The foremost difference was one of
archetypes: "The cultural archetype of Greece is philosophical, Rome's
is artistic and militaristic, China's is mystical, India's is spiritual, and that
of ours [Iranians] is religious and Islamic" (Shariʿati 1981a, 282). He
maintained that these differing archetypes have brought along different
cultural properties in the Occident and in the Orient: rationalism, materialism, objectivism, and profit-seeking in the former, and ecclesiastical,
collectivist, subjectivist, and moral traits in the latter. Ontologically,
then, the Occident has come to seek the "reality" that is, whereas the
Orient is still pursuing the "truth" that shall be.

Shariʿati attributed these larger cultural/ontological differences to
fundamental dissimilarities in the nature and function of religion and
politics in the Orient and the Occident. He charged that whereas in the
former, religion has promoted an activist approach, in the latter it has
fallen prey to the rulers and has sided with the oppressors against the
vanquished. Religious leaders in the Occident have become collabora-

tors with authorities, whereas in the Orient they have traditionally spear-headed rebellions against all sorts of injustice. Furthermore, Shari°ati maintained that whereas Christian churches have come to be the slum-ber-houses of spirit, Islamic mosques have remained the abode of pro-gressive revolutionary movements.

Shari°ati, alas, was being inconsistent, dishonest, and thoroughly ahistorical on this subject. Ironically enough, a man whom he adored as one of his main mentors, Louis Massignon, was a Franciscan tertiary and a Catholic priest of the Melkite Rite. As France's most celebrated Orientalist of the twentieth century, Massignon had embraced a Gan-dhian style of politics and was actively sympathetic toward the anti-colonial movements of the Third World (in particular the Algerian resistance, which was so dear to Shari°ati). Furthermore, during his Pari-sian sojourn Shari°ati was exposed to the ideas of liberation theology through the journal *Esprit* and, thus, knew all too well that his dichot-omy between Christian passivity and Islamic militancy was fraudulent. The fact that the journal and its founder, the Christian philosopher Emmanuel Mounier, had taken up the cause of the French resistance and had criticized Hitler's anti-Semitism as early as 1933 could not have escaped him. Finally, his inconsistency in praising oriental religious leaders as spearheads of rebellion is demonstrated in the following quotation.

We had put our faith in Confucius, the philosopher, who had spoken of man and the community but became a servant to the princes of China. As for Buddha, the great prince of the Banaras [Varanasi, city in India], he deserted us and turned within himself to reach the state of "Nir-vana"—which I do not know where it is—[thereby] suffering great pains to develop great ideas! Zoroaster, who was appointed to prophethood in Azerbaijan, left without speaking to us, the mourners and wounded of the tomb, and fled to Balkh [province in Afghanistan] where he aban-doned us in the safety of King Goshtasp's royal court. As for Mani, who spoke of light and assailing darkness, he dedicated his book to the Sas-anid king, Shapur, blessed his coronation, and was proud to accompany him in his sojourns to Sri Lanka, India, and Balkh. (Shari°ati 1982, 181–82)

Nevertheless, as an ideologue, Shari°ati chose to ignore these facts and inconsistencies to make Islam—really Shi°a Islam—unique. He was able to reinterpret Shi°ism's claims of historical persecution, its dis-course of martyrdom, and its futuristic language (promising eternal sal-vation, heaven, and immortal happiness for those who choose to confront the "unjust others") in a modernist vein. He accentuated the "historic-victim discourse" of Shiʿism and made it the object of his rhetorical trope. As Michel Foucault's genealogy of power has demonstrated, however, discourses are terrains in which power and authority are given to some and withheld from others. Embedded within Shiʿism's historic-victim discourse is a call for resistance to the unjust incursions of the other(s). Shariʿati's modernist interpretation of this discourse and the unique neologism that went along with it made it compatible with the dualistic Weltanschauung of orientalism in reverse. In response to the injustices of the shah's political and economic systems, Shariʿati was easily able to invoke the syntax, slogans, and imagery of a Shiʿism impregnated with nativism.

Shariʿati further deemed politics to have incarnated different qualities in the Orient and the Occident. In the Orient, he argued, political philosophy is based on spiritualism and not humanism. An important component of this oriental doctrine is the quintessential role of the leader. Shariʿati contended that in the Orient leaders are usually prophets who are mandated by divine commandments in contrast to the politicians who run Western societies based on man-made laws and constitutions. In other words, the basis of power in the Occident is political, whereas in the Orient it has remained antipolitical.

"The native has spoken," Shariʿati heralded in the pages of one of his most important works (1983a, 352). The accent on *native* is what ties Shariʿati's discourse to that of the secular intellectuals examined earlier. With Shariʿati, however, the terms of referentiality and the topics of discourse undergo a transformation. The language in which the *native* is demarcated, exonerated, challenged, and called into action, and the means and methodology through which the other is portrayed, vary immensely. Similarly, as the spokesman for a generation of religious intellectuals coming of age, Shariʿati embodied their pointed historical turn from the clerical class. As such, he and his generation attempted to address the dichotomy of Iran's cultural life in the 1960s and the 1970s whereby secular intellectuals and the establishment clerics largely overlooked developments within each others' camps. Standing at this midpoint, the religious intellectuals endeavored to confront, compete with, and/or make alliances with both their secular and clerical adversaries.

Shariʿati's life and works best illustrate this twofold striving. He reprimanded the secularists for their ignorance of metaphysical thought, their uncritical invocation of such foreign-made doctrines as Marxism and liberalism, and their lack of contact with the masses. Correspondingly, he castigated the clergy for their obscurantism, apolitical views, quietism, and their inattentiveness toward the important contributions and influences of modern sciences and technological breakthroughs.

Shari'ati believed that Islam and its leadership institution required a fundamental restructuring, nothing short of what Luther had initiated against Christian orthodoxy and the church hierarchy in the sixteenth century. He maintained that Islam, like all other religions, has been used differently throughout history. At times it has been the static and silent religion of the ruling classes, whereas at different junctures it has served as the seditious and combative religion of the dispossessed.[11] Searching the root causes of this political vulnerability, Shari'ati concluded that Islam needed to be reformed both theoretically and organizationally. Theoretically, it had to undergo a transformation process from a culture into an ideology, from a collection of assorted learning into an organized body of social thought. He maintained that Islam was neither a scientific specialization nor a culture but instead an idea, a belief system, and a feeling about how human societies must be governed. According to Shari'ati, it was only the latter concept of Islam that could lead to such social properties as awareness, commitment, and responsibility.

This theoretical metamorphosis, however, necessitated an organizational change in which more qualified and fitting agents of change would emerge in vanguard positions. Shari'ati advocated that the torch of leadership be transferred from the clerical establishment to the religious intellectuals. He charged that Islam as a mere culture had only produced clerics, whereas as an ideology it can produce warriors and intellectuals. The latter group, he argued, had the advantage of looking from a more objective view toward such critical issues as reinterpreting texts, demythologizing the past, incorporating the new, and abandoning the erroneous.

At the same time Shari'ati made it clear that the class most needed in the Third World is the class of committed intellectuals who speak of "truth" and "what ought to be" rather than scientists who only speak of "facts" and "how it is" (Shari'ati 1981a, 258). Shari'ati maintained that the greatest responsibility facing these intellectuals was to discover the real cause of their societies' stagnation and backwardness, to warn their compatriots about their ominous historical and social destiny, and, finally, to propose an appropriate solution. He wrote: "Similar to the prophets, the enlightened souls also neither belong to the community of scientists nor to the camp of unaware and stagnant masses. They are aware and responsible individuals whose most important objective and responsibility is to bestow the great God-given gift of 'self-awareness' (*khodagahi*) to the general public" (Shari'ati 1986, 5).

Shari'ati insisted, however, that Third World intellectuals had to dis-

11. For more on this issue see Shari'ati, n.d.

tinguish themselves from their European counterparts, who could generally be recognized by their belief in the following set of ideas: irreligiosity, nationalism, scientism, materialism, cosmopolitanism, antiaristocracy, antiarchaism, and antitraditionalism. He charged that those Islamic intellectuals who have advocated imitating Western models of development have failed to realize that "civilization and culture are not like radios, televisions, and refrigerators that could be imported, powered, and allowed to operate" (Shari'ati 1981b, 86). Incriminating them as alienated, *assimilés,* and uprooted individuals who have forfeited their characters and identity, Shari'ati contended that internationalism, humanism, and the ideal of universality are great lies promoted by the West, which aspires to negate the cultural character of oriental societies. In other words, the assimilé intellectuals of the Third World contribute to cultural imperialism and their own "ethnocide" at the hands of their Western adversaries. He was fond of quoting the following words of Sartre:

> The European elite undertook to manufacture a native elite. They picked out promising adolescents; they branded them, as with a red-hot iron, with the principles of Western culture; they stuffed their mouths full with high-sounding phrases, grand glutinous words that stuck to the teeth. After a short stay in the mother country, they were sent home, whitewashed. These walking lies had nothing left to say to their brothers; they only echoed. From Paris, from London, from Amsterdam we would utter the words "Parthenon! Brotherhood!" and somewhere in Africa and Asia lips would open ". . . thenon! . . . therhood!" (Sartre 1979, 7)

To offset this intellectual-cultural trend Shari'ati promoted the discourse of bazgasht beh khishtan (return to the self). This was a replica of Fanon's discourse of "return of the oppressed" but with a peculiarly Iranian twist. Whereas Fanon's discourse was nonreligious in spirit and placed the emphasis on the racial, historical, and linguistic features of Third World struggles, Shari'ati's discourse was religious in tone and placed its emphasis on "Islamic roots." Addressing the Iranian secularist advocates of "return," he wrote:

> When we say "return to one's roots," we are really saying return to one's cultural roots. . . . Some of you may conclude that we Iranians must return to our racial (Aryan) roots. I categorically reject this conclusion. I oppose racism, fascism, and reactionary returns. What is more, Islamic civilization has acted like scissors and has cut us off completely from our

pre-Islamic past. . . . Consequently, for us to return to our roots means not a rediscovery of pre-Islamic Iran but a return to our Islamic roots.[12]

Shari'ati's discourse of return embodies yet another example of the quest for authenticity undertaken by Iranian intellectuals. His crusade was launched with the aim of posing a challenge to several contending forces. First, Shari'ati wished to juxtapose Iran's Islamic heritage to the secular nationalists' glorification of pre-Islamic Iran. Second, he wanted to disarm his Marxist rivals with the reasoning that Islam was the commanding spirit of Iranian culture and that Marxism was an ideology repulsive to the masses. Third, Shari'ati hoped to establish that it was the ignorance, superficiality, and hypocrisy of the conservative clerics that was precipitating the flight of young Iranians from Islam and toward Western ideologies and culture.

This discourse, however, was both deceptive and intellectually flawed. The first problem concerns his predilection to use "return" as a transportational metaphor for communication. Return to what and communication with whom? A general common view assumes that by these Shari'ati meant return to the mythic past of early Islam and communicating with the disenfranchised masses whose cause he championed so fervently. I believe, however, that Shari'ati's discourse of bazgasht beh khishtan must be understood synchronically instead of diachronically because it was more a discourse of "re-turning" the present rather than "returning" to the past. Shari'ati was more a man of today than a partisan of yesteryear. His thought was contemporary in nature. Shari'ati relied heavily on the tenets of phenomenological epistemology and preferred sociology and other social science disciplines. He appealed to the authority of contemporary thinkers while he targeted young urban(ite) Iranians. He maintained relentless opposition to the shah's regime and unconditionally supported such anticolonialist struggles as that of the Algerians. Finally, his challenge to such secularist projects as Marxism and liberalism was rooted in the belief that they were formidable ideological contenders.[13]

Furthermore, Shari'ati's instrumentalist view of the role of religion in politics, his increasing abandonment of metaphysical notions, his em-

12. As quoted in Abrahamian 1989, 116.

13. Shari'ati considered his task of criticizing Marxism to be rather important. To discredit Marxism's philosophical postulates he drew upon classical Islamic doctrines and Sartre's critique of Marxism's one-dimensionality as well. Shari'ati's lecture series on "Islamology" (Shari'ati 1983c) constituted his mature attempt to present a philosophical and social rebuttal to Marxism. For young Shari'ati's reflections on the same subject, which tend to be pedestrian, see Shari'ati 1980.

phasis on practical reason instead of revelation, and, finally, the belief that traditional Islam was passé and had to be replaced by an ideological Islam all helped to bridge the gap between the secularists and the young militants who professed adherence to his ideas. Shari'ati's conscientious attempt for a reconstructed and radicalized Islam were not directed at the downtrodden but at the urban, middle-class Iranian youth who had become his most enthusiastic followers.[14] Realizing these important factors, Shari'ati sought to inject aspects of modernity into the traditional socioreligious relations and value systems of Iranian society. Hence, Shari'ati was speaking of "return" not as an Oriental but instead as a Third World intellectual. His disdain of the West was not that of an Islamic mystic unaware of the West but that of a disillusioned Western-educated intellectual. Akin to Fanon's discourse, he wrote: "Come, friends, let us abandon Europe; let us cease this nauseating, apish imitation of Europe. Let us leave behind this Europe that always speaks of humanity, but destroys human beings wherever it finds them" (Shari'ati 1979, 23).

Despite this and other similar rhetorical proclamations about Western-wrought calamities Shari'ati's thought was permeated by the prevailing presence of the West. Like the secular intellectuals before him, his epistemology, language, rivals, and reference points were all Western inspired. Shari'ati's quest for restoring the "authentic humanity" of Muslim natives and updating Shi'a concepts and values was rooted in Western concepts and frames of reference (Bayat-Philipp 1980, 165–67). Whereas the secularist Iranian intelligentsia, following Marx, regarded religion as the "opium of the masses," he and numerous other lay religious intelligentsia, following Weber, believed that Islam needed to be reconciled with the necessities of the age of modernity.[15] Shari'ati went as far as proclaiming the historical era in which Iran was living at the time to be one between the end of the Middle Ages and the beginning of the Renaissance (Shari'ati 1981a, 281). The inference that he thus drew, not surprisingly, was that Iran was in need of the likes of Luther and Calvin to spearhead Islamic Protestantism. His fascination with

14. As a gifted speaker, Shari'ati was no doubt the most successful Iranian intellectual to use oral discourse. The power of Shari'ati as an agile and spellbinding orator able to hypnotize his audience first became evident at Hoseyniyyeh-ye Ershad. This splendid religious-lecture hall which was founded by a wealthy bazaar merchant and philanthropist in northern Tehran in 1964, used to accommodate thousands of Iranian youth who would congregate there regularly to hear Shari'ati's blatant antiregime and anticlerical discourse (Chehabi 1990, 202–7).

15. Shari'ati, however, had no use for Max Weber's other dictum that "he who seeks the salvation of the soul, of his own and of others, should not seek it along the avenue of politics."

Protestantism is somewhat captured in the following quotation: "The Muslim intellectual should begin by [embracing] an Islamic Protestantism similar to that of Christianity in the Middle Ages, destroying all the degenerating factors which, in the name of Islam, have stymied and stupefied the process of thinking and the fate of the society, and giving birth to new thoughts and new movements" (Shari'ati 1986, 25). Needless to say, these types of proclamations did not sit well with many Shi'a clerics and their lay supporters who accused Shari'ati of blasphemy and branded him an infidel, a materialist, a Sunni, and a Marxist.[16]

In considering the overall contribution of Shari'ati, one does not need to be preoccupied with these trivial accusations. What is important to remember, however, is that Shari'ati comes across more as a polemicist rather than as a philosopher or a theologian. He was not well versed in the nuances of Islamic philosophy and did not share this discipline's historic penchant for political aloofness. This is reflected in his choice of revered historical figures. He was more fascinated with Islamic militants (Abuzar, Salman) than with philosophers (Avicenna, Farabi). Shari'ati considered philosophy and science to be forms of "consciousness," whereas he equated religion with "self-consciousness." Yet he was not interested in the *inter dicta* discourse and hair-splitting argumentation of theologians.

Shari'ati deserves credit for heralding the notion that the lay intelligentsia is as capable and, perhaps, even more successful than the ulema in addressing the perennial questions of Islamic thought. I consider his greatest asset as well as his most glaring liability to be his ability to bypass almost entirely the discursive reasoning of theologians and experts in jurisprudence. Although this detour made him popular with the younger generation, who did not appreciate the antiquated jargon of the ulema, it did not win him much support or respect among the clerical elements. In fact, his anticlerical discourse alienated many potential allies. Furthermore, from a secular perspective, Shari'ati can be criticized for his naïveté in wanting to imitate the Protestant Reformation. He was not willing to acknowledge that in an age of modernity and universal secularization, Islamic Protestantism was not capable of duplicating the revolutionary consequences of Luther's revolt. Finally, in his appeal to Luther, Shari'ati was oblivious of the fact (or rather found it convenient to forget) that Luther carried out his Protestant revolution with the direct assistance of the princess. Sure enough, however, as an opposition figure Shari'ati was not willing to forge an alliance with the shah to dislodge the clergy.

16. For one example of the conservatives' critique see Ansari 1972.

Mojahedin-e Khalq: The Religious Militants

The liberal outlooks of Bazargan and the modernist views of Shariʿati found their radical incarnation in the shape of the Sazman-e Mojahedin-e Khalq-e Iran (Organization of the Iranian People's Holy Warriors). Founded in 1965, it became "the first Iranian organization to develop systematically a modern revolutionary interpretation of Islam" (Abrahamian 1989, 1). The Mojahedin were able to transform the solitary utterances of discontented Iranian religious intellectuals into a collective voice. In the intellectual and political vacuum created by the departure of the Tudeh Party and the National Front from active political struggle such newly formed organizations as the Fedaʾiyan and the Mojahedin were able to move into the theater of Iranian political life. As representatives of the militant Left and the religious intellectuals, the two organizations developed an unsurpassed grip over their respective constituencies.

Unlike their Marxist counterparts, who came mainly from the ranks of the new technocratic middle class, the Mojahedin were predominantly recruited from the traditional and bazaar classes. Many were graduates of the Alavi schools, the provincial seminaries, high school Islamic councils, or the Hoseyniyyeh-ye Ershad lecture series. They had been involved in the activities of the National Front and/or the Nehzat-e Azadi (Liberation Movement). Like the Fedaʾiyan, however, Mojahedin's main source of constituency and recruitment was concentrated in the universities. This must be understood against the background of a change in the composition and class origin of the overall Iranian student body. As the modern upper and middle classes were becoming more prosperous, they developed a strong proclivity to send their children abroad for higher education. Meanwhile, the required countrywide university entrance examination (in which the class background of the candidates had little role to play) enabled many smart students from lower and traditional classes to gain admission. This latter group of students was more inclined toward careers in engineering and other hard sciences that would expedite their social mobility. Furthermore, the secularization of the educational system made it possible to interpret Islam in a new manner. As a result of these class, cultural, academic, and professional developments, many of Iran's rising intelligentsia were attracted toward an egalitarian, progressive, and scientific interpretation of Islam such as the one promoted by the Mojahedin.[17]

17. Abrahamian's occupational breakdown of the eighty-three martyrs that the Mojahedin suffered between 1972 and 1979 reveals the following known statistics: forty-four college students (with thirty-four of them majoring in the exact sciences); fourteen

Theirs was an Islam interpreted not by the distant ulema, with their cryptic language, but by the students' and young professionals' own highly educated and militant cohorts and colleagues.

As an active urban guerrilla organization, the ideological worldview of Mojahedin rested upon two of the main characteristics of Iranian social thought at the time: nationalism and populism. They perceived themselves as inheritors of the radical legacies left by the constitutionalist revolutionaries of the early 1900s, the radical movement of the late 1910s led by Mirza Kuchek-Khan, and the oil nationalization movement of the early 1950s. Internationally, they were inspired by the anticolonialist and anti-imperialist struggles in Algeria, Vietnam, Cuba, and Palestine. In the face of these revolutionary and nationalistic developments Mojahedin came to designate American imperialism as their principal enemy.

Unlike their secular counterparts, however, they claimed Islam to be the only ideology capable of mobilizing the masses for such a colossal struggle. In a Weberian manner they regarded Islam as a "this worldly" political ideology capable of fighting oppression and delivering freedom and democracy. Like the advocates of liberation theology in Latin and Central America, the Mojahedin began to circulate a populist interpretation of their religion. Such themes as resistance, martyrdom, revolution, and establishment of a classless society (*nezam-e towhidi*) dominated Mojahedin's discourse in the 1960s and the 1970s. These themes, however, demonstrate not only the "this worldly" but also the "third worldly" nature of Mojahedin's program. Similar to the claims put forward by other lay intellectuals, their allegiance to Shi'ism must be examined in light of the ideas, events, and individuals impacted by modern life and philosophy.

Perhaps the best example of the Mojahedin's ideological contemporaneity can be found in the pages of *Tabyin-e jahan* (Comprehending the world), the organization's foremost work on ideology. This book consists of a long series of lectures delivered in 1979 by Mas'ud Rajavi. The son of a government employee, Rajavi was born in Tabas in 1948 and attended primary and secondary schools in Mashhad along with such future Feda'i leaders as Mas'ud Ahmadzadeh and Amir-Parviz Puyan. He later attended Tehran University where he majored in political science. Rajavi joined the Mojahedin in 1967, became a member of its central committee in 1970, and was arrested and sentenced to life

---

engineers; five teachers; three accountants; two shopkeepers; one doctor; one army officer; one theology student; one factory worker; and one housewife (Abrahamian 1989, 167–68).

imprisonment in 1971. He was, however, released shortly before the triumph of the 1979 revolution and has emerged as the organization's preeminent leader ever since.

Organized as a set of pedagogical lectures, *Tabyin-e jahan* was intended to present Mojahedin's beliefs on the nature of *existence, humans, history,* and *epistemology* (Rajavi 1979, 1: 11). The greater bulk of this three-volume book, however, is devoted to the latter question as the author attempts to criticize August Comte's, Max Planck's, and Kant's positivism; William James's pragmatism; Freudian psychoanalysis; Darwinian evolutionism; along with a host of other Western "isms" such as scholasticism, scientism, empiricism, and rationalism. Rajavi's references in the book are revealing in themselves: Darwin, *Origin of Species;* Albert Einstein, *Essays in Science;* Erich Fromm, *Psychoanalysis and Religion;* Georges Gurvitch, *Dialectique et Sociologie;* Max Planck, *The Universe in the Light of Modern Physics* and *Where Is Science Going?;* Bertrand Russell, *The Scientific Outlook* and *History of Western Philosophy;* George Sarton, *The History of Science;* Omar Ouzegan, *Le Meilleur combat;* and Amir-Hoseyn Aryanpur, *Zamineh-ye jameʾehshenasi.*[18]

Rajavi saves his most extensive critical commentary for Marxist materialistic epistemology. The book's chief target is the Russian biochemist Aleksandr Ivanovich Oparin (1894–1980), whose materialistic theory on the origin of life, first formulated in 1922, transformed this problem from the domain of religious faith to one of natural science. According to Oparin, who was the first president of the International Society for the Study of the Origin of Life, the origin of life is an event regulated by natural laws and is an undeniable and indispensable part of the evolutionary process of the universe (Oparin 1961). By subjecting the materialistic doctrines of Oparin and a host of other orthodox Marxist thinkers to a religious critique the Mojahedin hoped to challenge the more vigorous presence of Marxism within Iranian intellectual circles. To do that they provided their members with a heavy dosage of materialistically inspired books. According to Mojahedins' own testimony, the organization's ideological reading list included Georges Politzer, *Elementary Principles of Philosophy;* Aleksandr Oparin, *Life, Its Nature, Origin and Development;* Stalin, *Dialectical Materialism;* and John Somerville, *Philosophy of Marxism: An Exposition* (Sazman-e Mojahedin-e Khalq-e Iran 1979, 150, 160). The necessity of a philosophical critique of Marxism

18. Aryanpur's book (1965), which was based on an adaptation of Ogburn and Nimkoff 1958, was the most popular university textbook on sociology in Iran of the 1960s and 1970s.

became even more pressing after 1975 when a sizable number of Mojahedin cadres converted to Marxism, thereby causing a split within the organization.

In their quest for a critical analysis of historical and dialectical materialism the Mojahedin drew upon works by both Iranian and Western critics of Marxism. Their discourse was mainly anchored in the theoretical line pioneered by Bazargan, Taleqani, Shari'ati, and the Algerian revolutionary thinker Omar Ouzegan. Rajavi acknowledges the impact on his own work of the first two thinkers by stating that in his youth he was particularly attracted to Bazargan's scientific defense and Ayatollah Taleqani's progressive and egalitarian interpretations of Islam (Rajavi 1984). The Mojahedin's predicament was twofold. First, they did not wish to participate in the myriad of nonscientific and conservative objections to Marxism raised by the ulema, whose logos they could not share; and second, the Mojahedin did not want to incur so much intellectual debt to the secular epistemology of the Left that they could no longer establish their own distinctive identity. Hence, they opted for a policy of selective acquisition, borrowing mainly from Marxism's principles of political economy. They concurred with such Marxist-Leninist principles as class struggle, the exploitative nature of capitalism, the need for socialization of the means of production and having a revolutionary vanguard, the necessity of fighting imperialism, and the appropriateness of a dialectical method of inquiry. The Mojahedin, however, remained skeptical of Marxism's philosophical postulates and rejected the latter's cardinal doctrine of historical materialism. They held firm to their beliefs in the existence of God, revelation, afterlife, spirit, expectation, salvation, destiny, and of people's commitment to these intangible principles.

All in all, Shari'ati, Mojahedin-e khalq, and other like-minded religious intellectuals succeeded in their task of formulating a revolutionary interpretation of Islam. They might not have been on a par with the ulema as accomplished Qur'anic scholars, but they were skillful men of ideology. Their ideology was not particularly philosophically consistent, yet it was capable of exhorting a great many Iranian youth to rediscover Shi'ism and return to the Muslim fold, which they were deserting in large numbers. While Shari'ati and the Mojahedin were concerned with the social, economic, and political realities of life in Iran, a second group of lay religious intellectuals were busy formulating a more philosophically articulate interpretation of Islam. Reflecting the diverse political spectrum that lay religious intellectuals occupied, a number of the more philosophically minded members of this class were extremely wary of the antiestablishment ideas of Shari'ati and the Mojahedin. It is to an examination of one such intellectual that I now turn.

Seyyed Hoseyn Nasr: The Theosophist Mandarin

Seyyed Hoseyn Nasr was born on 7 April 1933 in a family of religious scholars and physicians in Tehran. His father, Seyyed Valiollah Nasr, was a famous physician, literary scholar, educator, parliament deputy, and minister of education. On his maternal side, he is the great-grandson of the famous anticonstitutionalist cleric, Sheykh Fazlollah Nuri. After receiving his early education in Iran, Seyyed Hoseyn Nasr (hereafter S. H. Nasr) came to the United States where he earned a Bachelor of Science degree in physics from the Massachusetts Institute of Technology (MIT) in 1954. Later, he enrolled at Harvard University where he obtained a master's degree in geology and geophysics in 1956 and a doctorate in the history of science and philosophy in 1958. He then returned to Iran to begin work as an associate professor of history of science and philosophy at Tehran University (teaching such courses as history of Islamic philosophy and culture, history of science, criticism of philosophical texts in foreign languages, etc.). Nasr soon climbed the ladder of academic success by becoming a full professor, vice-chancellor and dean of the Faculty of Letters at Tehran University (1968–72), and chancellor of Aryamehr University of Technology (1972–75). In addition to visiting professorships at Harvard and Princeton, Nasr was appointed as the first Aga Khan Professor of Islamic Studies at the American University of Beirut during the 1964–65 academic year. Meanwhile, in addition to all his collegiate appointments, he served in the following capacities as: Iran's ambassador-at-large in cultural affairs (1975–79), the director of Queen Farah's Special Bureau (1978–79), the first chairman of the Board of Governors of the RCD (Iran-Pakistan-Turkey) Cultural Institute, a member of the National Cultural Council of Iran, a member of the Iranian Academy of Sciences, a member of the National Council of Higher Education of Iran, and, finally, the founder and first director of Anjoman-e Shahanshahi-ye Falsafeh-ye Iran (The Imperial Iranian Academy of Philosophy, 1975–78). In light of his high-profile position as a cultural Mandarin in the Pahlavi royal court, Nasr decided to leave Iran in 1979 for the United States where he is presently (1996) University Professor of Islamic Studies at George Washington University.

In his capacity as a university professor and an active member of the Iranian philosophical, political, and religious community since the 1950s S. H. Nasr has left an indelible mark upon philosophical deliberations in modern Iran. The radius of Nasr's philosophical influence, however, is not just limited to Iran. As the author of some twenty books and more than two hundred articles in Persian, English, French, and Arabic, he has certainly established himself as the foremost proponent of the traditionalist school of Islamic thought in the world today.

Nasr's intellectual voyage is rather fascinating. He had received a rigorous early education in Islamic and Persian literature. As a teenager, upon the death of his father, he went to the United States. Nasr chose to study physics at MIT to grasp the nature of physical reality. Yet, upon hearing a lecture by the English mathematician and philosopher Bertrand Russell (1872–1970) he was "shocked to discover that many leading Western philosophers did not consider the role of science in general and physics in particular to be the discovery of the nature of the physical aspect of reality at all" (Nasr 1994, xxviii). Meanwhile, the works of his Italian mentor at MIT, Giorgio de Santillana (1902–197?), introduced Nasr to the history of the strained relationship between philosophy, science, and religion in the West. At Harvard he pursued his newly found interest in the history of science, culminating with a dissertation entitled "Conceptions of Nature in Islamic Thought During the Fourth Century (A.H.): A Study of the Conceptions of Nature and the Methods Used for Its Study by the 'Ikhwan as-Safa, al-Biruni, and Ibn Sina." During his studies Nasr became acquainted with such renowned scholars as Richard N. Frye, Sir Hamilton Gibb (1895–1971), Etienne Gilson (1884–1978), George Sarton (1884–1956), Daisetz Teitaro Suzuki (1870–1966), and Harry A. Wolfson (1887–1974). He also began to read the works of Ananda Kentish Coomaraswamy (1877–1947), René Guénon (1886–1951), Frithjof Schuon (1907–   ), and Titus Burckhardt (1908–1984), respectively, an exceptional authority on Hindu thought and traditional art, a great traditionalist metaphysician, a leading authority on comparative religion, and a European convert to Sufism. These scholars, in turn, introduced him to the world of oriental, Hindu, and traditional Western metaphysics. Speaking of the cumulative impact of these influences, Nasr writes, "The Indian, and to the lesser extent Far Eastern, sojourn combined with the criticism of the modern world by Western traditional authors served more than anything else to wash away the dross of modern Western thought patterns upon my mind and soul" (Nasr 1994, xxviii).

Secured in his training in modern science and comparative religion, Nasr made an intellectual return to his homeland where he rediscovered Islamic Sufism and the sagacious theosophy of such thinkers as Avicenna (980–1037), Shehaboddin Sohravardi (1154–1191), and Sadroddin Shirazi (1571–1640), better known as Molla Sadra. Nasr maintained that Islamic philosophy began its thoughtful ontological quest with that genius Persian physician and philosopher-scientist, Avicenna (Ibn Sina), who in his *Mantiq al-Mashriqiyyin* (The wisdom of the Orientals) and the three visionary recitals spoke symbolically of the Orient as representing the world of light, ideas, and purity (see Cobin 1980). Nasr felt an immediate affinity for Avicenna's mystical theosophy, which aspired to transcend Aristotelian philosophy. In opposition to Aristotle, who viewed logic as the first principle and regarded the reality of things as beings-in-themselves, Avicenna believed that the existence of every object emanated from the existence of God and hence reason should be viewed only as a ground for transcending itself. Nasr resolved that Avicenna's ontological doctrines, so implanted with the other-ness of the divine, were transmitted through the illuminationist school of Islamic philosophy and were carried forward by such thinkers as Sohravardi, the master of the philosophy of *Ishraq* (illumination), and Molla Sadra, the greatest philosophical scion of seventeenth-century Persia.

Nasr further modeled his intellectual journey after that of these two philosopher-mystics. In his *al-Ghorbat al-gharbiyah* (The Occidental exile), Sohravardi narrates the arduous spiritual journey one has to undertake in order to gain esoteric knowledge and hence deliverance and felicity. This spiritual journey, however, is not the normally depicted vertical ascent. Rather, it takes place on a horizontal plane. By utilizing geographic symbolism, Sohravardi argued that the Orient or the East (place of the rising sun) represented knowledge, wisdom, and spirituality while the Occident or the West (place of the setting sun) symbolized darkness, materiality, and antispirituality. Nasr concluded from this allegorical tale that one must shed all material attachments and carnal desires to return to one's divine origin. He found further comfort in the transcendental theosophy of Molla Sadra, who elevated the pantheistic doctrine of Sohravardi to new intellectual heights. Furthermore, he could relate to Molla Sadra's metaphysical *verstehen* and found his illuminationist theosophy, in which reason and revelation were intertwined (with the latter having prominence), particularly appealing. Nasr writes:

> If I were to summarize my so-called "philosophical position," I would say that I am a follower of that *philosophia perennis* and also *universalis,* that eternal *sophia,* which has always been and will always be and in whose perspective there is but one Reality which can say "I." This sophia is based on a universal metaphysics with its applications to the domains of cosmology, psychology, art, etc. . . . But in practice, this sophia cannot be attained save with the aid of that macrocosmic manifestation of the Intellect, namely tradition or religion which alone provides the necessary

means to make the Intellect operative within man and to enable him to become transformed through knowledge until he himself becomes the embodiment of this sophia. (Nasr 1994, xxxi)

So to be delivered from his "occidental exile," Nasr resorted to a theosophic and gnostic interpretation of Islam and came to view mysticism as the main axis of his thinking and worldview (Nasr 1982–83). He abandoned rationalism for illumination, Cartesian thought for mediative thought, and modern science for traditional metaphysics. In a Neoplatonic fashion he proceeded to indict the intellectual heritage of the Renaissance and the ensuing age of modernity. Nasr considered the ascendancy of the humanist movement of the Renaissance, with its anthropocentric and universalist claims, to be the turning point in the philosophical estrangement of Western and oriental civilizations. This is the result of the fact that the Renaissance brought along the divorce of philosophy from ethics, science, and religion. First, Machiavelli (1469–1527) masterminded the emptying of politics from its classical ethical prudence. Then Galileo (1564–1642) forced the parting of ways between science and religion. Finally, Descartes (1596–1650) and Newton (1642–1727) shouldered the separation of philosophy from both religion and science.

Nasr was also critical of the entire civilizational design of modernity: its privileging of mind and body over the soul, its abandonment of mystical vision, its stripping of nature's divine essence, and its advocacy of science and secular knowledge as the remedies for universal social salvation. He also objected to the Enlightenment thinkers relinquishment of the medieval messianic time in favor of what Walter Benjamin has called a homogenous empty time (Benjamin 1973, 263–65). Like most other critics of modernity, Nasr assumed that an initial, positively valued state of affairs characterized by a harmony with God and nature was somehow eradicated by the onslaught of modernity. He alleged that this "new age," which is marked with "man's revolt against Heaven," "divorce of reason from the guiding light of intellect," and "shortage of virtue," has led to a morass of confusion, decadence, and unrighteousness.

Modern civilization as it has developed in the West since the Renaissance is an experiment that has failed—failed in such an abysmal fashion as to cast doubt upon the very possibility of any future for man to seek other ways. It would be most unscientific today to consider this civilization, with all the presumptions about the nature of man and the Universe which lie at its basis, as anything other than a failed experiment. (Nasr 1975a, 12)

Having concluded that modernity is the avatar of betraying revelation and a historical cul-de-sac, Nasr maintained that one should not repudiate the effects but the very foundations of modern Western civilization. After all, by turning away from the authentic and the divine, humankind has brought its present state of crisis upon itself. Nasr, who is fond of quoting the maxims of Plato ("Philosophy is the practice of death") and that of the thirteenth-century sufi mystic and poet Jalaloddin Rumi ("The leg of the syllogisers is of wood; a wooden leg is very infirm") argued that the way to salvation is not through the labyrinth of Nietzschean nihilism but through the sapiental theosophy of oriental mystics. In regard to the particular situation of Iran Nasr articulated his intellectual rebellion against an enticing yet intimidating West within the contours of the following fourfold strategy:

1. Reviving the authentic intellectual traditions of Persia by resuscitating Islamic philosophy and mysticism;

2. Admonishing Iranians about the nature of Western sciences, philosophy, and technology and the risks that their acquisition will pose to Iranian culture, thereby enabling Iranians to view the West from the vantage point of a critical outlook rather than an inferiority complex;

3. Informing Iranians about cultures and civilizations of Asia as a possible counterbalancing force to Western influence;

4. Attempting to delineate a way through which it would be possible to maintain Iranian cultural authenticity in the face of Western culture, technology, and sciences. (Nasr 1982–83, 47–48)

Nasr pursued the first leg of the above strategy through a relentless effort to demonstrate the affinity of Persians and Muslims for philosophy and metaphysical thought. In his academic capacity as a professor of philosophy he helped train many outstanding students, some of whom have become major exponents of Islamic philosophy both in and out of Iran. As a dean, vice-chancellor, and chancellor of two of Iran's leading universities, Nasr worked toward forging closer ties between the ulema and the university students and as such facilitated the entrance of a number of learned clergy into the Iranian academic environment. His numerous publications on the lives and thought of such philosophers as Molla Sadra, Sohravardi and other original Muslim thinkers constituted yet another contribution.

Nasr recalled that on the occasion of congratulating him for his selection to the prestigious Institut International de Philosophie he suggested to the queen that there was a need for forming a world-class institute devoted to Iranian/Islamic philosophy (Nasr 1990). Upon securing the queen's patronage and asking her to serve as the honorary chair of its Board of Trustees, Nasr founded the Anjoman-e Shahanshahi-ye Falsafeh-ye Iran (Imperial Iranian Academy of Philosophy) in the spring of 1974. The founding of this academy represented his most systematic attempt to rekindle an interest in Islamic philosophy. As its first president, Nasr defined the goals of the academy as follows:

> The goals of the academy are the revival of the traditional intellectual life of Islamic Persia; the publication of texts and studies pertaining to both Islamic and pre-Islamic Persia; making the intellectual treasures of Persia in the fields of philosophy, mysticism and the like known to the outside world; making possible extensive research in comparative philosophy; making Persians aware of the intellectual traditions of other civilizations in both East and West; encouraging intellectual confrontations with the modern world; and, finally, discussing from the point of view of tradition various problems facing modern man. (Nasr 1975b, 7–8)

Hoping to turn the academy into a first-rate intellectual center, the Board of Trustees helped to bring together a noteworthy corps of scholars from both the East and the West.[19] In addition to the regular publication of its journal, *Javidan Kherad (Sophia Perennis)*, during its four years of operation the academy organized a number of international conferences on philosophy and published numerous books on Islamic mysticism and philosophy. Its cooperation with two independent institutes, L'Institut Franco-Iranien[20] and the Tehran branch of McGill University's Institute of Islamic Studies,[21] led to the profusion of scholastically sophisticated Islamic texts in the mid-1970s.[22]

19. Some of the scholars affiliated with the academy included Seyyed Jalaloddin Ashtiyani, William Chittick, Henry Corbin, Mohammad-Taqi Daneshpazhuh, Reza Davari, Mehdi Ha'eri-Yazdi, Toshihiko Izutsu, Javad Mosleh, Ayatollah Morteza Motahhari, Nasrollah Purjavadi, and Seyyed Ja'far Sajjadi.

20. In 1946 the French philosopher and Islamist, Henry Corbin, was appointed by the French Foreign Ministry as the director of the Iranology Department of L'Institut Franco-Iranien in Tehran. Corbin inaugurated a series entitled Bibliothèque Iranienne, which published a number of texts on Islamic philosophy. Among those Iranian scholars who cooperated with Corbin in these series were Seyyed Jalaloddin Ashtiyani, Mohammad Mo'in, Mohammad Mokri, S. H. Nasr, and Morteza Sarraf.

21. The McGill University Institute of Islamic Studies, which is one of the leading centers of its kind in the world, was founded in 1952. The Tehran branch of the institute was established in January 1969. Under its Wisdom of Persia series, which was supervised by Mehdi Mohaqqeq and Charles J. Adams, the Tehran branch of the institute published more than twenty texts and studies related to Islamic philosophy and theosophy before the revolution. Besides Mohaqqeq, Mehdi Ha'eri-Yazdi and the Japanese philosopher Toshihiko Izutsu (1914–1993) were also affiliated with both the Montreal and Tehran branches of the institute.

22. For a detailed introduction to philosophical endeavors in prerevolutionary Iran see Nasr 1972.

Nasr was further influential because of his pivotal role in organizing regularly held private discussions and study groups. One of the most long-lasting and important of such gatherings was a series of private discussions between Henry Corbin (Islamic chair at the Sorbonne from 1954 to 1974) and Allameh Tabataba'i, beginning in 1958 and ending in 1977. The discussions, which were often held in the presence of a small distinguished audience,[23] basically revolved around issues pertaining to Islamic philosophy, the encounter of East and West, the relation of science to religion, Hindu and Islamic mythology, and comparative mysticism.[24] These gatherings, which were held independently from both the government and the seminaries, helped to bridge the gap between the more intellectually minded members of the clerical class and a particular group of university professors and religious intellectuals.

Nasr, who had studied for many years with such clerics as Allameh Tabataba'i, Seyyed Mohammad-Kazem Assar, and Ayatollah Seyyed Abolhasan Rafi'i-Qazvini, was interested in bridging the gap between them and the religious intellectuals. This put Nasr at odds with Shari'ati, who had adopted a blatant anticlerical discourse. A brief comparison of the ideas of these two individuals, who not only were born in the same year but who also belonged to the same intellectual class, can be somewhat revealing. Nasr and Shari'ati were highly articulate representatives of a generation of religious intellectuals who wanted to revive Islam and challenge Western thought. Each had studied with some of the towering intellectual figures of the West during the 1950s and 1960s. In their capacities as university professors and esteemed guest lecturers, both men promoted Islamic teachings passionately. Nasr and Shari'ati, nonetheless, differed in important ways. Whereas Nasr had undergone the tutelage of the traditional masters of Islamic thought, Shari'ati had no such formal education in traditional Islamic sciences. Whereas Shari'ati spoke the language of a sociologist of religion, Nasr conversed in the language of philosophy and theosophy. Shari'ati could not equal Nasr's solid grounding in comparative religion, whereas Nasr proved incapable of matching Shari'ati's familiarity with such social science disciplines as sociology. Furthermore, Nasr's status as a cultural figure of the Pahlavi regime was in total opposition to Shari'ati's antistatist views, leading to the exchange of such mutual accusations as a "reactionary arm-chair intellectual" and a "subversive Islamic-Marxist attempting to infiltrate

23. Some of the individuals present at this discussion were Seyyed Jalaloddin Ashtiyani, Badi'ozzaman Foruzanfar, Ayatollah Motahhari, S. H. Nasr, Daryush Shayegan, Isa Sepahbodi, and Mahmud Shahabi.

24. For a sample of these discussions see Tabataba'i and Corbin 1960 and Shayegan 1990.

the ranks of religious forces." The culminating point in the parting of ways of Nasr and Sharia'ti happened around 1970 when upon hearing a lecture in which Shari'ati compared Imam Hoseyn to Che Guevara, Nasr resigned from the Hoseyniyyeh-ye Ershad and was followed in so doing by Ayatollah Motahhari.[25] Nasr maintains that he nonetheless pleaded with the shah to release Shari'ati from prison after the latter was arrested in 1972 (Nasr 1990). He also reveals that Allameh Tabataba'i asked him to encourage Shari'ati to refrain from politics for a while and come to Qom to study philosophy with him (Nasr 1990). Needless to say, Shari'ati did not heed this advice.

The greatest disparity between these two thinkers must be seen in the different ways in which each interpreted Islam and encountered the West. Unlike Shari'ati, Nasr's critique of the West did not revolve around its imperialistic or colonialist ambitions and misdeeds. Instead, Nasr found the West guilty of having committed a much more serious sin, that of modernity.[26] Whereas Shari'ati drew inspiration from certain developments within the West (e.g., Luther's revolt, advancement of social sciences) and viewed Western society as a mixed bag from which one could pick and choose, Nasr believed in repudiating not the effects but the very foundations of modern civilization. Indeed, Nasr compared Western civilization to a beheaded rooster that flails frantically in all directions before it drops dead (Nasr 1993, 194). As such, Nasr was adamantly opposed to the modernism of Shari'ati, which in his view was reducing Islam to a mere ideology. He believed that in lieu of the clergy's largely ignorant attitude toward the West and the deceitful criticisms put forward by modernized Muslims (Shari'ati) who have found fault only with certain Western individuals and/or characteristics, a much more significant criticism must be levied against the modern West. According to him, anything short of an absolutely comprehensive critique of modernity and secularism, which were threatening the citadel of Islam in every respect, was a misdirected strategy.

In a preface to one of Nasr's books De Santillana, who used to teach Nasr history of science at MIT, took issue with some of the ideas of his former pupil. As the author of *The Crime of Galileo,* De Santillana could not agree with Nasr's justification for the silence of Muslim astronomy with respect to the Copernican system. He wrote "one might wonder whether the author [Nasr] is not making a virtue of necessity" and continued, "in passionately defending the essential wholeness and integ-

25. Shari'ati, Nasr, and Ayatollah Motahhari, along with a fourth cleric by the name of Ali Shahcheraqi, were the leading lecturers at the Hoseyniyyeh-ye Ershad.

26. For his elaborated views on modernity see Nasr 1976a; 1976b; 1987; 1989.

rity of his culture down to modern times, Nasr is willing to lay himself open to doubt." Finally, De Santillana took exception to Nasr's likening of Thomas Aquinas (1224/25–1274) to Mohammad Ghazali (1058–1111), the man most responsible for driving rationalist philosophy out of the mainstream of Islamic thought (De Santillana 1968, xi–xiii). In making these points the teacher showed that he had pondered more seriously than his student on why the bonds of faith and reason were loosened in the first place. Perhaps for De Santillana the burning of the Italian philosopher Giordano Bruno (1548–1600), the excommunication of Galileo (1564–1642) and Spinoza (1632–1677), and the forced recantation of the French naturalist Georges-Louis Leclerc De Buffon (1707–1788) were not issues to be simply ignored. Nor was De Santillana willing to overlook the lynching of Nasr's favorite thinker, Sohravardi, who was condemned to death at the mere age of thirty-eight by jurists in Aleppo, Syria, for his esoteric doctrines. I believe De Santillana is correct in saying that, in his enthusiastic attempt to vindicate the character of Islamic thought, Nasr is too willing to ignore and forgive the abominations and splits that have occurred in the history of Islamic societies. After all, the excommunication or banishment of such thinkers as Avicenna, Averroes (Ibn Rushd), Omar Khayyam, Jalaloddin Rumi, and the executions of such figures as Shamsoddin Mohammad ibn Makki, Zeynoddin ibn Ali, Mansur Hallaj, Eyn ol-Qozzat Hamadani, Sohravardi, and Seyyed Ali-Mohammad Shirazi (the Bab) cannot be easily overlooked in the name of expediency. Furthermore, the differences between the exnihilo arguments of the Ash'arites and the rationalist philosophy of the Mu'tazilites, the fundamental disagreements of Avicenna and Ghazali and the bitter Akhbari-Usuli dispute needs to be explicated in a nonpartisan, nonapologetic manner. Finally, one wishes that Nasr would have explained in a nontautological and critical manner the reasons and ramifications of Iranians' interest in the antiphilosophical and mystical ideas of Ghazali and Ibn al-Arabi (1165–1240) and their apathy toward the philosophical and sociological theories of Averroes (1126–1198) and Ibn Khaldun (1332–1406).

What is more troubling is Nasr's critique of modernity, however, which tends to be quite subjective and ahistorical. Nasr, who was formatively influenced by the writings of the French metaphysician René Guénon, appropriated such ideas of his as the "crisis of modernity," "fatalism of progress," and "tyranny of events."[27] In the tradition of

27. For Guénon's explication of these ideas see Guénon 1962. In 1970 Nasr wrote an introduction to the Persian translation of this book which had first appeared in the French edition in 1928.

Guénon, Nasr's traditionalist critique of modernity fails to appreciate the reasons for the philosophical uneasiness that launched the Enlightenment movement in the first place and the inventiveness that has since sustained it. Perhaps his elitist reading of philosophers and philosophy hampers his attempt to analyze causes leading to the rise of modernity. Nasr criticizes such central Enlightenment concepts as progress, reason, science, technology, and freedom of the individual from the vantage point of a revered past. His "theology of crisis," just like Guénon's metaphysical critique before him, tends to underestimate the complexities of modernity.[28] Both men find it difficult to recognize that modernity is not a historical parenthesis to be left behind. Nasr criticizes the age of modernity while he forgets that historical consciousness is itself a product of the modern subjective mind. As Jürgen Habermas has put it, "Modernity can and will no longer borrow the criteria by which it takes its orientation from the models supplied by another epoch; it has to create its normativity out of itself" (Habermas 1987, 7). Yet Nasr found it easy to preach the gospel of the West's decline from a theosophic position. One wonders whether Nasr's glorification of the antiquated religious cultures, both in the East and in the West, did not preclude him from deliberating on the reality of the state of intolerance, decadence, misery, repression, and ignorance that became the hallmark of those societies. After all, why did the Muslim states begin to dwindle long before the advent of Enlightenment thought? Why was it that the creative energies of Islamic, Buddhist, and Hindu civilizations corroded so dramatically even before the scientific discoveries of Copernicus, Galileo, Kepler, and Newton were to change the world?

Although Nasr is certainly not an advocate of what has come to be known as "Islamic fundamentalism," the stringent ramifications of his theosophic critique of modernity is rather alarming to those who consider modernity not as a "failed" but as an "unfinished" project. Although his diligent efforts over the last forty years to introduce the ideas of Muslim thinkers to the intellectual community of both the West and the East is certainly respectable, his self-appointed role as a cultural storekeeper of traditionalism is not without its pitfalls. Although his criticism of Western science and "scientism" is much more sophisti-

28. René Guénon's *The Crisis of the Modern World* was part of a series of critical books on the nature and destiny of Western civilization that appeared in the first four decades of the twentieth century. Other examples of this genre of books include Oswald Spengler, *The Decline of the West* (1918); Albert Demangeon, *The Decline of Europe* (1920); Julien Benda, *Treason of the Intellectuals* (1927); Johan Huizinga, *The Crisis of Civilization* (1928); José Ortega y Gasset, *The Revolt of the Masses* (1930); and Hilaire Belloc, *The Crisis of Our Civilization* (1937).

cated than that undertaken by the earlier generation of Muslim thinkers (Seyyed Jamal al-Din Afghani, *Rejection of Materialists*), his claim that "reason cut off from both the 'Intellect' and revelation, [is] nothing but a luciferian instrument leading to dispersion and ultimately dissolution" is bound to raise eyebrows (Nasr 1994, xxxii). Finally, many may object to the theosophic abstraction with which Nasr lays out his theology of crisis because it is always difficult to subject this analysis to the trials of inductive reasoning and methodological falsification.

In short, one can say that Nasr is representative of a generation of traditionalist religious thinkers who did not want to succumb to the ideas of modernity and secularism. Self-assured in his theosophic thinking, he had early on set himself the task of responding to the challenges posed to Islam by such doctrines as evolutionism, psychoanalysis, existentialism, historicism, and dialectical materialism (Nasr 1966, 6). Nasr helped to further strengthen the philosophical armor of nativism by demonstrating that the traditionalist culture of Iran was not yet incapacitated. Furthermore, by maintaining that non-Western cultures have not lost the battle of history to Western civilization, because the latter is suffering from a terminable disease, Nasr injected a dosage of optimism and pride into the philosophical veins of the Islamic community. Finally, by questioning the correctness of modernity's epistemological abandonment of traditional thinking he reassured the aficionados of nativism that their worldview was still relevant and, more importantly, operational.

Seyyed Fakhroddin Shadman
Courtesy of Seyyed Ziyaʾoddin Shadman

Ahmad Fardid
Courtesy of Mrs. Fardid

Jalal Al-e Ahmad
Courtesy of Simin Daneshvar

Ali Shari'ati
Courtesy of Mehran Boroujerdi

Seyyed Hoseyn Nasr
Courtesy of Seyyed Hoseyn Nasr

Ehsan Naraqi
Courtesy of Ehsan Naraqi

Hamid Enayat
Courtesy of Anna Enayat

Daryush Shayegan
Courtesy of Daryush Shayegan

Reza Davari
Courtesy of Reza Davari

Abdolkarim Sorush
Courtesy of Abdolkarim Sorush

6

Academic Nativism

The West is fast asleep, so wake it up
In drunkenness it's steeped, so shake it up
From the land of glitter all happiness has left
Chains abound, but of faith it is bereft
Naught but numbers fill the Western brain
For joy without anxiety you'll search in vain
The East has been corrupted, destroyed by the West
Which itself is helpless now, in a torture test
Twice it's waged a war, this century not half way
No longer has the West a message to convey
      —Hasan Honarmandi, "The West Is Fast Asleep"*

Academia

IN MANY WAYS the decades of the 1960s and the 1970s can be considered a turning point in Iran's intellectual history. As pointed out in chapter 3, during this time span new underground guerrilla organizations entered the political arena, promoting a novel approach to political struggle. In addition, great strides were made in the field of literature as elegant new styles and innovative writers (including many women) emerged. As the numbers of writers and intellectuals increased, book reading and publishing expanded accordingly. Translations of foreign works also flourished, resulting in the development of a more sophisticated reading audience. Modern social science centers and institutes were set up, and new philosophical and sociological styles of prose started to take shape. Finally, the return of many young professors from abroad improved academic standards. By the 1975–76 academic year, 3,037 (or 55.9 percent) of the 5,430 Iranian faculty members teaching at various Iranian universities and institutions of higher learning had received at least one degree from a foreign university.[1]

*Translation of epigraph courtesy of M. R. Ghanoonparvar.

1. My analysis of the data in *Vezarat-e Olum va Amuzesh-e Ali* 1976 revealed the following breakdown of where these scholars had received their education: 3 (.10 per-

Yet this period also represented the heyday of nativism and antiorientalism in Iran. During this time, the question of self and other came to the forefront of intellectual deliberations and stayed there for good. In 1962, sixteen years before the appearance of Said's *Orientalism,* Al-e Ahmad subjected Orientalists to virulent criticism in his essay, *Gharbzadegi.*[2] Then came Fakhroddin Shadman's virtuosic suggestion, in 1965, about establishing a field of study antithetical to Western orientalism called farangshenasi, or *gharbshenasi* (occidentalism). Shadman, Fardid, and Al-e Ahmad had managed to convince many of Iran's intellectuals that the prevalent social malady was no longer one of "backwardness," as thought by their nineteenth-century predecessors, but instead one of "Westoxication." As such, instead of promoting wholehearted imitation or catching up with the West, they called for its abandonment.

Although Shadman, Al-e Ahmad, and Fardid had laid the groundwork for a critique of Western colonialism, machinism, and humanism, they had said relatively little about Western scholarship and mode(s) of knowledge about the Orient. This task fell upon the shoulders of a second generation of intellectuals, mostly Western educated, eager to engage in a host of debates concerning *sharqshenasi* (orientalism) and gharbshenasi. This generation differed from its predecessors in a number of ways. First, they did not have the high esteem of such earlier scholars as Mohammad-Ali Foroughi, Allameh Mohammad Qazvini, Mojtaba Minovi, and Seyyed Hasan Taqizadeh for Western Orientalists and Iranologists.[3] Second, through studying with and exposure to the ideas of such Western thinkers as Georges Gurvitch (1894–1965), Carl Gustav Jung (1875–1961), Claude Lévi-Strauss (1908–   ), André Malraux (1901–1976), Maurice Merleau-Ponty (1908–1961), Jean Piaget

---

cent) in South America; 3 (.10 percent) in Australia; 12 (.40 percent) in the communist bloc; 34 (1.12 percent) in Asia; 107 (3.52 percent) in the Middle East; 1,050 (34.57 percent) in North America; and 1,828 (60.19 percent) in Western Europe. In other words, 94.76 percent of foreign-educated Iranian academics were graduates of North American and Western European universities. The top four countries of choice were the United States (1,025); France (758); West Germany (422); and the United Kingdom (364).

2. Al-e Ahmad (1984, 99) wrote: "I haven't the foggiest notion when Orientalism became a 'science.' If we say that some Westerner is a linguist, dialectologist, or musicologist specializing in Eastern questions, this is defensible. Or if we say he is an anthropologist or sociologist, that again is arguable to an extent. But what does it mean to be an Orientalist without further definition? Does it mean to know all the secrets of the Eastern world? Are we living in the age of Aristotle? This is why I speak of a parasite growing on the root of imperialism."

3. For two examples of this earlier generation's cooperation with, and reverence for, Orientalists see Monshizadeh 1949 and Afshar 1977.

(1896–1980), Jean-Paul Sartre (1905–1980), and others, they had become more sophisticated in their philosophical tastes. As such, this generation was not content to merely follow the positivist scholarship of such scholars as Qasem Ghani, Yahya Mahdavi, Gholamhoseyn Sadiqi, and Sirus Zoka', whom they would teasingly refer to as the "Anatole France generation." Lastly, having been influenced by the West's self-doubt (alluded to earlier), the gharbzadegi debate, the rise of post-colonial movements, and the rapid transformation of their own society, these intellectuals attempted to redefine the boundaries of the occidental other and the oriental self.

One such attempt was made in 1967 by Seyyed Abolhasan Jalili, a colleague of Fardid and Nasr at Tehran University.[4] In an address to the Twenty-seventh Congress of Orientalists in Ann Arbor, Michigan, Jalili justified the rationale for engaging in gharbshenasi (occidentalism) by purporting that "occidentalism can give to the Orient what orientalism was unable to deliver, that is, self-awareness. . . . Orientalism was an attempt to occidentalize the Orient. But what is occidentalism? Is it the exact opposite of orientalism? No, this is neither possible nor desirable. Occidentalism is an attempt to detach from the West and keep a distance from it so that we can get to know its essence through all of its various facets" (Jalili 1969, 55). According to Jalili, orientalism by its very nature was a Western-oriented field of study that under the pretext of scientific objectivity tried to promote a Western way of looking at things. Because, however, in the social sciences even scientific objectivity is grounded in a set of values, he argued, orientalists have consciously or unconsciously followed the colonialist frame of mind as well as its politics. What is important, based on the quotation by Jalili, is the extent to which a systematic critique of the West was viewed by Iranian intellectuals as a prerequisite to their own process of identity formation. It was logical for Jalili and others to move from a critique of Western technology to a critical appraisal of its body of knowledge on the Orient. Orientalism was, thus, coming under criticism not only as a handmaid of colonialism but also as a stumbling block to the modern quest for identity.

Almost at the same time that Jalili was defending the establishment

4. Jalili, a professor of philosophy at Tehran University, had returned to Iran in 1955 after completing his doctoral studies at the University of Paris with a thesis entitled "Foi et transcendance: Expérience existentielle du réel." Interested in the thought of German philosophers Martin Heidegger and Karl Jaspers, he used to teach courses on the history of Greek philosophy and on contemporary philosophical texts. In the 1970s he served in such capacities as chair of Tehran University's Faculty of Letters and Humanities. He also served as Iran's cultural attaché in France.

of occidentalism as a field of study in an academic convention at Ann Arbor, Michigan, another Iranian academic, Mohammad-Ali Eslami-Nadushan, was defending his ethical Third Worldist view of the world in a seminar with no other than Henry Kissinger in Cambridge, Massachusetts.[5] As a prominent scholar, writer, and translator, Eslami-Nadushan had been invited as the Iranian representative to the 1967 Harvard University International Summer Seminar.[6] His seminar paper entitled "The Modern Man and the Underdeveloped Man" embodied the moralistic sentiments of many Iranian intellectuals of that era. In that paper Eslami-Nadushan outlined the characteristics of two types of people in the modern world. He portrayed the "modern man" as one who is well-to-do, enjoys luxury goods, believes in following technicalism and technology, is alone, lacks peace of mind, and, finally, substitutes intelligence for wisdom. By contrast, he pictured the "underdeveloped man" as mystical, angry, absent, hungry, faithful, bitter, and subject to prejudice. Eslami-Nadushan believed that the two obstacles to world progress were the oppressive behavior of the industrial world and the inequality and injustice prevalent in the less-developed countries. He went on to suggest that the United Nations be replaced with an international autonomous organization in which the representatives of the peoples instead of governments would take part (Eslami-Nadushan 1977, 197–202; 206). In short, Eslami-Nadushan confronted Kissinger's power politics approach with the same idealism the Melians had articulated against the Athenians in the Peloponnesian War.

Yet a third French-educated scholar of this generation, Jamshid Behnam, engaged in criticism of the Western literary persona in order to demonstrate the moral bankruptcy of the West.[7] Recognizing the need to first clarify the term *West,* Behnam provided the following definition: "All countries that have based their economic, social and political system upon a European civilization that had inherited Greek philosophy,

5. Eslami-Nadushan had earned his Ph.D. in international law in 1954 from the University of Paris with a thesis dealing with the British Commonwealth and the Republic of India.

6. The Harvard Summer Seminar, which was directed by Kissinger, used to bring together rising literary, intellectual, and political figures from around the world to discuss a variety of issues. Other notable Iranians who in the 1960s participated in this seminar included Mohammad Mo'in, Sadeq Chubak, Jalal Al-e Ahmad, Shapur Rasekh, and Simin Daneshvar.

7. Jamshid Behnam, a 1958 economics Ph.D. from the University of Paris, served as a professor of demography at Tehran University from 1959 to 1974. He also served as the dean of Tehran University's Faculty of Social Sciences and the chancellor of Farabi University.

Roman statecraft, and Christian ecclesiasticism" (Behnam 1970, 27).[8] He then proceeded to argue that "none of the four mythical characters of Western civilization, that is, Faust, Hamlet, Don Juan, or Don Quixote, represent the material spirit of that civilization. Instead, each one of them is wandering in pursuit of a utopian end, totally alien from the economic principles of the West" (Behnam 1970, 33).

As demonstrated by the above examples, the Iranian critique of the West, for the most part, remained an ethical one. The West was criticized for its past colonialism and present imperialism, its excessive admiration of technology and rampant irreligiosity, its materialism and consumerism, and its abandonment of moral convictions and justice. Occidentalism as a discourse on the Western other was, thus, predicated upon a deeply rooted feeling of moral and cultural superiority of oriental civilizations. These predispositions, however, were rarely subjected to a critical scrutiny. More often than not, the knowledge of self was attained through a noncritical, nostalgic appropriation of one's own historic past. Whereas some took refuge in the glory of pre-Islamic Persia, others idolized the country's religious and mystical traditions.[9]

To further explicate the nature, intricacies, and pitfalls of Iranian intellectuals' predominantly ethical critique of the West and Western Orientalists, I concentrate on the works of three scholars, each of whom left his indelible mark on the course of these discussions. Ehsan Naraqi was a well-known public intellectual with close ties to the royal court. He, nonetheless, called for the indigenization of social sciences in Iran. Hamid Enayat, was an imposing political scientist and a pioneer critic of

8. Another definition of the West offered during this period reads as follows: "The totality of Western European and North American countries, which through the Industrial Revolution and liberal bourgeois regimes, were transformed into world powers, and made the countries of Asia, Africa, and Latin America into their own economic and political waste baskets; and began the era of world imperialism in history" (Ashuri 1967).

9. Two of the leading academic advocates of the glorification of the pre-Islamic period were Zabih Behruz (1890–1971) and Ebrahim Purdavud (1886–1968). Both men were specialists in the history of ancient Persia and in Zoroastrianism as well. Purdavud, a professor of the Avestan language at Tehran University, translated *Avesta* into Persian and in the 1940s formed an intellectual circle that included such figures as Mohammad Mo'in, Sadeq Hedayat, Mehdi Bayani, and Bahram Farahvashi. Behruz founded the Iran-Vij Society along with two professors of Old and Middle Persian at Tehran University, Mohammad Moqaddam and Sadeq Kiya. This society and its organ, *Iran-kudah*, promoted the legacy of the ancient Persian civilization. Behruz and Purdavud considered Arabic influence on Iranian culture and language as most destructive and as such devoted their lives to countering it in any way possible. Their nationalistic zeal was no doubt augmented by the fact that only a tiny vestige of that former Iranian splendor now existed.

Iranologist scholarship. Finally, I turn to an examination of the ideas of Daryush Shayegan, one of Iran's most remarkable philosophers.

Ehsan Naraqi: The Nativist Sociologist

One scholar who contributed immensely to the popularization of the nativist discourse in the 1960s and 1970s was Ehsan Naraqi. He was born into a family of religious scholars in Kashan in 1926. After finishing his high school education in Darolfonun, Naraqi went to the University of Geneva where he studied sociology with the celebrated Swiss psychologist Jean Piaget. Upon earning his bachelors degree in 1951, Naraqi returned to Iran where he was introduced to Gholamhoseyn Sadiqi, a famed sociologist and Mosaddeq's interior minister. Sadiqi arranged for Naraqi's affiliation with the statistics center of his ministry, which was an extension of the American Point Four aid program. After working with a group of competent statisticians, demographers, and engineers at this center for a while, Naraqi was motivated to proceed to Paris in 1954 to continue his doctoral studies in sociology. In 1956 he graduated from the Sorbonne after finishing a thesis entitled *Les methodes d'études de la population dans les pays à statistiques incomplètes ou dépourvus de statistiques notamment en Iran.* Soon after his second return to Iran, Naraqi joined the academic camp of such Francophiles as Gholamhoseyn Sadiqi, Yahya Mahdavi, and Ali-Akbar Siyasi who sponsored his academic career as an assistant professor of sociology at Tehran University beginning in 1957.[10] One year later, Naraqi, who offered such courses as sociology, anthropology, and social problems of Iran, made a lifelong dream come true when at the age of thirty-two he founded the Institute for Social Studies and Research (hereafter the institute) at Tehran University.[11]

10. Each of these three individuals played a crucial role in the development of sociology as an academic discipline in Iran. Sadiqi, a positivist sociologist in the tradition of Auguste Comte, had earned his Ph.D. from the University of Paris in 1938 with a thesis entitled *Les Mouvements religieux iraniens au II* et au III* siecle de l'hegire.* He was generally regarded as the father of sociology in Iran because he initiated and taught a course on the science of society at Tehran University beginning in 1940. After the coup that toppled Mosaddeq, Sadiqi spent a couple of years in prison and then retired from political life to pursue his scholarly career. Yahya Mahdavi, a philosopher by training, published a translated version of a book by Felicien Challaye in 1943. This translation was the first Persian textbook on sociology available in Iran. Finally, in his role as the chancellor of Tehran University from 1943 to 1955, Ali-Akbar Siyasi's patronage of this academic enterprise was rather important. Beginning in 1957, sociology was taught as a separate academic discipline at the undergraduate level at Tehran University.

11. Needless to say, Naraqi's matrilineal ties to the queen could not but help secure

What motivated Naraqi to set up this institute was his own life expe-riences. As a Tudeh Party activist in his youth, it was not lost on him that a good deal of modern social theory had entered Iran through the samizdat literature of this party and other underground political organi-zations. Needless to say, this theoretical literature was habitually ideolog-ical. Naraqi felt that the prognosis of and remedies for Iranian social ills offered by the Tudeh Party were not truly grounded in the realities of the society. His final intellectual break with Marxism, however, happened in 1948 after he witnessed how a veteran Yugoslav communist partisan, whom he had befriended in Geneva, was being pressured by the Soviets to denounce Marshall Tito for pursuing an independent path to com-munism (Naraqi 1994b). Afterward, Naraqi became a rabid anti-Com-munist.[12] The second defining influence on him was his intense studies with Piaget from 1947 to 1952. He recalls that he came away from this experience with a sense that the worldview and analytical methods of Piaget and his other mentors in Geneva were the by-products of a Western society and could not necessarily be generalized to all other societies. From that moment Naraqi became convinced that the methods of Western social sciences (with their particular set of philo-sophical and ethical baggage) could not be merely "applied" but had to be "adapted" to conditions of social research in Iran (Naraqi 1994b).

As such, Naraqi hoped that the institute would lay the foundations for a more indigenous and less ideological tradition of social research in Iran. Toward that goal he decided to undertake the following two initia-tives. First, the institute dispatched its researchers to the urban and rural regions of Iran so that they could live among the people whom they were studying. Second, Naraqi decided to invite foreign social scientists to share their expertise with their Iranian counterparts on how to do applied social research. He hoped that in this way Iranians could imitate the Japanese's method, namely, to bring the West to their country in-stead of Westernizing it (Naraqi 1996, 529).[13]

---

all the required permissions for setting up such an enterprise. In addition to directing the institute, Naraqi also served as an adviser on social affairs to the High Economic Council and was a member of the Council for Administrative and Training Reorganiza-tion in the 1960s.

12. Naraqi's sympathy for both Mosaddeq and Mosaddeq's arch enemy Ayatollah Seyyed Abolqasem Kashani, whose house Naraqi frequented in the early 1950s, dem-onstrates his attempt to find a viable and popular alternative to the Tudeh Party.

13. Meanwhile, Naraqi managed to maintain his ties with a host of international organizations. He has been affiliated with UNESCO, in various capacities, for the last five decades. In the late 1950s he served as a consultant to the organization's Social Science Department. In that capacity he studied such issues as the settlement of no-

As its able director for more than one decade, Naraqi managed to turn the institute into one of Iran's leading centers for applied social science research.[14] The affiliation of such leading social scientists as Nader Afshar-Naderi, Ahmad Ashraf, Daryush Ashuri, Jamshid Behnam, Ali-Mohammad Kardan, Amir-Hushang Keshavarz, Abbas-Qoli Khajehnuri, Baqer Parham, Majid Rahnama, Shapur Rasekh, and Firuz Towfiq with the institute lent it a great deal of prestige. The National Iranian Oil Company, the Central Bank, the Agricultural Bank, the Fisheries Organization, and numerous other governmental bodies contracted with the institute to undertake various studies. Its researchers studied such diverse subjects as the social-psychological dimensions of pregnancy, the carpet-weaving industry, real estate trends, demographic trends, the circulation pattern of oil revenues, the conditions of earthquake stricken regions, urban slums, and rural economies.

Naraqi's own research along with the cumulative findings of the institute's researchers convinced him that Iran's technocratic elites' obsession with modernization had led them to disregard totally the indigenous cultural characteristics of the country. He decided to lay out this charge in three consecutive books, which were all published between 1974 and 1977. *Ghorbat-e Gharb* (The alienation of the West), *Ancheh khod dasht . . .* ([Cherishing] one's own trove . . .), and *Tamaʿ-e kham* (Raw greed), respectively, deliberated on the intricacies faced by modern Iranian social scientists in applying their Western-imported knowledge to the domestic conditions at hand, the nature of Western society and technology, and Iranians' search for cultural identity in a rapidly changing world. In terms of where he stood vis-à-vis the shah's government, Naraqi was closer to the tradition of Shadman and Nasr than to that of Al-e Ahmad or Shariʿati. Although a part of the establishment, Naraqi was, nonetheless, critical of the shah's "haphazard modernization,"

---

madic populations and the social consequences of industrialization and urbanization in a host of Middle Eastern countries. In 1966 he undertook the United Nation's first worldwide study of the migration of scientific personnel from lesser-developed countries to the advanced industrial states, (the brain-drain problem), and in 1969 he became director of the Youth Division of UNESCO. In 1975 Naraqi returned to Iran to become the head of the Institute for Educational and Scientific Research and Planning. As part of this position, he "sat on various state councils dealing with educational matters" (Naraqi 1994a, vii). His high profile affiliation with the shah's regime landed him in jail for a few years after the 1979 revolution. Upon his final release from prison in 1983 Naraqi moved back to Paris where he is now a special adviser to the director general of UNESCO.

14. In addition to publishing a journal, *Olum-e Ejtemaʾi* (Social Sciences), the institute also published more than sixty books and monographs related to various social science disciplines.

"forced developmentalism," and "relentless Westernization." He believed that the shah and the ruling technocrats used the "sacred formula of growth as an excuse to imitate the West mindlessly in the economic domain" (Naraqi 1994a, 217).[15] Not being able to criticize the shah himself, Naraqi decided instead to lambaste the technocratic elite. Referring to a generation of technocrats occupying high positions within the Iranian administration, Naraqi often attacked these "Massachusetts-type" technocrats for their excessive scientism and cosmopolitanism and for their corresponding obliviousness to indigenous Iranian conditions, norms, and values (Naraqi 1977, 13).

Naraqi believed that the Judeo-Christian tradition of thought, as it has been practiced in the West, did not have much to offer the Orient in original thought. "The power of Western civilization arises from its submergence in reality. The glory of Eastern history, on the other hand, emanates from the eternal glow of truth." Yet, Naraqi was not willing to reject readily the prospects of a sort of cultural eclecticism as he wrote, "Today we inevitably have to articulate and unite Western reality with Eastern truth" (Naraqi 1976b, 7). The "reality" he spoke of was of Western science and technology, whereas the "truth" alluded to oriental faith, mysticism, and esoteric philosophy. Hence, according to Naraqi, Iranians needed to maintain their culture and civilization while they borrowed Western know-how. This borrowing, however, had to be done discriminatingly, particularly if Iranians were to avoid such harmful consequences of technologism and machinery as alienation and spiritual/cultural poverty. Echoing Al-e Ahmad, Naraqi argued that machinism had brought spiritual and cultural poverty to the West (Naraqi 1974, 173–74). In short, Naraqi felt that the infatuation of the Iranian technocrats with Western (primarily American) models of growth would lead them down a disastrous course. The solution, for him, was to temper industrialism and technology by injecting them with some of the spiritual values of non-Western societies.

If he was opposed to the captive mind-set of Iranian right-wing technocrats, Naraqi was even more antagonistic toward the adherents of left-wing ideologies. He did not shy away from any opportunity to attack the intellectuals on the Left. Not even his own colleagues were immune from Naraqi's criticism. A case in point is that of Paul Vieille, a French neo-Marxist scholar who was affiliated with Naraqi's institute for almost ten years. Upon returning to France in the mid-1970s Vieille,

15. It helps to remember that 77.8 percent of the ministers in the last cabinet of Amir-Abbas Hoveyda before the revolution had graduated from Western universities (Menashri 1992, 276).

who had conducted extensive research on Iranian villagers, published two books entitled *La Féodalité et l'etat en Iran* and *Pétrole et violence*. Naraqi chided his former colleague by claiming that a European like him could never understand Iran because Westerners' insistence on the "scientific" approach does not enable them to comprehend the "inner excitements" and "unique characteristics" of Iranian society (Naraqi 1976a, 274, 573)! Here Naraqi evoked the conventional nativist assumption that the natives' self-understanding is by its very nature more authentic than any representation that could be contrived by foreigners. Yet it was not lost on anyone that Naraqi's attack on Vieille, whose two books were banned in Iran by the SAVAK, was really a clever way of currying favor with the government. This case perfectly demonstrated how nativism was intertwined with the will to power. As Foucault and Said had aptly demonstrated, knowledge and power are intertwined. Notwithstanding Naraqi's aversion to addressing the domestic configuration of power relations in Iran, his discourse about the West and the self was, nonetheless, contaminated by these very power relations.

Hamid Enayat: The Pensive Political Scientist

While Ehsan Naraqi was fanning the flames of indigenization by managing applied sociological research, another academic, Hamid Enayat, was forewarning Iranian intellectuals about the perils, vulgarities, and excesses of this enterprise. Enayat was born in 1932 into a middle-class religious family in Tehran. He completed his primary and secondary education in his place of birth by attending a number of schools (including an Armenian and a Zoroastrian school) and finally graduated from Darolfonun. Enayat then enrolled at the Faculty of Law and Political Science at Tehran University from which he graduated first in his class in 1954. After working for a number of years as a translator for the Japanese Embassy in Tehran, he went to England in 1956 to continue his studies at the London School of Economics and Political Science. Having spent his formative intellectual years as an activist in the Tudeh Party, Enayat was deeply influenced by the oil nationalization campaign of Prime Minister Mosaddeq. He therefore decided to write his 1958 master's thesis on British public opinion and the Iranian oil crisis. His attempt to come to terms with the tumultuous politics of the Middle East in the 1950s was further enhanced by his 1962 doctoral dissertation in political science entitled *The Impact of the West on Arab Nationalism (1952–1958)*. After working for a couple of years for the BBC World Service in London, Enayat went to the Sudan where he spent the 1965–66 academic year as a lecturer in Islamic political thought at the University of Khartoum. In 1966 he returned to Iran where he began his career as an associate (and later full) professor of political science at Tehran University.[16] After the 1979 revolution, Enayat resigned from his position at the university and once again returned to England where he became a fellow of St. Anthony's College at Oxford University. In 1980 he succeeded the eminent historian Albert Hourani (1915–1993) as the second university lecturer in modern history of the Middle East at Oxford. Unfortunately, however, he did not last long in this position because he died suddenly of a heart attack on 25 July 1982 during a flight from France to England (Gheissari 1989).

In its obituary for Enayat, the *Times* (London) wrote: "He was a man uniquely qualified, by family background, education and the breadth of his experience of Islam, to explain to the English-speaking world the nature and probable direction of the Islamic movements of today. . . . He was at home in Cairo as well as Tehran." The obituary (apparently written by Albert Hourani) continued, "His books and articles in Persian are generally agreed to be written in a pure, elegant and original style; his translations of European thought . . . helped to create the philosophical idiom of [the] modern Persian" (*Times* 1982, 10). There is scarcely any exaggeration in the above description of Enayat. Competent in Arabic, English, French, German, and Pahlavi, Enayat translated several important works into Persian. Among these were Aristotle, *Politics,* David Hume, *The Natural History of Religion,* Walter T. Stace, *The Philosophy of Hegel,* Edmund Leach, *Lévi-Strauss,* Alasdair C. MacIntyre, *Marcuse,* parts of Alexandre Kojève, *Introduction à la lecture de Hegel,* parts of Immanuel Kant, *Grundlegung zur Metaphysik der Sitten,* parts of Will Durant, *The Story of Civilization,* and parts of G. W. F. Hegel, *Phänomenologie des Geistes, Vorlesungen über die Philosophie der Weltgeschichte,* and *The Philosophy of History.*[17]

In the 1970s Enayat found himself perforce in the middle of an intense discussion about the merits and vices of orientalism and Orientalists.[18] A moderate person by temperament, he proceeded to simultaneously and evenhandedly tackle the arguments of both sides of this

16. Immensely popular among his students, Enayat used to teach such courses as Western Political Thought, Government and Politics in the Middle East, Political and Social Developments in Iran, and Political Thought in Iran. He served as the chair of the Political Science Department from 1969 to 1975.

17. Enayat further contributed to the augmentation of the philosophical idiom of modern Persian through his work on the Committee on the Social Sciences of the Iranian Language Academy and as an editor at a number of publishing houses.

18. For three examples of the antiorientalist discourse see Ashuri 1972, Anjavi-Shirazi 1972, and Rasekh 1972.

divide. In an address to the Third Congress of Iranology held in Tehran in September 1972, Enayat criticized Western Iranologists for their Eurocentrism and colonialist mentality; excessive preoccupation with the minutiae of philology, archaeology, and the history of military and religious conflicts; lack of attention to the broader features of Iranian history and culture; and neglect of Islamic political philosophy. He complimented Soviet Iranologists, however, for the proper attention they had devoted to the social and economic causes of historical developments in Iran and for unearthing and elucidating certain unorthodox ideas and movements. Enayat did not, however, forget to criticize their Stalinist method of historiography, which was based on the deterministic belief that every society, irrespective of its unique qualities, must pass through the same stages of development (Enayat 1973, 15–17; Enayat 1990, 69–83).

Enayat was even critical of those Western Orientalists who were sympathetic to Iranian causes and "used the most colorful language in praise of Iranian culture."[19] Speaking of the latter group, he wrote:

> Great efforts are now being made by some Western scholars to combine their studies on Iran and Islam with sympathy and empathy through adopting such approaches as phenomenology, or by trying to analyze Islam from the "faith perspective" of its believers. However, in contrast to a few of my colleagues, I am not convinced that this change has come about because the light of Eastern wisdom has fallen on their perplexed Western hearts. I believe, rather, that here again the exigencies of governmental interests continue to determine the orientation and content of much of current Oriental studies. (Enayat 1973, 14–15)

In a later work he further criticized the mystical or romantic interest of Western scholars and artists in Eastern civilizations by writing:

> Their praise of the spiritualism, simplicity, unhurried pace of life and joys of contentment among Easterners has often found echo, if not faithfully reproduced, in much of the current Muslim theorizing on the virtues of modest national economies, free from the obsessions of rates of growth and fast development. However, this perverted Eastern attraction to itself through the West's condescending love for the exotic has been deservedly censured by the Martiniquan Frantz Fanon, whose ideas have

19. In this regard Enayat criticized the French Islamist Henry Corbin for "divorcing Shi'ism from its social and political context," took issue with Hamid Algar's positive portrayal of Iranian ulema under the Qajar era as vanguards of Shi'ite militancy, and objected to Maxime Rodinson's exaggerations in demonstrating the compatibility of Islam with capitalism (Enayat 1972b; Enayat 1975b, 89–99).

gained popularity among Muslim intellectuals opposed to cultural imperialism. (Enayat 1980, 22)

By referring to this "perverted Eastern attraction to itself through the West's condescending love for the exotic," Enayat proved that he was quite conscious of the fact that in the signification universe of orientalism in reverse, the Oriental makes a detour through the Western other to know itself. Enayat maintained that this situation can be explained as follows: Iranian (or oriental) intellectuals try to alleviate their present inferiority complex vis-à-vis the West through an uncritical glorification of their ancient past and culture. Ironically enough, however, Orientalists have inadvertently boosted this nativistic sentiment and have provided its proponents with ready-made arguments through their scholarly findings.[20] Speaking of the causes of the contemporary sense of self-consciousness and self-assertiveness on the part of Muslim countries, Enayat wrote:

> The oldest cause in chronological terms has come from Orientalism and other disciplines of Western scholarship which have provided such an immense wealth of data concerning the history, language, religion, social structure and geography of "Third World" countries in general. Drawing upon this wealth, an increasing number of Muslim universities and institutions have continued, with or without official sponsorship, to study their national cultures. Great efforts have been made to discover, preserve, and occasionally assess the heritage of the past. This has resulted in the growth of a reassuring sense of pride among the younger generation in Islam's historical achievement, which, although not always well-founded, comes as a fitting counterweight to the feelings of inferiority which overcame the Muslim literates towards the end of the last century. (Enayat 1980, 22)

Enayat had earlier found the same trend in Iran as well. "The discovery by Western Iranologists of many elements of our pre-Islamic cultural heritage has been responsible for the growth in Iran of a nationalistic urge for the exaltation of pre-Islamic civilization" (Enayat 1973, 11). Ever so worried about Iranian chauvinism, Enayat had forewarned his compatriots by writing: "Yet if the basic and implicit assumption of Oriental-

20. This fact can help explain why even in the midst of a rampant antiorientalist campaign in Iran in the 1960s and 1970s warm testimonies to certain types of orientalists never fell out of fashion with the higher echelons of the Iranian academic establishment. For example, in 1963 and 1977 Tehran University published two books in honor of French orientalists Henri Massé (author of *Persian Beliefs and Customs*) and Henry Corbin (author of *Avicenna and the Visionary Recital* and numerous other books on Islamic philosophy). See Tehran University 1963; 1977.

ism was that Western civilization was innately and eternally superior to Eastern civilization, our own Iranology ought not to commit the opposite error, and assume that everything pertaining to Iranian culture is a paradigm of perfection. It ought not to be forgotten that fanaticism begets fanaticism" (Enayat 1973, 10).

What distinguished Enayat from the other Iranian critics of orientalism was the fact that he was well aware of the historicity and epistemological defects of his colleagues' discourse. He considered the "absence of any background of criticism and evaluation of Western orientalism" to be a great shortcoming. Enayat attributed this theoretical poverty to the belatedness of the embryonic spirit of antiorientalism among Iranian scholars.

> While such critical analyses of Orientalism have been discussed in various Asian, African and Western academic or intellectual circles, the subject has received scant attention in Iran. . . . A whole set of psychological reasons ranging from our oft-vaunted tendency to welcome and tolerate alien intellectual trends, to our equally oft-deprecated infatuation with Western cultural trappings, come to one's mind in explanation of this phenomenon. But one particular historio-political explanation which should be of interest to us here is the fact that, contrary to most Asian and African countries, Iran never suffered colonization at the hands of Western powers. (Enayat 1973, 6).

Comparing Iran to its neighboring Arab states makes the significance of the last point more clear. In the Arab world, which fell under direct colonial rule, an antiorientalist intellectual trend appeared in the nineteenth and early twentieth century.[21] In Iran, however, it only began to assert itself vigorously in the aftermath of World War II.[22] Speaking of this contrast, a former director of the Center for Arabic Studies at the American University in Cairo noted:

> It should be appreciated that the anti-Orientalist movement in Iran is perforce roughly fifty to seventy-five years behind its Arab counterpart.

21. This trend can in large part be attributed to the rise of the Al-Salafiyya movement and its intellectual leader Mohammad Rashid Rida (1865–1935). Whereas Rida's mentor, Mohammad Abduh (1849–1905), had championed the cause of Islamic modernism and strived for an intellectual synthesis between Islam and Western thought, Rida himself adopted a more conservative perspective and called for a strict affirmation of Islam.

22. A notable exception in this regard was Seyyed Jamal al-Din Afghani (Assadabadi) who engaged the famous French orientalist, Ernest Renan (1823–1892), in a polemic concerning Europe's claim to a universalistic philosophy and its self-appointed mission to "civilize" the rest of the world.

Not only this, but it would appear to be moving in the opposite direction. While the Arab branch of the movement peaked in the early years of this century and has since wound itself down to relative oblivion, the Iranian movement, beginning in the early to middle decades, has gradually gathered strength and is now building up a crescendo. (Millward 1975, 52)[23]

Enayat did not share the antipathy of many of his colleagues toward the West. Nor was he comfortable with the overtly "polemical or ethico-political" thrust of the Iranian antiorientalist discourse. Like Shadman, he maintained that Iranian intellectuals did not even know the West because "99 percent of the major literary, philosophical, and scientific Western texts have not yet been translated into Persian" (Enayat 1990, 60).[24] Furthermore, Enayat was convinced that what the Iranian-educated public knew of the West has been transmitted to it either through second-rate translations and commentaries or through superficial and nonmeticulous observations of individuals who have traveled to the West. Considering these facts, Enayat claimed that Iranian intellectuals had not yet reached the stage where they could pass judgments on whether a Western philosopher was right or wrong in his or her opinion of Western society and culture (Enayat 1972a, 9). At their best, he argued, Iranian intellectuals could only be competent researchers who report on what occurs in Western philosophical and social science circles. To further support his charge Enayat reminded his colleagues that in their denunciation of the West they have only repeated the "moral and pseudo-mystical" criticisms of such Western thinkers as Voltaire, Montesquieu, Rousseau, Marx, Nietzsche, Spengler, Toynbee, and Heidegger without adding much of their own (Enayat 1990, 62).

Enayat believed that contrary to Japanese, Indian, Egyptian, and

23. Millward, who had visited Iran and had met with Al-e Ahmad, was one of a handful of Western scholars who took seriously the charges raised by Iranian intellectuals against orientalism and responded to them accordingly. For the most part, however, this important debate among the Iranian intelligentsia went unnoticed in the West.

24. There was a lot of merit to this charge. For example, as far as the towering figures of Western philosophical tradition were concerned, until the end of the 1960s, none of the major works of Hegel, Spinoza, Descartes, or Kant had been rendered into Persian. The Marxist literature was not doing any better because its scope was limited to a few clandestine translations such as Marx and Engels, *The Communist Manifesto*, Engels, *Anti-Duhring*, Georgii Plekhanov, *Role of Individuals in History*, and a brief summary of Marx, *Capital*. A cursory look at the works of such philosophically inclined translators as Ahmad Aram, Amir-Hoseyn Aryanpur, Daryush Ashuri, Najaf Daryabandari, Mahmud Human, Mohammad-Baqer Hushyar, and Mahmud Sana'i also reveals that they were not following any systematic agenda in their selection of books to translate.

Arab Christians of Lebanon and Syria, who had engaged in intense discussions on the intellectual legacy of their ancestors and the nature of their ties with the West, Iranian intellectuals, until very recently, had done neither. What made the matter worse, according to him, was that the Iranian-educated public seemed to be content with its superficial understanding of Western philosophy and its ignorance of intellectual trends in other Muslim countries.[25] In this spirit Enayat lauded Al-e Ahmad's *Gharbzadegi* for succeeding in "discrediting the contemptuous stance of Westernized Iranians towards their Islamic past" despite the book's numerous "stylistic inconsistencies, methodological flaws and errors of judgment" (Enayat 1974, 4). Yet Enayat was also quick to caution that by becoming the rhetorical stock-in-trade of intellectuals, gharbzadegi had become a justification for not getting to know the West in the first place. Once again echoing Shadman, he contended that gharbzadegi is not manifested in translating the masterpieces of Western culture into Persian but is rather apparent in Iranian's fragmentary knowledge and plagiaristic mimicry of the West (Enayat 1979, 15–16).

According to Enayat, the Iranian intellectuals' alienation from their Islamic heritage, which had resulted in a dearth of research on Islamic thought, was the other side of the intellectuals' ignorance of and inferiority vis-à-vis the West. Reporting on the status of social sciences in Iran in the early 1970s, Enayat (1974) wrote: "One sometimes even notes an open opposition on the part of some intellectuals to any scholarly study of the history of Irano-Islamic social and political ideas on the grounds that since such ideas have proved to be one of the major obstacles to the progress and awakening of the Iranians, any attempt at reviving interest in them would be a futile, pedantic exercise and a harmful distraction from the 'relevant' ideas of the modern world." Enayat was strongly opposed to such tendencies.[26] Addressing his compatriots, he wrote:

> Apart from its historical importance, a critical study of Shi'ite political ideas is particularly essential for us in evaluations of the place of Shi'ism in our nation's cultural heritage. Such an evaluation will enable us to decide a more important issue in Iran's social history, that is to say, whether some of the negative traits in our national character, such as

25. Enayat worked diligently to disrupt this state of lethargic serenity. See Enayat 1970; 1975a; 1979.

26. It is fair to say that a goodly number of Iranian secular intellectuals were rather unfamiliar, inattentive, or disinterested in the religious sentiments of their more traditional compatriots. These intellectuals' upper-class origins, elitist upbringing, Western training, and high academic or political positions often caused their estrangement from the popular masses.

fatalism, love of superstition, submissiveness in the face of oppression, and dissimulation, are, as has sometimes been claimed, the outcome of Shi'ite indoctrination, or whether they have been simply the by-products of sociopolitical circumstances. (Enayat 1973, 13)

Enayat himself took a gigantic step toward this "evaluation" by publishing *Modern Islamic Political Thought,* which proved to be his first and only book in English. In the acknowledgment section of this book he wrote: "The original idea of this book would never have been conceived were it not for my friendship with the late Murtada Mutahhari [Morteza Motahhari], Professor of Islamic Philosophy at Tehran University, a most original and creative thinker, a dedicated Muslim, and a humanist" (Enayat 1982, xi).[27] Enayat's book dealt with the attempts of Shi'a and Sunni modernist thinkers who wanted to move from "confrontation to cross-sectarian fertilization" while developing political doctrines appropriate for the modern age. Although Enayat comes across in this book as sympathetic (even at times apologetic) toward Islam and supportive of modernist interpretations, he is not able to hide some of his trepidation.[28] While reflecting on the nature of the postrevolutionary government in Iran, Enayat's trepidations were transformed into subtle criticisms as he took issue with the "fundamentalist," "autocratic," "patriarchal," and "non-democratic nature of the hierarchic government" that came to power (Enayat 1983, 204; Enayat 1986, 164–74).

Daryush Shayegan: The Gypsy Philosopher

A man who comes at the end of a generation of intellectuals critical of the West and manages to formulate one of the most philosophically refined expositions of the Orient/Occident problematic in Iran of the 1970s is Daryush Shayegan, a self-proclaimed philosophical gypsy. Shayegan was born on 24 January 1935 in Tehran to an Azar-i father and a Georgian mother. After attending the Saint-Louis school in Tehran, he went to Badingham College in England at fifteen to continue his high school studies. Upon earning his diploma in 1954 he moved to the University of Geneva to study medicine but soon switched to studying philosophy and political science. Meanwhile, he began to study Sanskrit under the tutelage of one of his Swiss professors. Having spent six years in Geneva, Shayegan then returned to Iran and began to teach the

27. Enayat had begun to take part in a discussion group on Islamic philosophy at the home of Ayatollah Motahhari in 1974.
28. For an uncharitable philosophical critique of Enayat's views on Islam see Dustdar 1991, 213–47.

Sanskrit language at Tehran University. In 1964 Shayegan left Iran once again to attend the Sorbonne where, through the guidance of Professor Henry Corbin, he continued his studies of Hinduism and Sufism. His studies at the Sorbonne included a master's degree and a doctorate in Indian Studies and Comparative Philosophy culminating with a dissertation entitled *Les relations de l'Hindouisme et du Soufisme d'après le "Majma al-Bahrayn" de Dara Shokuh*. Upon his return to Iran Shayegan was lured back to Tehran University by S. H. Nasr (then dean of the Faculty of Letters and Humanities) as an assistant professor of mythology, indology, and comparative philosophy, first in the Department of Philosophy, and later in the Department of General Linguistics and Ancient Languages. His affiliation with Tehran University lasted from 1962 until 1980, during which time he mainly taught courses on the Sanskrit language and literature and Indian religion and thought (including such schools of thought as Vedic and Upanishad philosophy, Buddhism, Yogism, Theosophy, etc.).[29] After the revolution, he left his position and returned to France where he directed the Paris branch of the Institute of Ismaili Studies for a while.

Shayegan is one of the few Iranian intellectuals who has balanced his interest in Western philosophy with an equal attention to Asian philosophy. Fluent in Persian, French, English, and German with a working knowledge of Latin, Sanskrit, Arabic, and Turkish, he was well qualified to found and direct the Markaz-e Irani-ye Motale'e-ye Farhangha (Iranian Center for the Study of Civilizations). This institute, which was established in 1977 under the supervision of the Farah Pahlavi Foundation, managed to bring together, among others, such scholars as Reza Alavi, Daryush Ashuri, Mir-Shamsoddin Adib-Soltani, Reza Davari, and Shahrokh Meskub. The aim of the center was to familiarize Iranians with the civilizations of Eastern and Asian countries such as China, Japan, India, and Egypt. Toward that end the center hosted an international symposium in Tehran in 1977 entitled, "Does the Impact of the Western Thought Render Possible a Dialogue Between Civilizations?"[30] In addition, in its two years of existence the center published more than twenty books on various aspects of Asian civilization. One of the most acclaimed books to be published was *Asiya dar barabar-e Gharb* (Asia facing the West), a collection of essays by Shayegan himself on the sociocultural mutations of the traditional societies of Asia.

He began his book with the following bold statement: "My research

29. For more on Shayegan's views on Indian philosophy see Shayegan 1967.

30. For the proceedings of this symposium see Centre Iranien pour L'Etude des Civilisations 1979.

of many years on the nature of Western thought, which in terms of dynamism, variety, richness, and mesmerizing power is a unique and exceptional phenomenon in our earthly world, made me conscious of the fact that the process of Western thought has been moving in the direction of gradual negation of all articles of faith that make up the spiritual heritage of Asian civilizations" (Shayegan 1977a, 3). The above assertion was based on Shayegan's unique reading of the ontological differences between oriental societies (the world of Islam, Buddhism, and Hinduism) and that of the West. He maintained that the essence of philosophy and science in Asian civilizations was altogether different from its counterpart in the West. Based on a set of ideas he had laid out in his previous works, Shayegan maintained that whereas occidental philosophy was based on rationalist thinking, oriental philosophy was grounded in revelation and faith.[31] As a result, Asian philosophy has an essentially different character (gnostic) and telos (salvation). Shayegan wrote: "If occidental philosophy is a question of existence and being and if philosophy answers 'why' questions, in Islamic mysticism the questioner is God, and humankind only answers" (Shayegan 1977b, 109). This explains the different paths upon which each has embarked. As a result of the active promotion of doubt, relativity, contestation and secularization of knowledge, Western philosophy became autonomous from religion. In the Orient, however, philosophy remained contemptuous of profanity because it began with prophecy and divine revelation and viewed all knowledge as sacred. Shayegan gives the example of Islamic theosophy, which is based upon belief in a set of esoteric truths supported by such axiomatic principles as prophecy, holiness, and celestial revelation. In this system of thought there cannot be any "unknowns" because the answers were supposedly provided long before the questions were formulated.

Shayegan then goes on to outline the differences on the status of science in Asian and Western civilizations:

> In the great Asian civilizations of Islam, Hinduism, and Buddhism science has always been subordinate to religion and philosophy. Science never obtained the independence and possession that it gained in Western culture and subsequently led to its mutiny against religion and philosophy, making humans into the sole owners and possessors of the universe. . . . In the Orient, science never developed in the same way it evolved in the West because the Orient never became mundane, and nature never got separated from the spirit governing it, and the manifestations of divine blessing never left the realm of our universe. The Orient never produced a

31. For an elaborate exposition of this thesis see Shayegan 1976.

philosophy of history because existence was never reduced to a mere subjectivity or a process such as in the philosophy of Hegel. (Shayegan 1977b, 108)

Having laid out his typology of contrasts, Shayegan proceeded to argue that Western philosophers' replacement of revelation by reason led them to the negation of all metaphysical values. As such, Shayegan declared, the West has been losing its spiritual trustworthiness since the sixteenth century when it substituted civil society for religious order. The outcome is the present crisis of the West, which has manifested itself in four forms: cultural decadence, the twilight of gods, the demise of myths, and the collapse of spirituality (Shayegan 1977a, 168). The main culprit, according to Shayegan, was an ascending mode of "technical thinking." Having been introduced to the ideas of Martin Heidegger through his mentor, Henry Corbin, Shayegan considered this mode of thinking to be the "inevitable end of Western thought." Like Heidegger, he believed that science and technology are not just an assortment of neutral tools and techniques but are the embodiment of a type of metaphysics of being that imprisons and subjugates by granting boundless power to procure. Reminiscent of French sociologist Jacques Ellul's (1964) characterization of a "technological society" based on automatism, self-augmentation, universalism, autonomy, and monism, Shayegan put forward a philosophical critique of technical thinking. He viewed "technical thought" as a by-product of the amalgamation of four descending movements of the spirit in the evolution of Western thought:

Technicalization of Thought. The process of descendance from intuitive insight to technical thought and of reducing nature into material objects.
Materialization of the World. The process of descendance from substantial forms into mathematical-mechanical concepts, which strips nature of all its mysterious and magical attributes.
Naturalization of Man. The process of descendance from spiritual drives to instinctive drives, which negates all the divine qualities of celestial man.
Demythologization. The process of descendance from resurrection and concern with future life [based on cyclical time] to historicism and a concept of time that is empty of any otherworldly meaning [based on linear time]. (Shayegan 1977a, 47–48)

Following Heidegger, Shayegan further claimed that nihilism is the logical outcome of modern technology. The nihilistic reverberation of technical thinking will no doubt lead to the gradual negation of all oriental articles of faith. He insisted that if Asian civilizations were to have any realistic hope of recapturing their pristine vigor and virtue, they had to avoid the deleterious symptoms of the four descending movements of Western thought. Considering their state of debility and languor, however, this was by no means an easy task. According to Shayegan, the hegemony of Western thought and the feebleness of Asian cultures had concocted a condition of "double illusions" for Asian intellectuals who feel that they are intellectually ahead of their particular societies and yet behind what is considered to be "the world culture." The result is that, while their ties with their native thought, religion, and culture have been severed, they have also failed to grasp the philosophical foundations of Western thought. He considered this condition of "double claustrophobia" to be part of the larger predicament faced by the survivors of the Asian civilizations who are living in a no-man's land between the agony of God and His imminent death. Shayegan regards gharbzadegi to be the commanding spirit of this transitional phase. Speaking of which, he wrote: "It is another side of unawareness about the historical destiny of the West . . . gharbzadegi equals ignorance about the West, not knowing the dominant elements of a way of thought that is the most dominant and aggressive worldview on earth" (Shayegan 1977a, 51). Hence, it was only logical for Shayegan to conclude that alienation from the authentic self and gharbzadegi were two sides of the same coin.

As an example of this "double illusion," Shayegan refers to the naïve hope of late-nineteenth and early twentieth-century Asian intellectuals who felt that they could acquire Western technology while maintaining their own cultural identity. "One cannot say that we borrow technology [from the West] but would abstain from its annihilating consequences because technology is a product of a transformation of thinking and the outcome of a process lasting a millennium" (Shayegan 1977a, 46). He considered Western technology and science to constitute an inseparable whole. To reject one was to reject the other. The solution, according to Shayegan, was to return to cultural spirituality, which represented the only effective weapon possessed by the Orient against the intrusive West. Viewing the Orient as the only remaining depository of humanity, authenticity, and spirituality, Shayegan criticized Asian intellectuals for not doing enough to introduce their cultures to one another. More importantly, however, he warned them in the strongest possible terms to safeguard their cultural identity, ethnic memories, and heritage in the face of the intellectual assault of Western thought: "Against a [Western] culture that is threatening our existence in the most aggressive way we have no right to remain silent" (Shayegan 1977a, 51). Shayegan was convinced that to maintain their cultural identity Asian intellectuals had to first engage in a dialogue with their ethnic memories and only then proceed to a dialogue with the West because ethnic memories could expedite the flourishing of Asia's ancient, glorious heritage. In the case of Iran he viewed Islam and, in particular, Shi'ism to be the constitutive source of Iranians' collective ethnic memory. For Shayegan, just as for Al-e Ahmad, Shari'ati, Nasr, Naraqi, and Enayat, Islamic Iran and Iranian Islam have been so mixed with one another (for more than fourteen centuries) that it is no longer possible to distinguish between the two. In a Hegelian style of historiography he wrote:

> Iran has had the same mission in the Islamic world as Germany has had in the West. If, according to Hegel, the Germans were the ones who kept alive the torch of Greek thinking, Iranians have been the guardians of the light of Asian legacy in Islam. Our modern nationalists, who deny Islam and this dimension of Iranian history and who as a result of their aversion to whatever is Islamic retreat to the history of pre-Islamic Persia [and, therefore] suffer from a type of mythomania, do not realize the fact that to deny Islam is to disavow fourteen centuries of Iranian civilization and thought. (Shayegan 1977a, 189)

Shayegan's upholding of Islam as Iranians' primordial source of identity led him to the same position previously undertaken by Al-e Ahmad. If Shi'ism was Iran's primary spiritual asset, then the ulema, by necessity, would be its most conscientious custodians. He concluded, "Today the class that is more or less the protector of the ancient trust and despite its weak health keeps alive the treasure house of traditional thought is to be found in the Islamic theological centers of Qom and Mashhad" (Shayegan 1977a, 296).

In the aftermath of the 1979 revolution Shayegan came to rethink many of his previous theoretical exhortations that were now turned into a disturbing political reality. He conceded that his book, *Asiya dar barabar-e Gharb*, suffered from a nostalgic disposition for traditional civilizations that were becoming defunct (Shayegan 1989). Proceeding to correct this earlier nostalgia, Shayegan also amended his brittle dualistic ontology:

> The deep shocks that the Iranian revolution caused in regard to our cherished ideas and values and our everyday practices lead us to reconceptualize the relationships among civilizations. We should not view these civilizations as two distinct geographical worlds constituting two opposite cultural poles. Instead, we should view them as two overlapping constellations whose stars are juxtaposed, creating eclectic and unclear concepts that to a sharp observer reveal the incompatibility of the fundamental ideas of each civilization. (Shayegan 1982, 200)

Furthermore, Shayegan parted ways with Fardid and Nasr's wholesale rejection of the West and modernity. Recognizing the resilience of cultures and civilizations, he declared that he does not subscribe to the thesis that the West is in decline or must be abandoned. Instead, he maintained that "nowadays the problems of the West are no longer limited to the West because they have become the problems of the planet earth. They are our problems as well. The advantage of this [modern] era is that this crisis can be solved through coordinating all efforts" (Shayegan 1994, 289).[32] Unlike Nasr, who believed an intellectual continuity is discernible throughout the annals of Iranian culture, Shayegan postulated that Iranian and other Asian civilizations had taken a vacation from history for the last few centuries and are now suffering from a kind of cultural schizophrenia. In an intrepid incrimination of Asian and African civilizations he wrote:

> For more than three centuries we, the heirs of the civilizations of Asia and Africa, have been "on holiday" from history. (Doubtless there are exceptions.) Having cemented the last stones into place on our Gothic cathedrals of doctrine, we sat back to contemplate our handiwork. We succeeded so well in crystallizing time in space that we were able to live outside time, arms folded, safe from interrogation. (Shayegan 1992a, 12)

He continued:

> The problem of the Islamic world resides in its cumbersome atavism, its defensive reflexes, its intellectual blockages and above all in the illusory pretensions that it possesses ready-made answers to all the world's questions. We need to learn a certain humility, a certain understanding of the relativity of values. (Shayegan 1992a, 28–29)

Shayegan maintained that just as a broken mirror fragments reality and distorts perceptions, the incompatible worldviews of Iranian (and other Asian) intellectuals who are trapped in a fault line have created a mental block. He considers intellectuals as ropewalkers who have to avoid the field of distortion underneath (Shayegan 1989). Returning to the theme of the last chapter of *Asiya dar barabar-e Gharb*, appropriately entitled "New Obscurantism," Shayegan maintains that the main task of oriental intellectuals is to gain a sort of self-consciousness and to begin to know the true foundations of Western thought. Shayegan, who like the French social philosopher, Michel Foucault, had come to express his admiration for the spiritual dimension of the Iranian revolution, engaged in a theoretical autocritique one decade later (Foucault 1979b;

32. For Shayegan's extensive elaboration on this issue see Shayegan 1992b.

Shayegan 1982). He also admitted that he had a utopic image of Islam and the ulema because of the small circle of people with whom he used to fraternize (Allameh Tabataba'i, Ayatollah Motahhari, Seyyed Jalaloddin Ashtiyani, Ayatollah Seyyed Abolhasan Rafi'i-Qazvini, and Ayatollah Elahi-Qomsheh'i) (Shayegan 1989).

The metamorphosis of Shayegan's views should not be discounted as the customarily moody vacillations of a philosophical nomad. His conceptual evolution is also symptomatic of the larger intellectual progression of the orientalism in reverse discourse. Shayegan is questioning the legitimacy of the bitter and contemptuous attitude of Iranian intellectuals. He is also cognizant of the epistemological poverty, dormant distortions, and menacing dead ends of nativism. Nonetheless, this is not to say that he represents a radical epistemological break with this project. Shayegan's philosophical expositions continue to demonstrate the preoccupation of Iranian intellectuals with the enigmatic question of other-ness. Shayegan's construction of the West is reminiscent of Georg Lukacs's *reification*. Lukacs, who was inspired by Marx's theory of *fetishism of commodities*, coined this term to describe the idea that humans come to perceive the products and realities "made" by themselves to have a separate existence from them. As the new objects, humans are then alienated from, controlled by, and live at the mercy of their own former products (Lukacs 1971, 83–110). Shayegan's grandiose postulation about the nature of things occidental has led him to a reification of the *West*. He does not consider the West as an assorted amalgamation of disparate entities and qualities but as an essence, or as a Hegelian *Geist*. Furthermore, like the other proponents of orientalism in reverse, Shayegan appropriated the Orientalists' postulate that primordial religion constitutes the "essential essence" or the "spirit" of the Orient.

Shayegan does not abandon his quest to tie modernity to tradition. For him the past is still just around the corner. Even if it is buried, it can still be exhumed. How? Through an ahistorical metaphysics of essence that links the mythopoetic worldview of the Oriental with the rational contemplative universe of the West. He sees Henry Corbin, a man totally committed to theosophical thought, as an example of a thinker who was able to make this journey by bridging Sohravardi's twelfth-century Persia and Heidegger's twentieth-century West (Shayegan 1990). Needless to say, this ontological eclectic syncretism of Shi'a Islam and continental philosophy is not without its shortcomings. At any given time Shayegan may arbitrarily adopt one or the other of these two modes of reasoning. For example, his definition of the *Orient* as the language of mythology, insight, symbolic forms, and a philosophy of being defined by a sense of submission in the altar of God and nature is completely mythopoetic.

Moreover, Shayegan contends that the traditional societies of Asia have fallen behind Western history and that this has become their predicament ever since. If so, how realistic is it to expect Asian civilizations to engage first in a dialogue with their own past and only then to engage in a dialogue with the West? Is it not true that there can no longer be any type of "pure" oriental selfhood or self-understanding because the knowledge of the self is tempered and tainted by dynamic and ongoing historical events, cultural collisions, and intellectual appropriations?

7

Debates in the Postrevolutionary Era

> And what work nobler than transplanting foreign thought
> into the barren domestic soil; except indeed planting
> thought of your own, which the fewest are privileged to
> do?
>
> —Thomas Carlyle

THE IRANIAN REVOLUTION of 1979 represented the first mass revolutionary movement in the modern age that led to the establishment of a theocracy. As is customary with every major revolution, this social upheaval fueled the development of thought in the postrevolutionary Iranian polity. The revolution presented Iranian intellectuals with serious theoretical challenges. While its enthusiastic supporters tried to present Islam as a distinct ideology capable of offering a viable philosophical alternative to the modern world, its zealous opponents needed to explain the reasons for the ascendancy of this much-ignored ideology. Its opponents, which included disillusioned and astounded Iranian intellectuals both inside and outside the country, experimented with seclusion, political marginality, exile, and expatriate life as short- and long-term remedies for the anguish that beset them.

The unfortunate course of events occurring in Iran since 1979 (the hostage crisis, Iran-Iraq war, execution of political opponents) have aborted any serious attempts to deconstruct postrevolutionary intellectual thought. The intellectual deconstruction of a revolution in the making requires much more time and serious critical inquiry into Iranian history, culture, politics, and religion than those that have proliferated up to now. With such a conviction in this chapter I endeavor to provide a glimpse of the intellectual panorama of postrevolutionary Iran through the exposition of a number of important theoretical debates taking place among its leading ideologues. My objective in this chapter is to correct a number of prevalent myths and fallacies concerning contemporary Iranian political culture. I contend that despite the many obstacles and restrictions put forward by the present regime in Tehran the 1980s and the 1990s indeed witnessed the prospering of political philosophy and jurisprudence in Iran. Intellectuals do play an important role in shaping the worldview of the Islamic Republic. Far from engaging in esoteric and trivial polemics, the discussions now taking place in Iran are philosophically sophisticated, intellectually sound, socially relevant, and politically modern.

The 1979 revolution brought something more consequential than the fall of the old regime. By politicizing the polity it forever changed the intellectual configuration of Iranian society. The theoretical ferment caused by the revolution and the outlandish events that ensued inevitably affected the course of intellectual deliberations among Iranian intellectuals. The new regime, unlike its predecessor, relied heavily on its propaganda and ideological state apparatuses, and its ideology could not remain secluded from the reverberating echoes of a changing time and new ideas. Meanwhile, the formation of a modern theocracy had confronted the new ruling elites with novel questions and challenges in terms of how to govern and what constitutes a revolutionary political culture. The essential needs of "governing" while remaining "revolutionary" required quick and immediate solutions to problems that did not previously exist. The revolution posed many serious questions to the Islamic ideologue. Is Islamic jurisprudence (feqh) capable of answering modern social and scientific challenges? Are technology, nationalism, and parliamentary democracy compatible with Islam? What can the Islamic Republic bestow upon the rest of the world? In addition, such previously asked questions as how to stop or reverse the advancing march of secularism and how to confront the "West" and its various philosophical schools of thought remained unresolved. In a politically repressive yet intellectually flourishing era these questions were bound to be answered differently by diverse people.

The above questions are illustrative of the kinds of continuities and discontinuities brought along by the revolution. Shortly after its triumph, the political culture of the revolution showed signs of disintegration. The Islamic regime soon began a war against intellectual dissent aimed mainly at its liberal and leftist opponents. It denounced the secular intellectuals and literati as a bunch of Westoxicated, alienated, imitating, and noncommitted individuals whom the revolution could do without. Those lay religious intellectuals, however, who were willing to accept the preeminence of the clergy were allowed to remain.[1] The anti-

---

1. Some of the more prominent members of this class of religious intellectuals were Hasan Ayat, Abolhasan Banisadr, Mehdi Bazargan, Mostafa Chamran, Reza Davari,

intellectual and populist rhetoric of the revolutionary administration also inundated such potential rivals as the Feda'iyan-e Khalq and the Mojahedin-e Khalq. The new regime naturally prized conformity and devotion more than dissent.

The untimely deaths or assassinations of such rising political and intellectual figures as Ayatollah Mahmud Taleqani, Ayatollah Mohammad Beheshti, and Ayatollah Morteza Motahhari provided a major intellectual vacuum among the ranks of the clergy. This predicament provided an opportunity for two lay religious intellectuals to emerge gradually as the unofficial leading ideologues of the new regime: Reza Davari-Ardakani (hereafter Davari) and Hoseyn Haj-Faraj-Dabagh (better known by his pen name, Abdolkarim Sorush).

Davari was born in Ardakan (near Esfahan) in 1933 and finished his primary and secondary education in his place of birth. He was hired as a teacher by the Ministry of Education in 1951. Three years later, he enrolled at the Faculty of Literature at Tehran University as an undergraduate and proceeded to earn his doctorate in philosophy from the same institution in 1967. Since his graduation, Davari has been a professor of philosophy at his alma mater, where he mainly teaches courses on the history of modern philosophy. After the revolution, while maintaining his academic post, he has served in such capacities as a researcher in the Iranian Academy of Philosophy; member of the Iranian Academy of Sciences; and editor of the journal *Nameh Farhang,* organ of the Ministry of Culture and Islamic Guidance. In addition, he has been a member of a number of scientific and academic delegations representing Iran in international conventions.

Abdolkarim Sorush was born in Tehran in 1945 and attended Tehran University as a student of pharmacy. He later went to the University of London where he first studied chemistry and then became interested in the history and philosophy of science. Sorush pursued his interest in the subject of indeterminacy in science by working on a dissertation dealing with the history of monomolecular reactions. Before the revolution he worked mainly in pharmaceutical jobs in Bushehr and Tehran. After the revolution, Sorush occupied the following posts: member of the High Council of Cultural Revolution (responsible for revising the academic curriculums of Iran's primary, secondary, and higher institutions of learning); university professor (teaching such subjects as philosophy of science and philosophy of history), researcher at the Iranian Academy of Philosophy, and member of the Iranian Academy of Sciences. Sor-

---

Hasan Habibi, Gholamali Haddad-Adel, Fakhroddin Hejazi, Mohammad-Javad Larijani Habibollah Peyman, Nasrollah Purjavadi, Abdolkarim Sorush, and Ebrahim Yazdi.

ush's main occupation, however, was that of a researcher at the Institute for Cultural Research and Studies.

Defining the West

One of the early disputes between Davari and Sorush started over such questions as "What is the 'West'? How should one analyze and encounter it? and Do we have anything to learn from or to offer to it?" Similarly to his colleague, S. H. Nasr, Davari believes that Iranian intellectuals need to indulge in a process of critical reflection on the very essence and reality of Western history. This critique, he maintains, must undermine Western thought by aiming at humanism and modernity as its most celebrated legacies. Influenced by the Hegelian philosophy of history, which spoke of the spirit, drive, impetus, stages, and design as well as the passions of agents and subjects of history, Davari opts to view the West as a "totality" and a "unified whole." For him the West is not just a political entity but an essence. "It is a way of thinking and a historical practice which started in Europe more than four hundred years ago, and has since expanded more or less universally. The West portrays the demise of the holy truth and the rise of a humanity which views itself as the sole possessor and focus of the universe. Its accomplishment is to possess everything in the celestial cosmos. Even if it were to prove the existence of God, it will be done not with the intention of obedience and submission but in order to prove itself" (Davari 1984a, 18).

Having constituted the West as the absolute other against which an Islamic identity must be constructed, Davari then moves to a repudiation of modernity and all that the latter stands for. He regards modernity as an eighteenth-century intellectual project that replaced the natural order of the medieval era in the name of science and history. Davari maintains that since its onset at the time of the Renaissance, humanism has served as the very essence of the West and, as a result, individuality and humanism should be regarded as the pivotal truths of modern Western history. Thus, he incriminates humanism not for being just another philosophy but for becoming the blueprint for another human; a human to whom all the philosophies, theories, logic, and new sciences must be subordinated (Davari 1983, 59).

Reflecting on the imposed and imported nature of modernity in Iran and the rest of the Islamic world, he writes:

Modernity is a tree that was planted in the West and has spread everywhere. For many years we have been living under one of the dying and faded branches of this tree and its dried shadow, which is still hanging over our heads. Although we have taken refuge in Islam, the shadow of this branch has still not yet totally disappeared from over our heads. In fact, neither we nor it have left each other alone. What can be done with this dried branch? (Davari 1983, 83)

Davari's answer is obvious. Not only the branch but also the tree of modernity itself must be eradicated. Davari advocated that this be done through the formation of a distinctive intellect, one that is distinguishable from and superior to the "Western intellect." He rejected the Western models of democracy, which are based on the separation of politics and religion, as decadent. Instead of believing in the free-thinking criticism of religion brought along by humanism as a life-stance, he declared that a virtuous society is one that is grounded in the axioms of guardianship and prophecy (Davari 1983, 85). Here, Davari drew upon the neo-Platonic ideas of Abu Nasr Farabi (878–950), who is generally regarded as the founder of political philosophy in Islam.[2] Farabi and other Muslim political thinkers viewed the prophets as being the true Platonic philosopher-kings.[3] The prophets' mandate, however, was not based on human intellect but instead on revelation.

Furthermore, Davari reprimanded the West for its abandonment of metaphysical philosophy, a discipline provoking the highest questions. He contended that this type of philosophy, which had originated with the ancient Greeks and culminated in the ideas of Hegel and Nietzsche, can no longer be rejuvenated in the West. Echoing Edmund Husserl's assertion that the Enlightenment cunningly subdued philosophy in the name of science, Davari maintained that Cartesian philosophy in the West became subordinated to "method" and "science." In other words, philosophy, which was once recognized as the queen of the sciences, was now reduced to a primer for a set of natural and social sciences.[4] Yet even worse was the fact that these new sciences opted for

2. Davari's doctoral dissertation dealt with the influence of Greek thought on the political philosophy of such early Islamic thinkers as Farabi. For his work on Farabi see Davari 1975a, 1975b.

3. S. H. Nasr writes: "Farabi sought to identify the figure of the prophet-king of Plato with the prophet and law-giver of the Abrahamic tradition and described the perfect state in which a single revealed law would reign supreme over the world" (Nasr 1964, 15).

4. In reflecting on Davari's charge it will be useful to remember the following words of Immanuel Kant (1963, 116) written in 1795: "Thus it is said of philosophy, for example, that she is the handmaiden to theology, and the other faculties claim as much. But one does not see distinctly whether she precedes her mistress with a flambeau or follows bearing her train."

the preponderance of materialism and rationalism and, consequently, ignored religion. He asked why it is that, with a few exceptions (e.g., Friedrich Wilhelm Schelling, Max Scheler, and Sören Kierkegaard), the West has of late not produced any religious philosophers? Finally, following a Heideggerian outlook, Davari charged that technology is not just a set of means but a way of thinking that, in no uncertain terms, today dominates our world (Davari 1990, 34–37). Far from making people into subjects, technology has led to their subjugation. In short, the agent of freedom has been turned into a medium of imprisonment.

Based on the above set of pathological symptoms, Davari claimed that Western civilization has now reached its termination point and is struggling against alienation, solitude, and solipsism. He cautioned Islamic intellectuals to recognize that the West must be viewed as a "totality," a "unified whole," and an "essence" from which the non-Western world cannot pick and choose. The only solution for the West, according to Davari, is to abandon its collective and individual egoism and humanism, to repudiate its skepticism, and to eradicate the rotten tree of modernity altogether. These tasks, however, cannot be accomplished through any process of cultural exchange. Davari maintained that in the West, where secularism and materialism run riotously, anything short of a revolutionary detachment from humanism and submission to God was bound to fail. He concluded that non-Western societies were not facing individual Westerners but a unified West. Davari, thus, suggested that Iranian intellectuals should not be concerned with the destiny of individual Westerners but with the destiny of the West itself.

Abdolkarim Sorush could not disagree more with what are for him Davari's sweeping abstractions. He rejected all the above formulations as discreditable historicist determinism. Sorush maintained, because intellect is unfettered, philosophy cosmopolitan, and knowledge without boundaries, that date and place of birth cannot serve as valuative criteria for measuring the accuracy and legitimacy of ideas (Sorush 1988a, 236). Addressing Davari, he asked: "Where do you draw the boundaries of the West? Is this moral decline present wherever there is the West or wherever there is the West is there a moral decline? Should we know the 'Western spirit' based on the West or should we distinguish the 'West' from the Western spirit?" (Sorush 1988a, 231).

Sorush contended that Davari's philosophical postulate about the West as a unified and totalizing entity is a Hegelian construct that left no room for a constructive dialogue nor a mutually beneficial exchange. He criticized Davari's propositions for coercing people either to accept fully or to reject fully the West. In contrast, Sorush maintained that the West did not constitute a unified whole and should not be viewed as such. He rejected the usage of such grandiose concepts as "Western philosophy," "Western art," "Western culture," "essence of the West," "destiny of the West," and "spirit of the West." Sorush insisted that the West does not constitute a homogeneous totality with well-defined cultural and intellectual boundaries. The non-Western societies cannot face the West but can only confront individual Westerners.

Sorush proceeds to tackle another fallacy. He insists that what comes from the West is not necessarily contaminating; one can embrace Western thoughts, politics, and technology without inflicting self-harm. For Sorush, the issue is not one of submission or denunciation, but one of analysis and nourishment. Unlike Davari, Sorush strongly believes in cultural exchange. In a round-table discussion devoted to the issue of dialogue between different religions, he spoke of the hindrances caused by dogmatism, certitude, and self-righteousness and instead promoted mutual recognition and cooperation. Sorush argued: "I do not believe that a religious government like the Islamic Republic of Iran has (or should have) the intention of converting the whole world to Islam and Islamic government. The first step should be to promote and respect religious thought [of whatever kind] around the world" (Nameh Farhang 1992, 10).

Sorush went so far as to say that Iranians are heir to three cultures: pre-Islamic Persian, Islamic, and Western. According to him, instead of privileging one over the others, Iranians should attempt to reconcile and recompose all three (Sorush 1990). For Sorush, the idea of "returning to self" is not as exclusive as that formulated by Ali Shari'ati before the revolution. Having acknowledged that they are the bearer of these diverse lineages, he maintained that Iranians can become more tolerant of their differences. In short, by identifying the Western heritage as one of the three pillars of Iranian historical memory, Sorush wished to turn a perceived handicap into a comparative advantage.

Sorush further disagreed with Davari's disapproving view of modernity and modernism. He maintained that the most consequential point of demarcation between the modern age and what preceded it has to do with the ushering in of a whole range of "logies" and "isms." The new epistemologies made it possible for Iranians to reflect critically and objectively on intellect, religion, knowledge, ideology, and worldviews. More importantly and paradoxically, they also provided Iranians with the necessary means to recognize the limits and transcend the boundaries of modernism (Sorush 1992, 12). Thus, Sorush accused Davari of suffering from a type of benightedness about the West and cautioned the Iranian intelligentsia not to blame, mourn, or abandon the West for the route it has taken or for what it has achieved. Instead, he argued, the Iranian intelligentsia should turn their attention to their own endemic problems and shortcomings.

Historicism versus Positivism

The translation and publication of Karl Raimund Popper, *The Open Society and Its Enemies,* in 1985 triggered another major debate in postrevolutionary Iranian intellectual circles.[5] The debate was not over Popper[6] (1902–1994) per se but over epistemological principles and political orientations as well. The appearance of this book sharpened the *positivism*[7] versus *historicism*[8] debate, which had already been launched with the translations into Persian of Immanuel Kant, *Critique of Pure Reason,* Friedrich Nietzsche, *Beyond Good and Evil,* René Descartes, *Discourse on Method,* and Emile Durkheim, *Rules of Sociological Method.*

Davari attacked this urgency to publish Popper's book as an attempt on the part of translators and publishers to promote "Western democracy" and a "rationalist movement" in philosophy. In regard to the first charge, he maintained that promoting Popper's dream of an open society is, in fact, a clever way of opposing the revolution because the political consequences of Popper's ideas were all too clearly in support of capitalism and Western political liberalism. Davari argued that Popper is a typical eighteenth-century intellectual for whom *freedom* is, in reality, "freedom from religion." He asked, rhetorically, how a man who is opposed to absolute faith and is so clearly against religious thought can be portrayed as a guardian of faith in a theocratic society such as Iran (Davari 1986, 12).

Davari then proceeded to assault Popper's positivist concept of sci-

5. In 1984–85 three translated versions of this book were published. The first translation by Ali-Asghar Mohajer was published in California by Melli Publishers in 1984. The second translation by Ezzatollah Fuladvand appeared in Tehran in 1985 through Kharazmi Press. In the same year Mohajer's earlier translation was reprinted by Enteshar Press in Tehran.

6. Popper was already known in Iran through these translations: Popper 1971; Popper and Marcuse 1979?; Magee 1980.

7. "The characteristic theses of positivism are that science is the only valid knowledge and facts the only possible objects of knowledge; that philosophy does not possess a method different from science; and that the task of philosophy is to find the general principles common to all the sciences and to use these principles as guides to human conduct and as the basis of social organization" (*Encyclopedia of Philosophy* 1972).

8. "Historicism is the belief that an adequate understanding of the nature of anything and an adequate assessment of its values are to be gained by considering it in terms of the place it occupied and the role it played within a process of development" (*Encyclopedia of Philosophy* 1972, s.v. *historicism*).

ence.[9] He claimed that although Popper is a specialist in the methodology of natural sciences, he did not understand the language of philosophers and, hence, distorted the ideas of Plato and Aristotle and those of Hegel and Marx as well. Davari reminded his critics that by claiming that science deals with what "is" while religion deals with what "ought to be," Popper indeed privileged scientific methodology (principle of refutability) over religious intuition.[10] Davari concluded by charging that the Iranian positivists' attempt to reconcile Popper's ideas with Islam went against the *shari'ah*, led to divisions within the ranks of the *umma*, and undermined one's obedience and reverence toward the Supreme Being (Davari 1985, 24).

Davari's critics retaliated by initiating a full-fledged attack on historicism. Following Popper, they came to define *historicism* primarily in a methodological sense to denote "the view that the main task of the social scientist is to discover the laws by which whole societies develop and, on the basis of these laws of historical development, to make predictions about the future" (Miller 1972, 797). They assailed the German historicist tradition of Nietzsche, Hegel, Marx, Mannheim, Heidegger, and, by association, Davari as well (see Ganji 1986). Sorush and his associates articulated their rebuttals on both epistemological and political levels. They first assailed the philosophical assumptions of Martin Heidegger's thought, whom Davari had previously hailed as the "great sage of our time" and "the pioneer of future philosophy" (Davari 1980, 210, 224). The critics charged that Heidegger's contention that the age of metaphysics has ended and that the age of "philosophy of Being" has begun neither acknowledged nor denied the existence of God. Furthermore, they charged that Heidegger's philosophical postulates were too speculative, mythological, and antiscientific.[11] The Iranian positivists thoroughly disapproved of Heidegger's embracing of ideal terms and mystical philosophy. To counter Heidegger's view that all science is philosophy, whether it knows and wishes it or not, they turned toward logical positivists whose aim was to remake philosophy in conformity

9. Davari maintained that Theodore Adorno and other philosophers of the Frankfurt School were correct in designating Popper as a positivist because he shared the positivist aim of remaking philosophy in conformity with the logic and epistemology of modern natural sciences. For a lucid account of the differences between Adorno and Popper see D'Amico 1990–91.

10. Sorush analyzed Popper's principle of refutability in a two-part article (Sorush 1987–88). He also translated parts of Popper's 1975 book, *Objective Knowledge*, in Sorush 1989.

11. There is a certain degree of merit in these charges because such an orientation is implied in Heidegger, *Being and Time*, and appears even more candidly in his later writings.

with the logic and epistemology of modern natural sciences. Like their European counterparts the Iranian positivists maintained that, instead of following the intangible Heideggerian strategy of deconstructing science, universe, and being, the intelligentsia must follow the task of logically analyzing scientific concepts, statements, and explanations. Toward that end they began to write and translate a number of books on the ideas of the Vienna Circle and other logical positivists,[12] helping to reenact the epistemological debates of Europe during the 1920s and 1930s.[13]

The critics also indicted Hegel and Nietzsche, whom Davari had previously identified as the two philosophers responsible for elevating Western philosophy to its pinnacle (Davari 1984b, 106–7). Hegel was criticized for his speculative philosophy of history with its heavy emphasis on determinism. Nietzsche was viewed as the exponent of nihilism and moral relativity.[14] Sorush and the other critics rejected Hegel, Nietzsche, and Heidegger for the political ramifications of their ideas as well. Hegel was viewed as an exonerator of the Prussian state, Nietzsche as an enemy of liberal democracy, and Heidegger as a defender of fascism. They charged that the political points of view of these three philosophers were a logical outcome of their philosophical postulates. Hegel's theory of state, Nietzsche's will to power, and Heidegger's existential phenomenology were all suspected of invoking totalitarianism. Turning the table on his critics, Davari retaliated by delineating the differences between Heidegger and Popper. Davari asserted that Heidegger was a thinker who was not liked and was being slandered by Western political propaganda, whereas Popper was becoming increasingly famous owing to that same machinery (Keyhan-e Farhangi 1992, 10). Hence, the Popper-Heidegger debate in postrevolutionary Iran became both an important epistemological and a pertinent political debate as well.

Traditional versus Dynamic Jurisprudence

The third and, perhaps, the most consequential debate began over the question of how to make shari'ah congruent with the needs and limitations of a theocratic state in the late twentieth century. The new revolutionary elites were faced with a wide range of social, economic,

12. For example, see Khorramshahi 1983; Adib-Soltani 1980; Naess 1974?; Barbour 1983; Hempel 1990; Popper 1991.
13. For two treatments of the original European debates see Landgrebe 1966; Adorno 1976.
14. As early as 1980, Sorush had criticized Hegel's historical determinism (Sorush 1980). For another criticism of Hegel see Ganji 1987.

and political issues for which there were no clearly defined answers. Birth control, polygamy, universal draft, universal education, criminal sentences for new crimes, taxes for economic development, housing shortages, subsidies for essential goods, mediation of contract disputes between workers and management, land reform, and, finally, the design and structure of government (the Islamic Republic, *velayat-e faqih*, elections) all constituted novel questions that needed to be resolved. The ulema became partly divided over these matters.[15]

The 1979 revolution and its aftermath rejuvenated some of these old debates and generated new controversies as well. The clerics were split into two major camps: those who sanctioned traditional jurisprudence (*feqh-e sonnati*) and those who advocated the need for a more dynamic jurisprudence (*feqh-e puya*) capable of dealing with the contemporary, public, and nonesoteric challenges facing the Islamic umma. This dispute first began over sociopolitical concerns and was gradually transformed into an epistemological polemic. Its focal point came in April 1988 when Sorush published the first of a series of articles entitled, "The theoretical constriction and expansion of shari'ah" in *Keyhan-e Farhangi*, a leading monthly cultural journal.[16] The public and open-ended nature of the articles generated fiery and contemplative rebuttals and rejoinders both by lay intellectuals and the clerics.[17]

Sorush's cardinal claim was that all sciences and fields of knowledge are in a state of constant transformation and that changes in any domain of learning are bound to cause modifications in the other domains as well, including jurisprudence. As an historian of science, he espoused the view that scientific discoveries have an impact on epistemology, which, in turn, causes a new philosophical understanding. This new understanding, Sorush maintains, subsequently affects humanity's knowledge of itself and its environment and finally leads to a transformation of religious knowledge (Sorush 1991b). As a historical illustration of this domino effect, he referred to scientific breakthroughs in mathema-

---

15. In one instance a land reform bill that had the endorsement of such prominent leaders as Ayatollah Beheshti, Ayatollah Hoseyn-Ali Montazeri, and Ayatollah Meshkini was suspended as a result of the concentrated opposition of the more conservative clerics who denounced the bill's sponsors as violating Islamic principles (Bakhash 1984, 201–11).

16. These articles, which appeared in installments between April 1988 and May 1990, were later published by Sorush as a 349-page book. See Sorush 1991b.

17. The argumentative nature of Sorush's articles and the controversies it helped to set in motion proved too much to bear for his opponents. *Keyhan-e Farhangi* was forced to close down in June 1990. It reopened in 1991 under a "new" editorial board. The old editorial board founded a new independent monthly journal, *Kiyan*, in which Sorush and like-minded lay intellectuals more freely express their opinions.

tics that transformed the discipline of logic and, in turn, humanity's understanding of philosophy, revelation, and theology.

Following the method of logical reasoning, Sorush asserted that as a human science *feqh* is, by its very nature, hermeneutical and speculative. Because science and philosophy are continuously evolving, comprehension of the shariʿah (which is based on the sacred text and the sunna) should follow suit. Sorush came to the conclusion that because philosophy and the natural sciences are always unfinished and in quest of perfection; jurisprudential theory is also deficient, mortal, and fleeting.

Equipped with such a heuristic premise, Sorush proceeded to criticize the seminarians for their closed or narrowly defined intellectual points of view and their systematic neglect of nonjurisprudential disciplines. Moreover, he found fault with the traditional jurists' obliviousness to modern strides in scientific and social sciences. Accusing the jurists of bigotry, Sorush charged them with paying only lip service to the privileged position of science in Islam. He claimed that they, in fact, avoided or rejected scientific theories with the bogus claim that these theories undermine the certitude and indisputability of sacred beliefs.[18] Advocating a total reversal, Sorush contended that religious cognizance should become contemporaneous. By this he meant that the shariʿah should not contradict modern scientific findings. He asserted that shariʿah should acquiesce to the assistance offered by the natural and social sciences in formulating its reasoning. He challenged jurists to respond to the theoretical questions of the modern era and to react to the practical challenges of the age of modernity. In other words, Sorush championed the idea that instead of loitering aimlessly in isolation religious scholars should participate in the permanent dialogue and intellectual exchange conventional among scientists.

Borrowing an inference from sociology of knowledge, Sorush further claimed that the Islamic jurists' divergent interpretations of the shariʿah

18. This debate originally began in 1980 when the Islamic Republican government began its campaign of "cultural revolution." The campaign was undertaken to purge opposition forces from the university campuses and to revise the academic curriculums of universities, high schools, and elementary schools. At this juncture social sciences were coming under severe criticism for being unscientific, Western-oriented, relativistic, and capable of undermining religious beliefs. Sorush responded by defending social sciences in a series of magazine interviews. Since then he has followed up his counter-effort, among other things, by translating the works of these Western philosophers: Alan Ryan, *The Philosophy of the Social Sciences* (London: Macmillan, 1970), which was published in Iran in 1988; Edwin Arthur Brutt, *Metaphysical Foundations of Modern Physical Sciences* (London: Routledge and Kegan Paul, 1959), whose Persian translation appeared in 1991; and Daniel Little, *Varieties of Social Explanation: An Introduction to the Philosophy of Social Science* (Boulder, Colo.: Westview Press, 1990), which came out in Tehran in 1994.

were certainly the result of their contrasting understanding of nature, anthropology, and jurisprudence. He charged that just as the *fatva* (religious edict) of a rural jurist differs from that of an urbanite (each reflecting the respective social environment), so the Islam of a philosopher contrasts with that of a mystic. Sorush's conclusive remark was that the field of *tafsir* is far from an exact science and must indeed be approached as an inexact, inconsistent, and controversial arena of human inquiry.

Sorush was joined in his attack on feqh-e sonnati by, among others, a brilliant cleric by the name of Hojjatoleslam Mohammad Mojtahed-Shabestari. Born in Tabriz in 1936, Mojtahed-Shabestari graduated from the Qom Seminary after eight years of rigorous study. Fluent in German, English, and Arabic, he served as the director of the Islamic Center of Hamburg, West Germany, for nine years immediately before the revolution and, for a brief time in 1979, published a high-quality biweekly entitled *Andisheh-ye Eslami*. In a series of articles that were published concurrently with Sorush's essays Mojtahed-Shabestari, who is presently a professor of theology at Tehran University and a member of the Iranian Academy of Sciences, raised similar themes and concerns. In a remarkably candid criticism of the educational curriculum of Iran's theological seminaries, he wrote:

> The fact that our seminaries have separated their path from that of the social sciences and are minding their own business without any awareness of the developments in these disciplines has brought us to the present condition in which we have no philosophy of civil rights or philosophy of ethics. [Furthermore] we have neither a political nor an economic philosophy. Without having a set of solid and defendable theories in these fields, how can we talk of universal or permanent laws and values? How can we [even] gain admission to international scientific communities? (Mojtahed-Shabestari 1988, 11)

Mojtahed-Shabestari proceeded to counsel the clergy that, unless they reconciled their differences with the modern social sciences, their intellectual turmoil was bound to persist. According to him, if the clergy emerged from their sequestered intellectual circles, they would realize that the theoretical and practical challenges posed by the modern age have not all been settled. This revelation would then convince the clergy that they could no longer take refuge in the verdicts of past jurists. Instead they would realize that the gates of *ejtehad* must remain open and that individuals must be granted a bigger role in regulating their social lives. Reminiscent of Popper's assertion that the main question is not "who should rule" but "how to rule," Mojtahed-Shabestari maintains that the Qur'an and the sunna actually emphasize the "values of government" and not necessarily the "forms of government." Because managing a society requires science and planning, he proposed that the task be entrusted to those who are qualified, namely politicians and economists. Meanwhile, the foqaha should be preoccupied with promoting values derived from the Qur'an.

In another essay Mojtahed-Shabestari drew parallels between the way Christianity and Islam each encountered modernism. He maintained that as a result of their contemplative encounter with modern science and philosophy, both Protestant and Catholic theology were able to produce such celebrated thinkers as Karl Barth (1886–1968), Paul Tillich (1886–1965), Rudolf K. Bultmann (1884–1976), and Karl Rahner (1904–1984). By contrast, Mojtahed-Shabestari contended that fearing the prospect of cultural as well as political colonization, most Muslims adopted an approach of absolute negation vis-à-vis the European world. As a result of this unwillingness to encounter Western ideas, the Islamic world has been in a state of lethargy, unable to confront the challenges of modern science and philosophy (Mojtahed-Shabestari 1992, 12). The tacit implication of this analogy leads this author to believe that Mojtahed-Shabestari called for nothing short of a philosophically informed Islamic Protestantism. His reference to Bultmann who, under the influence of Heidegger, set himself the task of demythologizing Christianity and called for the reconciliation of reason and faith is of special interest when one considers the overtly Aristotelian character of Islamic philosophy and theology.[19]

Sorush and to a lesser extent Mojtahed-Shabestari (because of his clerical status) came under severe criticism by a host of clerics and lay adversaries. These critics charged that by relying on the ideas of Popper (falsification principle), Imre Lakatos (research programs), and Carl G. Hempel (paradox of confirmation)[20] Sorush and his colleagues were in-

19. For Mojtahed-Shabestari's view on the emergence of secularism in the West see Mojtahed-Shabestari 1986, 19.

20. Popper's falsification principle proposes that the criterion of demarcation between science and pseudoscience is not empirical verifiability (as suggested by the inductive reasoning of logical positivists) but falsifiability by observation. Popper's famous example that one cannot deduce from the repeated observation of white swans that *all* swans are white captures the spirit of his theory of refutation. Popper believes that science is revolution in permanence. The scientific enterprise advances as falsified theories fall by the wayside and disprovable theories march forward. In short, Popper considers only those theoretical assertions whose nature allows them to be falsified as cogent. Imre Lakatos, a Hungarian disciple of Popper, argued that science progresses more gradually than Popper's conjecture, refutation, and theory elimination plot leads one to believe. Lakatos maintains that in the scientific community one deals with a

deed undermining the canons of Islamic faith.[21] The traditionalists objected that Sorush's postulate about the steady transformation and interconnectivity of all sciences would lead to "relativity of knowledge" and skepticism, both of which they regarded as Popperian axioms. One critic went as far as to say that Sorush's ideas were more horrifying and damaging than the ideas of Marx and Freud because he was assaulting the ideological foundations of the Islamic government from within.[22] Furthermore, the traditionalists protested that to sanctify the proposition that the shari'ah is subject to contrasting hermeneutical interpretations is tantamount to granting people the right to present their own interpretations of it (Sobhani 1988, 11). The outcome would be the same in feqh as in science: a state of anarchy and divisiveness. In short, whereas Sorush and other advocates of feqh-e puya emphasized epistemological flux, the proponents of traditional feqh insisted on the fixity of sacred scriptures.

In response to Sorush's central thesis that feqh is epistemologically related to the other sciences, the critics declared that this one-way dependence is neither possible nor desirable because feqh and philosophy are two different domains of knowledge, each with its own separate methodologies. This group also maintained that Sorush's theory tacitly privileged the human sciences over the word of God. As such, they proceeded to remind Sorush that although all sciences are suppositional and speculative in nature, divine wisdom flies on the wings of conviction. More importantly however, these critics feared the immensely radical implications of Sorush's theory. Because the amplitude and specialized nature of the modern sciences no longer allows for individuals to have extensive knowledge in all disciplines, the present structure and

---

series (or succession) of theories rather than with one isolated theory. The proponents of these series of theories are connected to one another within a web of research programs. Lakatos likens science to a battleground of competing research programs where victory (progress) is achieved piecemeal when one advances from one research program to another. For further explanations of these ideas see Popper 1959; Lakatos 1978; Hempel 1945.

21. For a representative sample of these criticisms see the following works: Makarem-Shirazi 1989; Larijani 1989; Karimi 1990. The exchange between Sorush and Ayatollah Makarem-Shirazi was particularly important because it signaled the continuity of the struggle between lay religious intellectuals and the more traditionally minded clerics. Three decades earlier, Makarem-Shirazi, a prolific writer and prominent member of the Qom seminary, had echoed similar charges against Sorush's predecessor, Ali Shari'ati.

22. When the editors of *Keyhan-e Farhangi* refused to publish his lengthy rebuttal, he expanded it into a 337-page book and published twenty thousand copies (Ghaffari 1989).

educational curriculum of the theological seminaries must be fundamentally altered. Sequentially, the present conventions and protocols of religious authority and emulation must also be modified as clerics become narrowly focused experts rather than broad-minded scholars. This would surely undermine and make obsolete the position of marjaʿ-e taqlid (source of emulation). Sorush's clerical opponents feared that they would lose their present positions of prominence and would be increasingly forced to relinquish authority to their more-qualified lay adversaries.

Differing from these traditionalists, Davari has let it be known that he disagrees with Sorush on this issue as well. Davari believes that in the age of postmodernity, when all the philosophical axioms of modernity have been called into question, the attempt by Sorush and his colleagues to modernize feqh is doomed to fail. He reprimanded Sorush and his colleagues for the ill-conceived nature of their project by reminding them that Westerners did not modernize their beliefs but abandoned one, medieval metaphysics, in favor of another, positive science (Davari 1992, 12). Furthermore, Davari considered the application of the methodologies of modern sciences to feqh as a sign of intellectual confusion, which robs feqh of its innermost values. He asked, What is the need for religion if it has to conform to scientific methods? In short, Davari considered Popperian epistemology to be "an ill-shaped and ugly garment for feqh" (Davari 1991).

I have so far proposed that postrevolutionary Iran's intellectual community has been seized by a theoretical ferment—a ferment that is continuing with no apparent end in sight. It has also been argued that much of this intellectual contention revolves around a complex set of epistemological discords. Although at times both sides have resorted to crude accusations and misrepresentation of the other's position, these quarrels for the most part have been theologically and philosophically well informed. The debates taking place in Iran today differ from the one that took place in Europe in the 1930s and 1940s because of Iranians' new preoccupation with the proper place of Islam in the postmodern world. More importantly, these debates are taking place at a time when the cumulative effect of the literature on linguistic philosophy, poststructuralism, postcolonialism, cultural relativism, Eurocentrism, and end-of-ideology has questioned not only the (neo)positivist paradigm but the very project of Enlightenment itself. As a result, the present intellectual quarrels in Iran display the agony, eclecticism, and advantages of the turbulent age in which everyone lives. Celebration of and identification with scientific accomplishments are promoted at the same time when others point to the impasse, blind alleys, and fin de siècle attitude of the age of (post)modernity.

In view of this, Davari's critique of the basic ontological assumptions of Western thought should not be too easily dismissed. In addition, his call for transcending modernity deserves serious contemplation. This, however, does not mean that his grandiloquent postulates should be accepted at face value either. Ostensibly influenced by Heidegger's statement, "We are latecomers in a history now racing toward its end," Davari proclaims that the history of the West has come or is coming to an end. I find this and similar propositions to be both meretricious and fatalistic. Although he speaks of "Western history," Davari is not willing to place himself within any such historical categorization. He wishes to criticize the West from the vantage point of an observer standing outside the perimeters of history. Furthermore, in asserting that the West is left with no other option but to turn toward the East for an intellectual loan, Davari seems to have forgotten the comments of his sagacious guru, Heidegger, who in an interview with *Der Spiegel* once proclaimed:

> It is my conviction that a reversal can be prepared only in the same place in the world where the modern technological world originated, and that it cannot happen because of any takeover by Zen-Buddhism or any other Eastern experiences of the world. There is need for a rethinking which is to be carried out with the help of the European tradition and of a new appropriation of that tradition. Thinking itself can be transformed only by a thinking which has the same origin and calling. (Heidegger 1976, 281)

Finally, Davari's facile dismissal and blanket distrust of positivism and modern sciences will not do. By their systematic questioning these sciences have forced into destitution or ameliorated various philosophical assertions. Philosophy needs to stand up to the important challenges posed by modern social and natural sciences.

I believe the endeavor by Sorush and his colleagues to vindicate a hermeneutical approach to Islamic jurisprudence is a herculean task worthy of considerable attention. Contrary to the efforts of such individuals as Mehdi Bazargan, Sorush is not attempting to reconcile science and Islam nor to justify a scientific approach to religion.[23] Indeed, he believes one has to move beyond these types of attempts by placing the emphasis on religious knowledge (*ma'refat-e dini*) and comprehension of religion (*fahm-e din*) rather than religion in abstraction. As such, Sorush does not talk about reconciliation of science and religion but about using science to better comprehend religion. Sorush asserts that religion is capable of presenting science with all sorts of issues, approaches,

23. For Sorush's view of Bazargans undertaking see Sorush 1988a, 376–80.

anomalies, and discoveries. Thus, his basic argument is that one's understanding of religion cannot be separate and incompatible with one's understanding of nature and natural sciences.

Furthermore, Sorush differed in his approach from such predecessors as Ali Shari'ati and Ayatollah Morteza Motahhari who devoted their lives to bridging the gap between tradition and progress. Sorush maintained that the intellectual tension in the works of these two thinkers emanated from their belief in the immutability of religion, on the one hand, and their desire to make religion compatible with the modern world, on the other. He believed that the key to this puzzle is to distinguish the permanence of shari'ah from the fluctuating nature of religious knowledge. Sorush claimed that while the sacred text and the sunna are always constants, religious knowledge is a part of the larger domain of human knowledge in which there is a permanent process of intellectual give and take.

Calling attention to this delicate distinction constitutes Sorush's major contribution to the course of intellectual deliberations in postrevolutionary Iran. He maintained that whereas shari'ah itself is divine, its comprehension is not; whereas shari'ah is a tradition, its cognition constantly becomes contemporary; whereas shari'ah is sublime, religious knowledge is mundane and human; and, finally, faith or conviction is different from religious knowledge. He wrote, "I regard this epistemological distinction to be my most important achievement" (Sorush 1991a). Needless to say, he received reprimands from parts of the clerical officialdom who feared the subversive ramifications of his project of hermeneutical reading, understanding, and criticism.

Notwithstanding the dogmatic criticisms of the traditionalists, it is still possible to raise a few objections to Sorush's arguments. It seems that he has overlooked a number of crucial differences between religion as a worldview and science as an approach. As a worldview, religion comes to know the world a priori. The world it wants to comprehend is an invention of religion itself. In it, humankind's relation to the universe has already been specified, and questions have all been answered (Dustdar 1981, 5–15). The religious worldview does not seek questions, but "the truth." It attempts to transcend everyday realities in the hope of discovering "larger truths." Its interest, however, lies not so much in a praxis based on these larger truths but in accepting and cultivating a conviction in them.

The scientific outlook, by contrast, sees the world a posteriori. The world it wants to understand is not a creation of itself because it regards nature as an independent entity. Whereas the religious worldview attempts to arrive at knowledge and conviction through a return to specific sacred texts, science strives to identify facts through a procedure relying on deduction and observation. The latter approach interrogates common wisdom by constantly constructing hypotheses and subsequently testing for their conformity with reality, whereas the religious perspective tries to criticize everyday realities based on bigger and immutable sets of truths. In short, the model of the scientific community is "a community of disputatious, quarreling 'truth-seekers' dedicated to validity-enhancing belief change" (Holzner, Campbell, Shahidullah 1985, 310). The frontiers of religious exploration, by contrast, far surpass that of science because its telos is to acquire or reassert faith and to develop a value system based on ethical obligations in order to arbitrate human conduct.

As for Sorush's criticism of historicism, he mainly used the term in a methodological sense. If one were to define "historicism" in an epistemological sense, however, to denote the view that all human knowledge is essentially relative to time and place, then much of Sorush's own hypothesis can be viewed as "historicist."[24] For example, his belief in the idea of the accumulation and successive approximation of knowledge toward truth is itself a shadowy replica of the eighteenth-century Enlightenment idea of progress, which fits well within the confines of Hegel's philosophy of history. Sorush's assertion about the impact of the social milieu on the theological judgment of Islamic jurists is also in conformity with the Hegelian notion that the ordering principles or categories of the mind vary with a succession of epochs and cultures.

Finally, it is fair to say that despite sharing some of the scientific and philosophical interests of positivists Sorush is far from being a convert. Although he shares the positivists' critique of Hegelian historicism (belief in intractable laws of human history), Sorush's notion of history is more indebted to the speculative and idealist motif of Arnold Toynbee and Robin G. Collingwood.[25] Unlike logical positivists he does not have an unquestioning faith in science and empirical verifiability, nor does he share the antimetaphysical orientation of Ernst Mach (1838–1916), who served as the icon of the Vienna Circle. Sorush regards religion and mysticism along with science and philosophy as four legitimate modes of attaining knowledge. For him, the perfect person is one whose conscience has been set ablaze by these "four tables of paradise" (Sorush

24. The historicist's critique of positivism centers around the following three points: no direct awareness of pure sense-data; the historicity of the human mind; and the relativity of truth.

25. Toynbee's idea of an attainable ecumenical brotherhood among the major world religions and Collingwood's thesis that one cannot make any claims to an aggregate knowledge of history are both appealing to Sorush.

1986, 35). Sorush's writings are replete with metaphysical argumentation and allegories.[26] Sorush's commitment to metaphysics obliges him to try to reconcile skepticism and conviction, the scientific and the sacred, and the mundane and the sublime. Needless to say, this eclecticism allows for a degree of intellectual tension in his epistemology and Weltanschauungen. Nowhere is this tension more evident than in his roundabout discussion of technology. While upholding it against the traditionalists, he prescribes only a limited consumption of technology (Sorush 1988a, 274–327).

Sorush's hermeneutical probing of feqh faces formidable obstacles and has yet to prove successful. It has surely, however, kicked open Pandora's box.

26. For his overtly metaphysical writings see Sorush 1977; 1988b.

8

Epilogue

Should this torture then torment us since it brings us great pleasure.

—Goethe, *Faust*

TO RECAPITULATE the overall thesis of this book I argued that modern Iranian intellectuals' concept of "self" has been historically constrained by their perception of a dominating Western other. Faced with this predicament, some advocated an imitation of Westernization and modernism either entirely or selectively. Other intellectuals pursued a renaissance of the glorious past by taking nostalgic lapses into the psychology of antiquated heroes. Still others aspired to a middle ground by trying to contemporize traditions. As previously shown, in the last five decades Iranian intellectuals (however inconsistently) have mainly opted for this middle ground option. They rejected the apish imitation of the West as fraudulent and the renaissance of the past as archaic. Nonetheless, the formidable ideological permeation of the West led many Iranian intellectuals, in search of indigenization and authenticity, to turn toward nativism and Islamicism.

Similar to their counterparts in the rest of Asia, prototypical Iranian intellectuals no longer resort to the language of Confucius, Buddha, or Prophet Mohammad. What captivates these disgruntled Third World natives is not *fatalism* or *nirvana* but resistance and activism. Their appeal to the ideas of Rousseau, Marx, Heidegger, Sartre, and the like, therefore, should not be considered counterintuitive. It is, indeed, through the eyes of this latter group that the Iranian intellectuals castigate the West and the age of modernity. They identify with Rousseau's call for social justice, Marx's analysis of class struggle, Heidegger's critique of technology, and Sartre's call for committed intellectuals. The cultural-ideological dilemma of the Iranian (and to generalize, most Third World) intellectuals emanates from their excruciating role as intermediaries between two cultures. This dilemma is, thus, not reducible to a matter of class interest.

Following Foucault and Said, I further demonstrated that modern Iranian intellectuals' understanding of the West was attained in terms of their own subjectivity. It was very difficult for them to study the laws of a civil society, the exploits of technology, the essence of humanism, the doctrine of secularism, and the paradigm of modernity in their own right. These phenomena were always criticized through the lens of prejudice for the types of mishaps, impediments, doubts, fragmentations, inconveniences, and alienation that their imported or imposed status brought for a society such as Iran. Irrespective of their position on the ideological spectrum, twentieth-century Iranian intellectuals accepted, for the most part, Western civilization as their culture of reference in the process of identity formation. Their precepts of self-evaluation, language, modes of thinking, value judgments, and political alternatives were all influenced by their encounter with the West. In other words, these intellectuals waged their philosophical war against the West with weapons borrowed from that same adversary. In their attempt to evade Eurocentrism, alas, they succumbed to nativism. "Reaction against" rather than "action for" became the fixed hallmark of the intelligentsia's identity discourse. Critiques of submission and mimicry often led to demagogy and obscurantism rather than authenticity and freedom. The resulting portrait, hence, was one of a distorted imagery, an essentialist and dichotomized worldview, and cultural schizophrenia.

As the dominant intellectual project of the post–World War II era, nativism, as embodied in the two discourses of Westoxication and return to the self, epitomized this new quest. The first diagnosed the intellectuals' dilemma, whereas the second prescribed a solution. The partisans of both discourses, however, had to walk a delicate line between rationalism and mysticism, secularism and religion, elitism and populism and, finally, progress and reaction. Nativism proved capable of articulating all these elements. Despite their different languages and political platforms, both the Islamic and the secular segments of the Iranian intelligentsia could identify with at least one of the elusive battle cries of nativism. It appealed to all those intellectuals who were obsessed with such essential questions as national independence, anti-imperialist struggle, and indigenous alternatives. At the same time, nativism left plenty of room for the clerical and religious intellectuals, who tended to emphasize the Islamic nature of the struggle against the shah's "alien," "corrupt," and "anti-Islamic" regime. In short, the combative and assertive nature of nativism could accommodate both the principles of Third World populism as well as the messianic and elitist themes of Shi'ism.

To understand how nativism was able to emerge as the sole ideological candidate suited to unite most segments of the intellectual polity, one must look broadly at the Iranian sociopolitical milieu since the middle of the nineteenth century. This marked the beginning of the time when the challenge of Western civilization inspired the ideals of awakening and modernity. Convinced of the inferiority and intellectual stagnation of the Iranian society, the early proponents of Westernization championed the cause of creating a modern, strong, and developed country through such ideas as liberalism, secularism, nationalism, or socialism. A few generations later, however, they became disillusioned and cynical. The restoration of autocratic rule after the Constitutional Revolution (1905–1911), the forced abdication of Reza Shah in 1941 under the pressure of the Allied powers, the infamous 1953 coup toppling Mosaddeq, and the reign of native colons under Mohammad-Reza Shah was enough to turn the tide for many intellectuals. Advocating a course reversal, they argued that Iranians needed to recapture their pristine and "authentic" identity. Pointing their accusatory finger at the West's prevalent spiritual stagnation, they reminded their compatriots that as Iranians they could (or, better yet, should) take pride in their literature, art, architecture, mysticism, and spirituality. After all, they asked, are not these the celebrated highlights of Iranians' moral fiber? It was within this ambiance that calls for authenticity and rediscovery of the lost self dislodged the earlier cries for law and liberty. The lack of ideological hegemony by the Pahlavi regime contributed immensely to the rise of nativism as a counterdiscourse. The populist connotation of nativism with its admixture of anti-Westernization, antidictatorship, antidependency, and Third Worldist rhetoric easily captivated the post-1953 generation of Iranians still grappling with the outcome of the coup against Mosaddeq. In addition, the fact that *secularism* as temporal consciousness was lagging far behind *secularization* as a socioeconomic process contributed to the effectiveness of the appeal of nativism to the repositories of traditional and religious values.[1] The candid tone of nativism proved quite seductive because it called for *collective consciousness* at a time when many people could not bear the agony of the transitional phase to a runaway capitalist and industrialist society (with its unavoidable atomism and insecurity). Finally, the distinctive features of Iranian Shi'ism,

---

1. For more elaboration on the themes of secularism and secularization see Boroujerdi 1994a.

clergy, and the lay religious intellectuals facilitated the unrivaled popularity of nativism as an alternative paradigm.

Under the sheltering umbrella of nativism the two discourses of Westoxication and return to oneself were able to furnish the theoretical exigency for the formation of an Islamic intellectual movement. The 1979 revolution transformed these discourses from being the acculturated response of disenchanted intellectuals to becoming the hegemonic discourse of a revolutionary elite. The former uneasy squabbles of a number of critical intellectuals were now transformed into the theoretical stockpile of a revolutionary polity. In the hands of the new revolutionary elite, nativism took up a sacerdotal character and was used blatantly and brutally to coerce and to block other discursive practices.

Yet despite its triumphant political status nativism remains intellectually tormented. It is based on too many untenable, questionable ontological and epistemological premises to sustain itself for long. Its nostalgia for the past, attachment to things native, idealization of identity, and ethical-romantic rejection of modernity (to say nothing of the reign of terror and political repression it has set in motion) are all problematical. Nativism commits the same mistake as orientalism proper. It renders the "other" opaque and undertakes an essentialist and unabashed criticism of that other while refraining from a harsh scrutiny of its own cherished assumptions.[2] The fondness of many Iranian intellectuals for Heideggerian thought emanated from this yearning for wholeness. These intellectuals could easily relate to Heidegger's redolent romanticism and daring antimodernism because they themselves were affronted by and contemptuous of the modern age.

Today, in the closing years of this aging century, the West and modernity have replaced the Arabs and Islam as the favorite scapegoats of the Iranian intelligentsia. Yet history teaches that although Iranians showed enmity toward the Arabs, they nevertheless converted to the religion that the latter brought. Can the same happen with the West and modernity? In other words, can the Iranians continue to denounce the West while absorbing the paradigm of modernity? This time the answer is a qualified maybe. Throughout history Iranians have experienced two

2. Addressing herself to this issue, Val Moghadam (1989, 88) writes: "In this new nativist discourse, cultural dependence, Orientalism, neo-colonialism and cognitive imperialism are blanket terms for any concept, practice or institution that originates in the 'West'. What is privileged is 'authenticity', what is sought for is 'identity'. This is often translated into a rejection—as alien and culturally inappropriate—of Marxism, feminism, democracy, socialism, secularism. What is indigenous and therefore good? 'Islam'."

sides of Western civilization: colonialism and imperialism, on the one hand, and its modern thought, science, and technology, on the other. Although they have rightfully criticized colonialism and imperialism, their rejection of modernity has often been hyperbolic, hypocritical, and futile. In an age when globalization of Western capitalism and modernity has become a reality, Iranian intellectuals need to emerge from their self-made chrysalis. They need to recognize their theoretical lacuna and intellectual stagnation. Moreover, they need to realize that they cannot continue to clear their consciences cheaply either through totalizing or reducing the West and its multifaceted elements and experiences.[3] Considering the absurdity of trying to block ideas, many of Iran's intelligentsia need to realize that they can no longer stroll vicariously in the museum of the past with its assortment of heroes, demi-gods, and memoirs. Indeed they would do well to recall the dictum of Francis Bacon concerning the need to eradicate the idols of the mind. It is also incumbent upon them to remember Samir Amin's maxim that "history is filled with the corpses of societies that did not succeed in time."

Nativism is both guilty of scapegoatism and of having chimerical hopes, which have made it such a superficial palliative. One should also acknowledge, however, that as the articulation of the utopian strivings of Iranian intellectuals, nativism has also contributed positively to the transient phase of national self-consciousness in Iran.[4] Gone are the days of ignorant rejection and laudatory embracement of the West. Iranian intellectuals' present understanding of the West is much more complex than it used to be. Days of servile adulation for the West are now over, and the legitimacy of Fanon's "walking white lies" has come to an end. Meanwhile, the works of such intellectuals as Enayat, Shayegan, and Sorush demonstrate that the superfluous calls for repudiating and demeaning the West or uncritically exalting Iran's Islamic and pre-Islamic past are beginning to be seriously called into question. Now more than ever, Iranian intellectuals need to critically reevaluate the legitimacy of their own intellectual predecessors and social heritage.

---

3. As Edward Shils has brilliantly put it: "modern society is no lonely crowd, no horde of refugees fleeing from freedom. It is no *Gesellschaft*, soulless, egotistical, loveless, faithless, utterly impersonal and lacking any integrative forces other than interest or coercion. It is held together by an infinity of personal attachments, moral obligations in concrete contexts, professional and creative pride, individual ambition, primordial affinities and a civil sense which is low in many, high in some, and moderate in most persons" (Shils 1957, 131).

4. As Said (1993, 229) has aptly put it, "moving beyond nativism does not mean abandoning nationality, but it does mean thinking of local identity as not exhaustive, and therefore not being anxious to confine oneself to one's own sphere, with its ceremonies of belonging, its built-in-chauvinism, and its limiting sense of security."

They must also reevaluate the legitimacy of those of the West. Nothing should be allowed to pass unchallenged. Iranian intellectuals are privileged enough to live simultaneously in two disparate life-worlds: the historic and the (post)modern. Their present distorted imagery can become an advantage if they adopt a more nuanced perspective. While enervated by their past theoretical poverty, they can still become puissant by synthesizing the various streams of thought present around them. After all, it may still be possible to combine what Mircea Eliade described as the archaic person's interest in *cosmos* and the modern person's interest in *history*. The essential question presently confronting Iranian intellectuals, however, is how to transcend the dichotomous thinking that traps them either in a state of fraudulent "modernism" or a nativistic impasse.

Appendix

Glossary

Works Cited

Index

APPENDIX

Catalogue of Iranian Intellectual
and Political Figures

THE DATA PRESENTED in this appendix have been collected from numerous sources (oral history archives, obituaries, biographies, university yearbooks, almanacs, encyclopedias, books, journals, personal interviews, correspondence with family members, etc.). The format in which the above information is presented is as follows: last name, first name; city of birth, years of birth and death according to Shamsi and Gregorian calendar dates; country, institution, degree (or type), major, and year of graduation for the highest level of education obtained; and work for which known. All information I was able to include in the various categories is included in each entry. Entries are by people's real names, but variant transliteration or pen names are listed in parentheses. The symbol * indicates Muslim lunar (Hijri Qamari) calendar dates when applicable.

Abedzadeh, Haj Ali-Asghar
    Mashhad, 1290–1365/1911–1986
    Iran, Mashhad Seminary, Religious Education, 194?
    Merchant, religious activist, philanthropist

Afghani (Asadabadi), Seyyed Jamal al-Din
    Asadabad, 1254–1314*/1838/39–1897
    Iraq, Religious Education, 185?
    Writer, Pan-Islamic political activist

Afshar-Naderi, Nader
    Khorasan, 1305–1358/1926–1979
    France, University of Paris, Ph.D., Social Science, 1964
    Professor of social science at Tehran University, expert on Iranian
        tribes

Ahmadzadeh, Mastureh
  Mashhad, 1324–   /1945–
  Iran, Mashhad University, M.D., Medicine 1973/74
  Feda'i guerrilla, physician

Ahmadzadeh, Mas'ud
  Mashhad, 1325–1350/1946–1972
  Iran, Tehran University, B.A., Mathematics, 1969
  Feda'i guerrilla and theoretician

Ahmadzadeh, Taher
  Mashhad, 1300–   /1921–
  Iran, Secondary Education
  Small landowner, political activist, first postrevolutionary governor of
    Khorasan

Akhavan-Sales, Mehdi
  Mashhad, 1307–1369/1928–1990
  Iran, High School Diploma, 194?
  Poet, scholar

Akhundzadeh, Mirza Fath-Ali
  Nuka, Azerbaijan, 1227–1295*/1812–1878
  Traditional Education
  Playwright, writer, colonel in the Russian army

Alavi, Bozorg
  Tehran, 1283–   /1904–
  Germany, University of München, B.A., Education, 1928
  Writer, founding member of Tudeh Party, professor of Language and
    Literature at Humboldt University 1953–1978

Alavi, Reza
  Ahwaz, 1314–   /1935–
  USA, Harvard University, B.A., History, 1957
  England, Oxford University, B.A., Indian Classical Languages, 1963
  Scholar, Cultural Counselor of Iran in India, adviser to ministers of
    science and culture

Al-e Ahmad, Jalal
  Tehran, 1302–1348/1923–1969

Iran, Tehran Teachers' College, M.A., Persian Literature, 1946
Writer, political activist, social critic

Alibaba'i, Ahmad
Tehran, 1303–1375/1924–1996
Iran, Secondary Education
Bazaar merchant, political activist (a founding member of Nehzat-e
Azadi organization), philanthropist

Amini, Ali
Tehran, 1284–1371/1905–1992
France, University of Paris, Ph.D., Law, 1932
Politician (Majles deputy, 1947–49; minister of finance, 1953, 1955;
ambassador to USA, 1958–59; prime minister, 1961–62)

Amini, Yadollah (Maftun)
Shahindezh (Tabriz), 1305–   /1926–
Iran
Poet

Amir-Kabir, Mirza Taqi Khan
Hazava (Farahan), 1222–1268*/1807–1852
Iran, Traditional Education
Politician (prime minister)

Anjavi-Shirazi, Seyyed Abolqasem
Shiraz, 1300–1372/1921–1993
Switzerland, University of Geneva, B.A.?, Political Science, 194?
Literary scholar, writer, folklorist

Aram, Ahmad
Tehran, 1281–   /1902–
Iran, B.S. (unfinished), Medicine, 1924?
Translator, teacher, civil servant (Ministry of Culture)

Arani, Taqi
Tabriz, 1281–1318/1902–1940
Germany, University of Berlin, Ph.D., Chemistry, 1927
Professor, scholar, Marxist theoretician, spititual mentor of the Tudeh
Party founders

Aryan, Sa'id
  Mashhad, 13??–1350/19??–1972
  Iran, Mashhad University, B.A., English Language and Literature
  Feda'i guerrilla

Aryanpur, Amir-Hoseyn
  Tehran, 1303–   /1924–
  Iran, Tehran University, Ph.D., Philosophy of Education and Persian
    Literature, 1960
  Scholar, professor, translator

Ashraf, Ahmad
  Tehran, 1313–   /1934–
  USA, New School for Social Research, Ph.D., Sociology, 1971
  Scholar, professor

Ashraf, Hamid
  Tehran, 1325–1355/1946–1976
  Iran, Tehran University, B.S. (unfinished), Mechanical Engineering
  Feda'i guerrilla

Ashtiyani, Seyyed Jalaloddin
  Ashtiyan, 1304–   /1925–
  Iran, Qom Seminary, Religious Education
  Professor of Theology at Mashhad University, scholar

Ashuri, Daryush
  Tehran, 1317–   /1938–
  Iran, Tehran University, B.A., Economics, 1964
  Lexicologist, essayist, translator, editor

Assar, Nasir
  Tehran, 1305–   /1926–
  Iran, Tehran University, B.A., Law, 1945
  Politician (deputy prime minister and director of the Endowments
    Organization, 1962–72; director of CENTO, 1972–75; deputy
    minister of foreign affairs for political affairs, 1975–78)

Assar, Seyyed Mohammad-Kazem
  Najaf, 1264–1353/1885–1975
  Iran and Iraq, Religious Education, 192?

Theologian, jurist, professor of Islamic philosophy at Tehran University

Ayat, Hasan
Najafabad, 1317–1360/1938–1981
Iran, Tehran University, M.A., Sociology, 1961
Scholar, political activist

Azhang, Bahman
1324–1350/1945–1972
Bandar Pahlavi, Mashhad University, B.A., English Literature 1968
Feda'i guerrilla

Azizi, Mohsen
1284–1372/1905–1994
France, University of Paris,, Ph.D., Literature, 1938
Professor at Tehran University

Bahar, Mehdi
Mashhad, 1299–   /1920–
France, M.D., Medicine, 195?
Physician, writer

Bahar, Mehrdad
Tehran, 1308–1373/1929–1994
England and Iran, Tehran University, Ph.D., Persian Language, 1965
Scholar, professor of pre-Islamic Persian languages at Tehran University

Bahar, Mohammad-Taqi
Mashhad, 1264–1330/1886–1951
Iran, Traditional Education, 190?
Poet, scholar, journalist, professor, politician (Majles deputy; minister of education, 1946)

Baheri, Mohammad
Shiraz, 1298–   /1919–
France, University of Paris, Ph.D., Law, 1954
Professor of Law at Tehran University (1957–78), politician (minister of justice, 1962–63, 1978–79; deputy minister of court, 1964–77; secretary-general of the Rastakhiz Party, 1977–78)

Bahonar, Ayatollah Mohammad-Javad
  Kerman, 1312–1360/1933–1981
  Iran, Tehran University, Ph.D., Theology, 196?
  Theologian, politician (prime minister)

Banisadr, Abolhasan
  Hamadan, 1312–   /1933–
  France, University of Paris, Ph.D., Economics, 196?
  Scholar, politician (foreign minister; first president of the Islamic Re-
    public)

Baqa'i-Kermani, Mozaffar
  Kerman, 1291–1366/1912–1987
  France, University of Paris, Ph.D., Philosophy, 1935
  Professor, politician (co-founder of Hezb-e Zahmatkeshan-e Melat-e
    Iran, Majles deputy)

Baraheni, Reza
  Tabriz, 1314–   /1935–
  Turkey, Istanbul University, Ph.D., English Literature, 1960
  Writer, literary critic, poet, professor at Tabriz and Tehran univer-
    sities

Bayani, Khanbaba
  Hamadan, 1288–   /1909–
  France, University of Paris, Ph.D., History, 1937
  Professor

Bayani, Mehdi
  Hamadan, 1285–1346/1906–1968
  Iran, Tehran University, Ph.D., Persian Literature, 1945
  Professor, librarian (founder and director of Iran's National Library;
    director of the Royal Library, 1956–68)

Bazargan, Mehdi
  Tehran, 1286–1373/1907–1995
  France, Ecole Centrale des Arts et Manufactures, B.S., Mechanical
    Engineering, 1935
  Writer, professor, politician (leader of Nehzat-e Azadi; first prime
    minister of the Islamic Republic of Iran)

Beheshti, Ayatollah Seyyed Mohammad
  Esfahan, 1307–1360/1928–1981

Iran, Tehran University, Ph.D., Theology, 1959
Theologian, political activist

Behnam, Jamshid
Istanbul, 1309–   /1930–
France, University of Paris, Ph.D., Economics, 1958
Scholar, professor of demography at Tehran University (1959–74), chancellor of Farabi University, 1975–79, senior staff member of UNESCO

Behrangi, Samad
Tabriz, 1318–1347/1939–1968
Iran, Tabriz University, B.A., English, 196?
Teacher, social critic, folklorist, writer, translator

Behruz, Zabih
Neyshapour, 1269–1350/1890–1971
Egypt, England (Cambridge University), Arabic Literature and mathematics, 192?
Scholar, satirist

Beyza'i, Bahram
Tehran, 1317–   /1938–
Iran, Tehran University, Film and Theater, 196?
Playwright, scriptwriter, filmmaker

Borqeh'i, Ayatollah Seyyed Ali-Akbar
Qom, 1279–1367/1900–1988
Iran, Religious Education, 192?
Theologian, political activist

Borujerdi, Ayatollah Hoseyn
Borujerd, 1254–1340/1875–1961
Iran and Iraq, Religious Education, 19??
Leading theologian

Chamran, Mostafa
Tehran, 1311–1360/1933–1981
USA, University of California at Berkeley, Ph.D., Electrical Engineering, 1962
Political activist, minister of defense in the postrevolutionary government

Chubak, Sadeq
  Bushehr, 1295–   /1916–
  Iran, High School Diploma, 1937
  Novelist, short-story writer

Daneshpazhuh, Mohammad-Taqi
  Amol, 1290–   /1911–
  Iran, Traditional Education
  Scholar, bibliotist, bibliographer, professor at Tehran University

Daneshvar, Simin
  Shiraz, 1300–   /1921–
  Iran, Tehran University, Ph.D., Persian Literature, 1949
  Novelist, translator, professor at Tehran University

Darvishiyan, Ali-Ashraf
  Kermanshah, 1320–   /1941–
  Iran
  Novelist

Daryabandari, Najaf
  Abadan, 1308–   /1929–
  Iran, Abadan Razi High School, High School Diploma, 1947
  Translator, author, literary critic

Dashti, Ali
  Karbala, 1273–1360/1895–1982
  Iraq, Traditional Education, 1918
  Scholar, journalist (founder and publisher of *Shafaq-e Sorkh* newspaper,
    1922–35), politician (Majles deputy; ambassador to Egypt, 1948–51;
    ambassador to Lebanon, 1963; senator, 1953–79)

Davar, Ali-Akbar
  Tehran, 1264–1315/1885–1937
  Switzerland, University of Geneva, B.A., Law, 1920
  Journalist, politician (Majles deputy; minister of justice, 1927–34, fi-
    nance, 1932–37)

Davari-Ardakani, Reza
  Ardakan, 1312–   /1933–
  Iran, Tehran University, Ph.D., Philosophy, 1967

Scholar, editor, professor of philosophy at Tehran University (1967–present)

Dehkhoda, Ali-Akbar
Tehran, 1258–1334/1879–1956
Iran, School of Political Science, B.A., Political Science, 190?
Scholar, poet, social critic, Majles deputy, director of the School of Political Science (1924–41), etymologist, encyclopedist

Dehqani, Ashraf
Tabriz, 1327/8–   /1949–
Iran, Secondary Education, 196?
Feda'i guerrilla

Dehqani, Behruz
Tabriz, 1317/8–1350/1939–1971
Iran, High School Diploma, 195?
Teacher, Feda'i guerrilla

Derakhshesh, Mohammad
Tehran, 1294–   /1915–
Iran, Daneshsara-ye Ali-ye Tehran B.A., Geography, 1940
Teacher (founder of Iran Teachers' Association), politician (Majles deputy, minister of education, 1961–62)

Dowlatabadi, Mahmud
Dowlatabad (Sabzevar), 1319–   /1940–
Iran, Self-educated
Novelist

Dustdar, Aramesh
Tehran, 1310–   /1931–
Germany, University of Bonn, Ph.D., Philosophy, 1971
Professor of philosophy at Tehran University, scholar

Elahi-Qomsheh'i, Mohyeddin-Mehdi
Qomsheh, 1280–1352/1901?–1973
Iran, Religious Education
Professor of theology at Tehran University, poet

Enayat, Hamid
   Tehran, 1311–1361/1932–1982
   England, University of London, Ph.D., Political Science, 1962
   Scholar, translator, professor of political science at Tehran University
      (1966–79), university lecturer in modern Middle East history at
      Oxford University (1980–82)

Eraqi, Haj Mehdi
   Tehran, 1309–1358/1930–1979
   Iran, Elementary school?
   Broker in the Tehran bazaar, member of Feda'iyan-e Eslam

Eslami-Nadushan, Mohammad-Ali
   Nadushan (Yazd), 1304–   /1925–
   France, University of Paris, Ph.D., International Law, 1954
   Scholar, writer, translator, professor of literature at Tehran University
      (1969–79)

E'temadzadeh (Behazin), Mahmud
   Rasht, 1293–   /1915–
   France, Engineering, 1938
   Translator, fiction writer, Tudeh Party leader

Falsafi, Nasrollah
   Tehran, 1280–1360/1901–1981
   Iran, Darolfonun, High School Diploma, 1919
   Professor of history at Tehran University (1936–61), author, transla-
      tor, civil servant (Iran's cultural attaché in Italy, 1956–61)

Farahvashi, Bahram
   Tehran?, 13??–1371/19??–1992
   France, University of Paris, Ph.D., 1962
   Professor at Tehran University

Fardid, Ahmad
   Yazd, 1291–1373/1912–1994
   France and Germany, Philosophy
   Scholar, professor of philosophy at Tehran University

Farrokh, Mahmud
   Mashhad, 1274–1360/1895–1981
   Iran, Traditional Education, 192?
   Poet, scholar, textual editor, civil servant

Farrokhi-Yazdi, Mohammad
  Yazd, 1267/68–1318/1889–1939
  Iran, Traditional Education, 19??
  Writer, poet, Majles deputy

Farrokhzad, Forugh
  Tehran, 1314–1345/1935–1967
  Iran, 9th grade, 1952
  Poet

Forughi (Zoka'olmolk), Mohammad-Ali
  Tehran, 1254–1321/1876–1942
  Iran, Darolfonun, Literature and Philosophy, 1901
  Scholar, politician (Majles deputy, prime minister), belletrist

Foruzanfar, Badi'ozzaman
  Bashruyeh (Tabas), 1279–1349/1900–1970
  Mashhad, Traditional Education, 192?
  Professor and dean of theology at Tehran University, poet, senator

Ghani, Qasem
  Sabzevar, 1272–1331/1893–1952
  Lebanon, American University of Beirut, M.D., Medicine, 1919/20
  Scholar, translator, politician (ambassador to Turkey, Egypt; minister
    of health, culture; Majles deputy)

Golpayegani, Ayatollah Mohammad-Reza
  Golpayegan, 1277–1372/1899–1993
  Iran, Religious Education, 1919
  Leading theologian

Golshiri, Hushang
  Esfahan, 1322–   /1943–
  Iran, Esfahan University, B.A., Persian Literature, 196?
  Novelist, literary critic

Golsorkhi, Khosrow
  Tehran, 1319/20–1352/1941–1974
  Iran, Tehran University, B.A., Literature, 196?
  Poet, art critic, political activist

Habibi, Hasan
  Tehran, 1314/15–   /1936–
  France, University of Paris, Ph.D., Sociology, 196?
  Scholar, politician (Majles deputy, minister of education, justice, first
    vice-president, Iran's representative at the UNESCO Executive
    Council)

Haddad-Adel, Gholamali
  Tehran, 1323/24–   /1945–
  Iran, Tehran University, Ph.D., Philosophy, 197?
  Professor, scholar, civil servant

Ha'eri-Yazdi, Ayatollah Abdolkarim
  Yazd, 1239–1315/1860–1937
  Iran and Iraq, Religious Education, 18??
  Leading theologian, religious leader (founder of Feyziyyeh Seminary
    in Qom)

Ha'eri-Yazdi, Mehdi
  Qom, 1301/2–   /1923–
  Iran, Tehran University, Ph.D., Theology?, 1952
  Canada, University of Toronto, Ph.D., Philosophy, 1979
  Scholar, theologian, professor of philosophy at Tehran University

Haj-Seyyed-Javadi, Ali-Asghar
  Qazvin, 1304–   /1925–
  France, University of Paris, Ph.D., Philosophy, 1951
  Writer, journalist, political activist

Hakim, Ayatollah Mohsen
  Najaf, 1267–1349/1888–1970
  Iran and Iraq, Religious Education
  Theologian

Hakimi, Abolfazl
  Mashhad, 131?–   /193?–
  Engineering
  Scholar, political activist (leading member of Nehzat-e Azadi orga-
    nization)

Hazhir, Abdolhoseyn
  Tehran, 1281–1328/1902–1949

Iran, School of Political Science, B.A., Political Science, 1923
Politician (minister, prime minister)

Hedayat, Sadeq
    Tehran, 1281–1330/1903–1951
    Iran, Ecóle St. Louis, High School Diploma, 1925
    Novelist, fiction writer, literary critic, folklorist

Hejazi, Fakhroddin
    Sabzevar, 1307/8–   /1929–
    Iran, B.A., Persian Literature
    Scholar, publisher, politician

Hejazi, Mohammad
    Tehran?, 1279–1352/1901–1974
    France, Literature and Philosophy
    Writer, politician

Hekmat, Ali-Asghar
    Shiraz, 1272–1360/1893–1981
    France, University of Paris, B.A., Literature, 1932
    Scholar, professor, chancellor of Tehran University (1935–38), politi-
        cian (minister of culture; foreign minister)

Hezarkhani, Manuchehr
    Tehran, 1313–   /1934–
    France, M.D., Pathology, 1965
    Physician, writer, translator, political activist

Hojjati-Kermani, Hojjatoleslam Mohammad-Javad
    Kerman, 1310/11–   /1932
    Iran, Religious Education, 195?
    Theologian, politician (member of the Assembly of Experts, Friday
        prayer leader in Kerman, Majles deputy)

Homa'i, Jalaloddin
    Esfahan, 1278–1359/1899–1980
    Iran, Traditional Education, 19??
    Scholar, poet, theologian

Homayun, Daryush
    Tehran, 1307–   /1928–

Journalist, editor-in-chief of *Ayandegan,* daily newspaper (1967–77), politician (deputy secretary-general of the Rastakhiz Party, 1967–77; minister of information and tourism, 1977–78)

Hoveyda, Amir-Abbas
Tehran, 1298?–1358/1920–1979
Belgium, University of Brussels, B.A., Political Science, 1942
Politician (prime minister, 1965–77)

Human, Mahmud
Tehran, 1287–1359/1908–1980
France, University of Paris, Ph.D., Philosophy, 1954
Professor of philosophy, translator

Jahanbeglu, Amir-Hoseyn
Tehran, 1302–1370/1923–1991
France, University of Paris, Ph.D., Economics, 1949
Scholar, professor of economics at Tehran University

Jalili, Seyyed Abolhasan
Tehran, 1305/6–   /1927–
France, University of Paris, Ph.D., Philosophy, 1955
Professor of philosophy at Tehran University, Iran's cultural attaché in France

Jazani, Bizhan
Tehran, 1316–1354/1937–1975
Iran, Tehran University, B.A., Political Science, 195?
Marxist theoretician and revolutionary

Kafa'i, Ayatollah Ahmad
Mashhad, 1261–1350/1882–1971
Iran, Religious Education, 19??
Theologian

Kardan, Ali-Mohammad
Yazd, 1306–   /1927–
Switzerland, University of Geneva, Ph.D., Philosophy of Education, 1957
Professor, scholar

Kashani, Ayatollah Seyyed Abolqasem
 Tehran, 1261–1340/1882–1962
 Iraq, Najaf Seminary, Religious Education, 191?
 Religious and political leader, Majles deputy

Kasravi, Ahmad
 Tabriz, 1269–1324/1890–1946
 Iran, Religious Education
 Historian, journalist, political and social thinker, lawyer

Kazemiyyeh, Eslam
 Mashhad, 1311–   /1932–
 Iran, Tehran University, B.A., Persian Literature, 1956/57
 Story writer, teacher, journalist, political activist

Kazemzadeh-Iranshahr, Hoseyn
 Tabriz, 1262–1341/1884–1962
 France, University of Paris, B.A.?, 191?
 Literary scholar

Kermani, Mirza Aqa Khan
 Mashiz (near city of Kerman), 1270–1314*/1853/54–1896
 Iran, Traditional Education, 187?
 Political thinker and revolutionary

Keshavarz, Amir-Hushang
 Tehran, 1311–   /1933–
 Iran, Tehran University, M.A., Anthropology, 1969
 Scholar

Khadivjam, Hoseyn
 Mashhad, 1306–1365/1927–1986
 Iran, Traditional Education
 Literary researcher, writer, translator

Khajehnuri, Abbas-Qoli
 1294–1372/1915–1993
 France, University of Paris, Ph.D., Statistics, 1956
 Professor of statistics, founder of Institute for Statistical Training

Khamenei, Ayatollah Seyyed Ali
 Mashhad, 1318–   /1939–
 Iran, Mashhad Seminary, Religious Education, 1968

Theologian, president (1981–89) and the leader of the Islamic Republic of Iran (1989–Present)

Khanbaba-Tehrani, Mehdi
Tehran, 1313–   /1934–
Germany, Goethe University, M.A., Law, 1971
Political activist (leading member of the confederation of Iranian students in Europe), journalist, translator

Kho'i, Ayatollah Abolqasem M.
Azerbaijan, 1280/81–1371/1900–1992
Iraq, Religious Education
Leading theologian

Kho'i, Esma'il
Mashhad, 1317–   /1938–
England, University of London, M. Phil., Philosophy, 1966
Poet, lecturer in philosophy

Khomeini, Ayatollah Ruhollah
Khomein, 1281–1368/1902–1989
Iran, Qom Seminary, Religious Education, 1926
Leading theologian, political activist, leader of the 1979 Islamic revolution and founder of the Islamic Republic of Iran

Khorramshahi, Baha'oddin
Qazvin, 1324–   /1945–
Iran, Tehran University, M.A., Library Science, 1973
Scholar, translator

Kimiya'i, Mas'ud
Tehran, 1322–   /1943–
Iran
Film director, screenplay writer

Kiya, Sadeq
Tehran, 1299–   /1920–
Iran, Tehran University, Ph.D., Persian Literature, 1941
Professor, deputy minister

Larijani, Mohammad-Javad
Najaf, 1330–   /1951–
USA, University of California at Berkeley, Ph.D., Mathematics, 197?

Politician (Majles deputy, deputy foreign minister, adviser on national security to President Rafsanjani)

Mahdavi, Yahya
Tehran, 1287– /1908–
France, University of Paris, Ph.D., Philosophy, 1933
Professor of philosophy at Tehran University

Mahdavi-Damghani, Ahmad
Mashhad, 1305– /1926–
Iran, Tehran University, Ph.D., Literature, 1963
Professor at Tehran and Harvard Universities, scholar, civil servant

Mahfuzi, Ali-Reza
Rudsar, 1335– /1956–
Iran, Pars Institute, B.S. (unfinished), Physics and Mathematics, 197?
Feda'i guerrilla

Majidi, Abdolmajid
Tehran, 1307– /1929–
France, University of Paris, Ph.D., Law, 195?
Politician (minister of labor, 1969–72; director of the Plan and Budget Organization, 1972–77; director of the Queen Farah Foundation, 1977–79)

Makarem-Shirazi, Naser
Shiraz, 1305– /1926–
Iran (Mashhad and Qom Seminaries) and Iraq (Najaf Seminary), Religious Education, 1940s
Theologian, political activist (member of the Assembly of Experts), religious writer

Malek, Hoseyn
Arak, 1300– /1921–
France, University of Paris, Ph.D., Rural Sociology, 1960
Writer, political activist and theoretician

Maleki, Khalil
Tabriz, 1280–1348/1901–1969
Germany, University of Berlin, B.S., Chemistry, 192?
Scholar, leading political thinker and activist (co-founder of Hezb-e Zahmatkeshan-e Melat-e Iran)

Mansur, Hasan-Ali
   Tehran, 1302–1343/1923–1965
   Iran, Tehran University?, B.A., Political Science, 194?
   Politician (prime minister)

Marʿashi-Najafi, Ayatollah Shahaboddin
   Najaf, 1273/74–1369/1895–1990
   Iraq, Najaf Seminary, Religious Education
   Leading theologian

Matin-Daftari, Ahmad
   Tehran, 1275–1350/1897–1971
   Switzerland, University of Lausanne, Ph.D., Political Science, 1930
   Professor, politician (senator, prime minister)

Mehrjuʾi, Daryush
   Tehran, 1319–   /1940–
   USA, University of California at Los Angeles, B.A., Philosophy, 1966?
   Film director, translator, screenplay writer

Meshkat, Seyyed Mohammad
   Birjand, 1280–1359/1901–1980
   Iran, Religious Education, 192?
   Theologian, bibliognost, professor of Islamic jurisprudence at Tehran
      University

Meskub [Meskoob], Shahrokh
   Babol, 1304–   /1925–
   Iran, Tehran University, B.A., Law, 194?
   Scholar, translator

Milani, Ayatollah Mohammad-Hadi
   Najaf, 1272/73–1354/1894–1975
   Iraq, Religious Education, 19??
   Theologian

Minovi, Mojtaba
   Tehran, 1282–1355/1903–1977
   Iran and England, 193?
   Professor, literary scholar, civil servant (cultural attaché)

Mirzazadeh [M. Azarm], Ne'mat
  Mashhad, 1317–   /1939–
  Iran, High School Diploma, 195?
  Poet, writer, political activist

Mofatteh, Ayatollah Mohammad
  Hamadan, 1306/7–1358/1928–1979
  Iran, Tehran University, Ph.D., Theology, 19??
  Theologian, political activist

Mohaqqeq, Mehdi
  Mashhad, 1308–   /1929–
  Iran, Tehran University, Ph.D., Theology and Persian Literature, 1959
  Scholar, professor at Tehran and McGill Universities

Mo'in, Mohammad
  Rasht, 1297–1350/1917–1971
  Iran, Tehran University, Ph.D., Persian Literature and Language, 1943
  Scholar, professor of Persian literature at Tehran University, encyclo-
    pedist

Mojtahed-Shabestari, Hojjatoleslam Mohammad
  Tabriz, 1315–   /1936–
  Iran, Qom Seminary, Religious Education, 195?
  Scholar, professor of theology at Tehran University, member of the
    Academy of Sciences

Mo'meni, Hamid
  1322–1354/1943/34–1976
  Iran, Tehran University, B.A., Economics, 1972/73
  Feda'i guerrilla

Monshizadeh, Davud
  Tehran, 1293–1368/1914–1987
  Germany, University of Berlin, Ph.D., Literature and Philosophy,
    1943
  Professor at Munich and Uppsala Universities, political activist
    (leader of Sumka Party)

Montazeri, Ayatollah Hoseyn-Ali
  Najafabad, Esfahan, 1300/1–   /1922–
  Iran, Esfahan Seminary, Religious Education, 1952

Leading theologian, political activist (member of Council of Islamic Revolution; speaker of the Assembly of Experts)

Moqaddam, Mohammad
Tehran, 1287–   /1908–
USA, Princeton University, Ph.D., Linguistics, 1938
Scholar, professor of ancient Persian languages at Tehran University (1939–68)

Mosaddeq, Mohammad
Tehran, 1261–1345/1882–1967
Switzerland, University of Neuchâtel, Ph.D., Law, 1914
Politician (provincial governor, Majles deputy, minister of foreign affairs, prime minister, 1951–53)

Mosleh, Javad
Shiraz, 1297/98–   /1919–
Iran, Traditional Education, Theology and Literature, 19??
Theologian, professor of philosophy at Tehran University

Motahhari, Morteza
Faryman, 1298–1358/1920–1979
Iran, Qom Seminary, Religious Education, Theology, 1952
Leading theologian, scholar, professor of Islamic Philosophy at Tehran University (1954–76), political activist (founder of the Society of Militant Clergy, member of the Council of the Islamic Revolution)

Nabdel, Ali-Reza
Tabriz, 13??–1350/19??–1972
Iran, Tehran University, B.A., Law, 196?
Feda'i guerrilla

Naderpur, Nader
Tehran, 1308–   /1929–
France, University of Paris, B.A., French Language and Literature, 1952
Poet, social and literary critic

Nafisi, Sa'id
Tehran, 1274–1345/1895–1966
France and Switzerland, 19??
Professor at Tehran University, scholar, translator, belletrist

Na'ini, Ayatollah Mohammad-Hoseyn
   Na'in, 122?–1315/1850–1936
   Iran, Religious Education, 18??
   Theologian

Naraqi, Ehsan
   Kashan, 1305–   /1926–
   France, University of Paris, Ph.D., Sociology, 1956
   Professor of sociology at Tehran University (1957–79), director of
      the Institute for Social Studies and Research (1958–79), scholar,
      advisor to the secretary-general of UNESCO (1983–Present)

Nasiriyan, Ali
   Tehran, 1313–   /1934–
   Iran
   Theater and film actor, theater director, playwright

Nasr, Seyyed Hoseyn
   Tehran, 1312–   /1933–
   USA, Harvard University, Ph.D., Philosophy, 1958
   Professor of philosophy at Tehran, Temple, and George Washington
      universities, chancellor of Aryamehr University of Technology,
      1972–75; director of Iranian Academy of Philosophy, 1975–78

Nasr, Seyyed Valiollah
   Kashan, 1255–1324/1876–1946
   Iran, old medical school of Tehran, M.D., 190?
   Physician, scholar, professor, politician (minister of culture)

Natel-Khanlari, Parviz
   Tehran, 1292–1369/1914–1990
   Iran, Tehran University, Ph.D., Persian Literature, 1943
   Scholar, poet, professor of Persian literature at Tehran University,
      politician (senator, minister of education)

Nateq, Homa
   Reza'iyeh, 1314/15–   /1936–
   France, University of Paris, Ph.D., History, 1967
   Professor of history at Tehran and Paris Universities, scholar, political
      activist

Navvab-Safavi, Seyyed Mojtaba
   1301/2–1344/1923–1956

Iraq, Najaf Seminary, Religious Education, 194?
Founder of the Feda'iyan-e Eslam organization

Nuri, Sheykh Fazlollah
1259–1327*/1843–1909
Iraq, Najaf Seminary, Religious Education, 18??
Leading theologian, political activist

Pahlavi, Farah
Tehran, 1317–   /1938–
France, Ecole d'Architectures, B.A. (unfinished), Civil Engineering
Empress of Iran

Pahlavi, Mohammad-Reza
1298–1359/1919–1980
Switzerland and Iran, Military academies, 1936
King of Iran (1941–1979)

Pahlavi, Reza
Savad Kuh, 1256–1323/1878–1944
No formal education
King of Iran (1925–1941)

Pahlbod, Mehrdad
1300–   /1921–
Iran, High School Diploma, 193?
Minister of culture and arts (1964–78)

Pakdaman, Naser
Tehran, 1311–   /1933–
France, University of Paris, Ph.D., Economics, 1965
Professor of economics at Tehran University, scholar, political activist
    (founder of the Organization of University Professors, 1978)

Paknezhad, Shokrollah
13??–1361/19??–1982
Iran
Political activist (leader of the Palestine Group)

Parham, Baqer
Rodbar, 1313–   /1934–
France, University of Paris, Ph.D., Sociology, 1974

Translator, scholar, social activist (founding member of the Writers'
Association of Iran)

Parvin-Gonabadi, Mohammad
  Gonabad, 1282–1357/1903–1978
  Iran, Traditional Education, 192?
  Scholar, translator, professor of literature at Tehran University, Majles
    deputy

Peyman, Habibollah
  Shiraz, 1314–   /1935–
  M.D., Dentistry, 19??
  Scholar, political activist (founder of the Movement of Militant Mus-
    lims), dentist

Pishdad, Amir
  Tehran, 1309–   /1930–
  France, University of Paris, M.D., Medicine, 1961
  Professor of medicine at University of Paris, political activist (found-
    ing member of the League of Iranian Socialists in Europe)

Purdavud, Ebrahim
  Rasht, 1264–1347/1886–1968
  Lebanon, France, Germany, India, Law and pre-Islamic Persian his-
    tory and language, 1930s
  Professor of pre-Islamic Persian history and languages at Tehran Uni-
    versity, poet

Purjavadi, Nasrollah
  Tehran, 1321/22–   /1943–
  Iran, Tehran University, Ph.D., Philosophy, 197?
  Scholar, philosopher, editor of *Nashr-e Danesh* magazine

Puyan, Amir-Parviz
  Mashhad, 1324/25–1350/1946–1971
  Iran, National University, B.A., Literature, 196?
  Feda'i guerrilla and theoretician

Qazvini, Allameh Mohammad
  Tehran, 1256–1328/1877–1949
  Iran, Traditional Education
  Scholar, belletrist

Qotbzadeh, Sadeq
   Esfahan, 1315–1361/1936–1982
   USA, B.A. (unfinished?)
   Political activist (organizer of Iranian students in United States and
      Europe, director of the Iranian National Radio and Television,
      minister of foreign affairs)

Radi, Akbar
   Rasht, 1318–   /1939–
   Iran
   Playwright

Rahimi, Mostafa
   Na'in, 1305–   /1926–
   France, University of Paris, Ph.D., Law, 195?
   Essayist, translator

Rahnama [Rahnema], Majid
   Tehran, 1303–   /1924–
   France, University of Paris, Ph.D., Law and Economics?, 1948
   Professor at Tehran University, scholar, politician (ambassador to
      Switzerland, 1965–67; minister of science, research, and higher ed-
      ucation, 1967–71; deputy prime minister, 1972–77)

Rajavi, Kazem
   Mashhad?, 1314–1369/1935–1990
   France, University of Paris, Ph.D., Law, 1964
   Professor, lawyer, political activist

Rajavi, Mas'ud
   Tabas, 1327–   /1948–
   Iran, Tehran University, B.A., Political Science, 1970/71
   Leader of the Mojahedin-e Khalq organization

Rasekh, Shapur
   Tehran, 1303–   /1924–
   Switzerland, University of Geneva, Ph.D., Sociology, 1958
   Professor of sociology at Tehran University (1958–1979), scholar,
      civil servant (secretary of state for economic and social planning),
      consultant to UNESCO

Rashed, Hoseyn-Ali
   Torbat-e Heydariyeh, 1284–1358/1905–1979

Iran and Iraq, Religious Education, 1934
Preacher, Majles deputy

Razmara, Ali
Tehran, 1280–1329/1902–1951
France, Ste. Cyr, Military Academy, 1929
General, politician (prime minister, 1950–51)

Rezazadeh-Shafaq, Sadeq
Tabriz, 1274–1350/1895–1971
Germany, University of Berlin, Ph.D., Philosophy, 1928
Professor, scholar, politician (senator)

Ro'ya'i, Yadollah
Damghan, 1311–   /1932
Iran, Tehran University, Ph.D., Law?, 196?
Poet, civil servant

Sa'adati, Kazem
1319–1350/1940–1971
Iran
Feda'i guerrilla

Sadiq, Isa
Tehran, 1273–1357/1894–1978
USA, Columbia University, Ph.D., Philosophy, 1931
Scholar, professor, university chancellor, politician (senator, minister)

Sadiqi, Gholamhoseyn
Tehran, 1284–1370/1905–1991
France, University of Paris, Ph.D., Sociology, 1938
Scholar, professor of sociology at Tehran University, politician (minister of interior, leading member of the National Front)

Sadr, Ayatollah [Imam] Musa
Qom, 1307–1357?/1928–1978?
Iran, Tehran University, B.A., Political Science, 195?
Iraq, Najaf Seminary, Religious Education, 1959
Theologian, political activist (leader of the Movement of the Deprived [AMAL] in Lebanon)

Sa'edi, Gholamhoseyn
  Tabriz, 1314–1364/1935–1985
  Iran, Tehran University, M.D., Psychiatry, 196?
  Psychiatrist, short-story writer, playwright, dramatist, political activist

Safa, Zabihollah
  Shahmirzad (Semnan), 1290–   /1911–
  Iran, Tehran University, Ph.D., Persian Literature, 1943
  Scholar, professor of Persian literature at Tehran University (1943–
    69)

Safa'i-Farahani, Ali-Akbar
  Gilan, 1318–1349/1939–1971
  Iran, Tehran University, B.S.?, Engineering, 196?
  Feda'i guerrilla

Saffari-Ashtiyani, Mohammad
  Tehran, 1313–1351/1934–1972
  Iran, Tehran University, B.A., Law, 1960
  Feda'i guerrilla

Sahabi, Ezzatollah
  Tehran, 1309–   /1930–
  Iran, Tehran University, B.S., Electrical Engineering, 1952
  Engineer, political activist (Majles deputy, minister in the Provisional
    Government), editor of *Iran-e Farda* magazine

Sahabi, Yadollah
  Tehran, 1285–   /1906–
  France, University of Lille, Ph.D., Geology, 1936
  Professor at Tehran University (1936–6?), political activist (leading
    member of Nehzat-e Azadi, minister for revolutionary projects in
    the Provisional Government)

Sa'idi-Sirjani, Ali-Akbar
  Sirjan, 1310–1373/1931–1994
  Iran, Daneshsara-ye Ali-ye Tehran, B.A.?, 195?
  Scholar, poet, novelist, belletrist

Sajjadi, Seyyed Ja'far
  Esfahan, 1303–   /1924–
  Iran, Tehran University, Ph.D., Theology, 1960?

Scholar, translator, professor of literature and theology at Tehran University (1962–79)

Sana'i, Mahmud
Arak, 1297–1364/1919–1985
England, University of London, Ph.D., Psychology, 194?
Professor, translator, cultural attaché

Sepahbodi, Isa
Hamadan, 1296–1357/1917–1978
France, University of Rouen, Ph.D., French Literature, 194?
Scholar, professor of French language and literature at Tehran University

Sepanlu, Mohammad-Ali
Tehran, 1319–   /1940–
Iran, Tehran University, B.A., Law, 196?
Poet, writer

Sepehri, Sohrab
Kashan, 1307–1359/1928–1980
Iran, Tehran University, B.A., English, 195?
Poet, painter

Shadman, Seyyed Fakhroddin
Tehran, 1286–1346/1907–1967
France, University of Paris, Ph.D., Law, 1935
England, London School of Economics and Political Science, Ph.D., History, 1939
Professor of history at Tehran University (1950–67), scholar, civil servant, politician (minister of agriculture, finance, justice)

Shafi'i-Kadkani, Mohammad-Reza
Kadkan (Neyshapur), 1318–   /1939–
Iran, Tehran University, Ph.D., Persian Literature, 1969
Poet, scholar, professor of Persian literature at Tehran University

Shahabi, Mahmud
Torbat-e Heydariyeh, 1282–1365/1903–1986
Iran, Traditional Education
Scholar, professor of jurisprudence at Tehran University

Shahid-Sales, Sohrab
    Tehran, 1323–   /1944–
    France, l'Institut des Hautes Études Cinématographiques (IDEC),
        B.A.?, 1968
    Film director

Shahidi, Seyyed Ja'far
    Borujerd, 1297–   /1918–
    Iran, Tehran University, Ph.D., Persian Language and Literature, 1961
    Scholar, translator, professor of Persian literature at Tehran Univer-
        sity

Shajariyan, Mohammad-Reza (Siyavash)
    Mashhad, 1308/9–   /1930–
    Iran
    Singer, musician, music teacher

Shakeri, Khosrow
    Tehran, 1317–   /1938–
    France, University of Paris, Ph.D., History, 1980
    Political activist (leading member of the Confederation of Iranian
        Students), scholar, professor, publisher of historical documents

Shamlu, Ahmad
    Tehran, 1304–   /1925–
    Iran, 11th grade, 194?
    Poet, scholar, translator, literary critic

Shanehchi, Mohammad
    Mashhad, 1301–   /1923–
    Iran, Secondary Education
    Broker in the Tehran bazaar, political activist (member of Nehzat-e
        Azadi organization; chief aid to Ayatollah Talegani, 1978–79)

Shari'ati, Ali
    Mazinan, 1312–1356/1933–1977
    France, University of Paris, Ph.D., Hagiology, 1963
    Professor of Islamic history at Mashhad University, scholar, religious
        thinker and activist

Shari'ati, Mohammad-Taqi
    Mazinan, 1286–1366/1907–1987

Iran, Mashhad Seminary, Religious Education, 1934
Scholar, exegete, teacher, high school principal, political activist

Shari'atmadari, Ayatollah Mohammad-Kazem
Tabriz, 1282/83–1365/1904–1985
Iran, Religious Education
Leading theologian

Shari'at-Sangalaji, Ayatollah Mirza Reza-Qoli
Sangalaj (Tehran), 1269–1322/1890–1944
Iran, Religious Education
Reformist theologian

Shayegan, Daryush
Tehran, 1313–   /1935–
France, University of Paris, Ph.D., Philosophy, 1968
Scholar, professor of Indology and comparative philosophy at Tehran
University (1968–80), director of the Iranian Center for the Study
of Cultures (1977–79)

Sheybani, Abbas
Tehran, 1309/10–   /1931–
Iran, M.D.?, Medicine
Politician (a leading member of Nehzat-e Azadi organization, mem-
ber of the Assembly of Experts, Majles deputy, minister of agricul-
ture), chancellor of Tehran University

Sho'a'iyan, Mostafa
Tehran, 1315–1354/1936–1976
Iran, Tehran University, B.S., Engineering, 196?
Welding engineer, teacher, political thinker and activist

Siyasi [Siassi], Ali-Akbar
Yazd, 1274–1369/1895–1990
France, University of Paris, Ph.D., Literature, 1931
Scholar, professor, chancellor of Tehran University (1943–55), politi-
cian (minister of culture, 1942–43, 1947–48; foreign minister,
1949)

Soltanpur, Sa'id
Mashhad, 13??–1360/19??–1981
Iran, Secondary Education, 19??
Poet, playwright, political activist

Sorush, Abdolkarim
Tehran, 1324–   /1945–
England, University of London, Ph.D., Philosophy of Science, 1979
Scholar, professor at Tehran University, translator, theoretician

Surki, Abbas
Shahrood, 1315–1354/1936–1975
Iran, Tehran University, B.A., Political Science, 19??
Feda'i guerrilla

Tabari, Ehsan
Sari, 1295–1368/1917–1989
Iran, Tehran University, B.A., Law, 19??
Scholar, Tudeh Party leader and theoretician

Tabataba'i, Allameh Mohammad-Hoseyn
Tabriz, 1282–1360/1903–1981
Iraq, Najaf Seminary, Religious Education, 1934
Leading theologian, philosopher, exegete

Takhti, Gholamreza
Tehran, 1309–1346/1930–1968
Iran, Secondary Education?
Athlete (wrestling champion)

Taleqani, Ayatollah Mahmud
Taleqan, 1290–1358/1911–1979
Iraq, Najaf Seminary, Religious Education, 193?
Leading theologian, exegete, political activist (co-founder of the
    Nehzat-e Azadi organization, member of the Assembly of Ex-
    perts)

Taqizadeh, Seyyed Hasan
Tabriz, 1257–1348/1878–1970
Iran, Traditional Education, Physics, Medicine, 1899?
Scholar, politician (ambassador, Majles deputy, minister, senator)

Taqva'i, Naser
Abadan, 1320–   /1941–
Iran
Filmmaker, short-story writer

Tavakkoli, Hamid
  Sabzevar, 1325–1350/1946/47–1972
  Iran, Mashhad University, B.A., History, 197?
  Feda'i guerrilla

Tonokaboni, Fereydun
  Tonokabon, 1316–   /1937–
  Iran, Persian Literature
  Novelist, teacher

Towfiq, Firuz
  Tabriz, 1313–   /1934–
  Switzerland, University of Geneva, Ph.D., Social and Economic Sciences, 1964
  Political activist, scholar, director of Iran's Statistical Center, minister of housing

Yalfani, Mohsen
  Yalfan (Hamadan), 1322–   /1943–
  Iran, B.A.
  Playwright

Yazdi, Ebrahim
  Qazvin, 1310–   /1931–
  Iran, Tehran University, Ph.D., Pharmacology, 195?
  Professor of medicine, cancer researcher, politician (deputy prime minister for revolutionary affairs, minister of foreign affairs in the Provisional Government, Majles deputy, 1980–84)

Yushij, Nima
  Yush, 1274–1338/1895–1960
  Iran, Secondary Education
  Poet

Zoka', Sirus
  Tabriz, 1305–   /1926–
  France, University of Paris, Ph.D., Law, 1954
  Writer

Glossary

Allameh: honorific title given to a great scholar of Islamic sciences

Anjoman-e Hojjatiyyeh: a conservative association that spearheaded an anti-Baha'i campaign beginning in the 1950s

anjomanha-ye tafsir-e Qur'an: societies formed to interpret Qur'anic exegesis

Ayatollah: "sign of God," a title conferred upon a leading Shi'ite *mojtahed*

Baha'is: adherents of a splinter movement from Shi'ism led by Baha'ullah (1817–1892), who advocated the spiritual unity of humankind and was viewed by his followers as the manifestation of God on earth; considered by many Muslims as apostates

bazgasht beh khishtan: return to the self

dasteh: group(s) of people who beat themselves with their hands or chains during religious processions as a sign of mourning

ejtehad: exercise of independent reasoning in the (re)interpretation of Islamic law

falsafeh: philosophy

faqih (pl. **foqaha**): jurist, an expert in Islamic jurisprudence

Farang: Europe, Occident, West

farangshenasi: Occidentalism

Farhangestan: the Iranian Academy

fatva: binding religious edict issued by a qualified *mojtahed*

Feda'i (pl. **Feda'iyan**): one who sacrifices himself

Feda'iyan-e Eslam: militant Islamic organization known for carrying out political assassinations in the 1940s and 1950s

Feda'iyan-e Khalq: Organization of the Iranian People's Self-Sacrificing Guerrillas

feqh: (Islamic) jurisprudence

feqh-e puya: dynamic jurisprudence

feqh-e sonnati: traditional jurisprudence

fokoli: one who is overdressed; often used as a derogatory term

Gharb: the West
gharbzadegi: Westoxication

hey'at: group, bands organized by believers during religious processions
Hojjatoleslam: "proof of Islam," clerical rank immediately below *Ayatollah*
Hoseyniyyeh: a mosque/teaching complex
howzeh: a center of theological learning, seminary

Imam: spiritual leader, for Ja'fari Shi'ites one of the twelve infallible heirs to the Prophet descended from Ali
Iranshenasi: Iranology

Majles: the Iranian parliament
marja'-e taqlid: "source of emulation," the highest ranking *faqih*
marja'iyyat: the Shi'a principle of emulating a living *mojtahed*
mojahed (pl. **mojahedin**): holy warrior
Mojahedin-e Khalq: Organization of Iranian People's Holy Warriors
mojtahed: one who exercises *ejtehad*
Muharram: the first month of the Islamic year

Nehzat-e Azadi: The Liberation Movement of Iran

Qur'an: the holy book of Islam

Ramadan: the ninth month of the Islamic year when Muslims fast from dawn to sunset
rowzeh khani: a ritualistic mourning ceremony involving homilies about the venerable lives of the Shi'ite imams
rowshanfekr (pl. **rowshanfekran**): intellectual, intelligentsia, enlightened thinker

SAVAK: Shah's notorious secret police
seyyed: a descendant of the Prophet
shari'ah: the canonical law of Islam
Shi'a: the partisans of Ali
showra: council
sunna: the body of Islamic custom and practice based on Prophet Mohammad's words and deeds

tafsir: interpretation and commentary on the Qur'an
talabeh (pl. **tollab**): theology student(s)
ta'ziyeh: a passion play enacting Imam Hoseyn's martyrdom in Karbala

ulema: the collective term for religious leaders
umma: the Islamic community

velayat-e faqih: the doctrine of guardianship of the jurisconsult; popularized by Ayatollah Khomeini

Works Cited

Abrahamian, Ervand. 1982. *Iran Between Two Revolutions*. Princeton, N.J.: Princeton Univ. Press.

———. 1989. *Radical Islam: The Iranian Mojahedin*. London: I. B. Tauris.

Adib-Soltani, Mir-Shamsoddin. 1359/1980. *Resaleh-ye Viyan* (The Vienna thesis). Tehran: Markaz-e Iran-ye Motale'e-ye Farhangha.

Adorno, Theodore. 1976. *The Positivist Dispute in German Sociology*. Translated by Glyn Adey and David Frisby. New York: Harper Torchbooks.

Afshar, Iraj. 2535/1977. "Minovi va mostashreqin" (Minovi and orientalists). *Sokhan* 25, no. 9:904–9.

Ahmadzadeh, Mas'ud. 1353/1974. *Mobarezeh-ye mosallahaneh, ham esteratezhi ham taktik* (Armed struggle, both a strategy and a tactic). 4th ed. N.p.: Sazman-e Jebheh-ye Melli-ye Kharej az Keshvar.

Akhavan-Sales, Mehdi. 1976. "Seven Poems by Mehdi Akhavan Sales." Translated by Leonardo P. Alishan. *Literature East and West* 20, nos. 1–4:130–43.

Akhavi, Shahrough. 1980. *Religion and Politics in Contemporary Iran: Clergy-State Relations in the Pahlavi Period*. Albany: State Univ. of New York Press.

———. 1983. "Shariati's Social Thought." In *Religion and Politics in Iran*, edited by Nikkie R. Keddie, 125–44. New Haven, Conn.: Yale Univ. Press.

Alatas, Syed Farid. 1993. "On the Indigenization of Academic Discourse." *Alternatives* 18:307–38.

Alavi, Reza. 1985. "Science and Society in Persian Civilization." *Knowledge: Creation, Diffusion, Utilization* 6, no. 4:329–49.

Al-e Ahmad, Jalal. 1344/1962. *Gharbzadegi* (Westoxication). Tehran: Ravaq.

———. 1345/1966. "Goftogu ba yek farangi-ye az Farang bargashteh va dar jostojuy-e zaban-e Baluchi baramadeh" (Conversation with a Westerner who has turned away from the West and is exploring Baluchi language). *Jahan-e Now* 1, no. 1:83–95.

———. 1357/1978. *Dar khedmat va khiyanat-e rowshanfekran* (On the service and treason of the intellectuals). 2 vols. Tehran: Kharazmi.

———. 1982. *Iranian Society: An Anthology of Writings by Jalal Al-e Ahmad*. Compiled and edited by Michael C. Hillmann. Lexington, Ky.: Mazda.

———. 1984. *Occidentosis: A Plague from the West*. Translated by R. Campbell and edited by Hamid Algar. Berkeley, Calif.: Mizan.

Al-e Ahmad, Shams. 1369/1990. *Az cheshm-e baradar* (From the eye of the brother). Qom: Ketab-e Sa'di.

Algar, Hamid. 1972. "The Oppositional Role of the ulama in Twentieth Century Iran." In *Scholars, Saints and Sufis: Muslim Religious Institutions in the Middle East since 1500,* edited by Nikkie R. Keddie, 231–55. Berkeley: Univ. of California Press.

———. 1990. "Ayatollah Hajj Aqa Hosayn Tabataba'i Borujerdi." In *Encyclopaedia Iranica,* edited by Ehsan Yarshater, 376–79. Vol. 4. New York: Routledge and Kegan Paul.

Alibaba'i, Ahmad. 1991. Interview by author. 13–14 June, Fairfax, Va.

Amin, Samir. 1989. *Eurocentrism.* New York: Monthly Review Press.

Amir-Arjomand, Said. 1984. "Traditionalism in Twentieth-century Iran." In *From Nationalism to Revolutionary Islam,* edited by Said Amir Arjomand, 195–232. Albany: State Univ. of New York Press.

———. 1988. *The Turban for the Crown: The Islamic Revolution in Iran.* New York: Oxford Univ. Press.

Amuzegar, Jahangir. 1977. *Iran: An Economic Profile.* Washington, D.C.: Middle East Institute.

Anderson, Benedict. 1991. *Imagined Communities: Reflections on the Origin and Spread of Nationalism.* Rev. ed. London: Verso.

Anjavi-Shirazi, Seyyed Abolqasem. 1351/1972. "Ellat-e vojudi-ye esteshraq va mostashreq" (Raison d'être of orientalism and orientalists). *Negin* 8, no. 85:5–8.

Ansari, Mohammad Ali. 1351/1972. *Defa' az Eslam va ruhaniyyat: Pasokh beh doktor Ali Shari'ati* (In defense of Islam and the religious establishment: A response to Dr. Ali Shari'ati). Qom: Mehr-e Ostvar.

Aryanpur, Amir-Hoseyn. 1344/1965. *Zamineh-ye jame'ehshenasi* (Introduction to sociology). Tehran: Entesharat-e Daneshgah-e tehran.

Ashraf, Ahmad. 1970. "Historical Obstacles to the Development of a Bourgeoisie in Iran." In *Studies in the Economic History of the Middle East: From the Rise of Islam to the Present Day,* edited by M. A. Cook, 308–32. Oxford: Oxford Univ. Press.

Ashuri, Daryush. 1345/1967. "Hushyari-ye tarikhi, negareshi dar *Gharbzadegi* va mabani-ye nazari-ye an" (Historical awareness: A look at *Gharbzadegi* and its theoretical foundations). *Barrasi-e Ketab* (Feb.): 2–33.

———. 1351/1972. *Iranshenasi chist? va chand maqalah-ye digar* (What is Iranology? And a number of other essays). 2d ed. Tehran: Agah.

———. 1989. Interview by author. 29 May, New York, N.Y.

Assar, Nasir. 1982. "The Reminiscences of Nasir Assar." Interviewed by Ardeshir Aqevli. Transcripts of tape recording, 2 Dec., Washington, D.C. *Oral History of Iran Collection.* Foundation for Iranian Studies, Bethesda, Md.

Association Internationale des docteurs de l'Université de Paris. 1967. *Bibliographie analytique des thèses (1899–1965).* Paris: Association Internationale des Docteur de l'Université de Paris.

Azizi, Mohsen. 1938. "La domination arabe et l'épanouissement du sentiment

national en Iran, étude politique et sociale sur l'Iran musulman, 650–900."
Ph.D. diss., Univ. of Paris.

al-Azm, Sadik Jalal. 1972. *The Origins of Kant's Arguments in the Antinomies.* Oxford: Clarendon Press.

———. 1981. "Orientalism and Orientalism in Reverse." *Khamsin,* no. 8:5–26.

Baheri, Mohammad. 1983–84. "The Reminiscences of Mohammad Baheri." Interviewed by Shirin Sami'i. Transcripts of tape recording, Dec. and Feb., Cannes. *Oral History of Iran Collection.* Foundation for Iranian Studies, Bethesda, Md.

———. 1990. Interview by author. 15 June, Roslyn, Va.

Bakhash, Shaul. 1984. *The Reign of the Ayatollahs: Iran and the Islamic Revolution.* New York: Basic Books.

Banu'azizi, Ali. 1362/1983. "Alunakneshinan-e khiyaban-e Profesor Berown" (Hut dwellers of Professor Brown street). *Alefba* (Paris), 2d ser. no. 3:53–65.

Barbour, Ian G., ed. 1362/1983. *Elm va din* (Science and religion: New perspectives on the dialogue). Translated by Baha'oddin Khorramshahi. Tehran: Markaz-e Nashr-e Daneshgahi.

Bayani, Khanbaba. 1937. "Les Relations de l'Iran avec l'Europe Occidentale a l'epoque Safavide (Portugal, Espagne, Angleterre, Hollande et France.)" Ph.D. diss., Univ. of Paris.

Bayat-Philipp, Mangol. 1980. "Shi'ism in Contemporary Iranian Politics: The Case of Ali Shari'ati." In *Towards a Modern Iran: Studies in Thought, Politics and Society,* edited by Eli Kedourie and Sylvia G. Haim, 155–68. London: Frank Cass.

———. 1982. *Mysticism and Dissent: Socioreligious Thought in Qajar Iran.* Syracuse, N.Y.: Syracuse Univ. Press.

Beblawi, Hazem, and Giacomo Luciani, eds. 1987. *The Rentier State: The Political Economy of Public Finance in the Arab Countries.* London: Croom Helm.

Behnam, Jamshid. 1348/1970. "Gharb, kodam Gharb?" (West, which West?). *Farhang va Zendegi,* no. 1:27–33.

Behrangi, Samad. 1348/1969. *Kand-o kav dar masa'el-e tarbiyati-ye Iran* (An inquiry into the educational problems of Iran). Tehran: Shabgir.

———. 1976. *The Little Black Fish and Other Modern Persian Short Stories.* Translated by Mary and Eric Hoogland. Washington, D.C.: Three Continents.

———. 2537/1978. *Majmu'eh-ye maqalehha* (Collection of essays). 2d ed. Tehran: Entesharat-e Donya va Entesharat-e Ruzbahan.

Benard, Cheryl, and Zalmay Khalilzad. 1984. *"The Government of God": Iran's Islamic Republic.* New York: Columbia Univ. Press.

Benda, Julien. 1927. *La Trahison des clercs.* Paris: Grasset.

Benjamin, Walter. 1973. *Illumination.* London: Fontana.

Berkes, Niyazi. 1964. *The Development of Secularism in Turkey.* Montreal: McGill Univ. Press.

Berlin, Isaiah. 1962. "Does Political Theory Still Exist?" In *Philosophy, Politics and Society* (2d ser.), edited by Peter Laslett and W. G. Runciman, 1–33. Oxford: Basil Blackwell.

———. 1978. *Russian Thinkers.* New York: Viking Press.

Berman, Marshall. 1988. *All That Is Solid Melts into Air: The Experience of Modernity.* New York: Penguin Books.

Bill, James A. 1972. *The Politics of Iran: Groups, Classes and Modernization.* Columbus, Ohio: Charles E. Merrill.

Binder, Leonard. 1965. "The Proofs of Islam: Religion and Politics in Iran." In *Arabic and Islamic Studies in Honor of Hamilton A. R. Gibb,* edited by George Makdisi. Leiden, The Netherlands: E. J. Brill.

Blacker, Carmen. 1964. *The Japanese Enlightenment.* Cambridge: Cambridge Univ. Press.

Boroujerdi, Mehrzad. 1992. "Gharbzadegi: The Dominant Intellectual Discourse of Pre- and Post-revolutionary Iran." In *Iran: Political Culture in the Islamic Republic,* edited by Samih K. Farsoun and Mehrdad Mashayekhi, 30–56. London: Routledge.

———. 1994a. "Can Islam be Secularized?" In *In Transition: Essays on Culture and Identity in Middle Eastern Societies,* edited by M. R. Ghanoonparvar and Faridoun Farrokh, 55–64. Laredo: Texas A&M International Univ.

———. 1994b. "The Encounter of Post-revolutionary Thought in Iran with Hegel, Heidegger and Popper." In *Cultural Transitions in the Middle East,* edited by Şerif Mardin, 236–59. Leiden, The Netherlands: E. J. Brill.

Brinton, Crane. 1965. *The Anatomy of Revolution.* New York: Vintage Books.

Brodsky, Theda. 1967. "The Teaching of Literature in Iran." *Literature East and West* 11, no. 2:177–80.

Calhoun, Craig J. 1983. "The Radicalism of Tradition: Community Strength or Venerable Disguise and Borrowed Language?" *American Journal of Sociology* 88, no. 5:886–911.

Centre Iranien pour L'Etude des Civilisations. 1979. *L'Impact de la pensée occidentale rend-il possible un dialogue réel entre les civilisations?* (Does the impact of Western thought render possible a dialogue between civilizations?). Paris: Berg International.

Charnay, Jean-Paul. 1973. "The Arab Intellectual Between Power and Culture." *Diogenes,* no. 83:40–63.

Chehabi, H. E. 1990. *Iranian Politics and Religious Modernism: The Liberation Movement of Iran under the Shah and Khomeini.* Ithaca, N.Y.: Cornell Univ. Press.

Clifford, James. 1987. "Of Other Peoples: Beyond the 'Salvage' Paradigm." In *Discussions in Contemporary Culture,* edited by Hal Foster, 121–30. Seattle, Wash.: Bay Press.

Cohn, Bernard S. 1980. "History and Anthropology: The State of Play." *Comparative Studies in Society and History* 22, no. 2:198–221.

Corbin, Henry. 1325/1946. *Ravabet-e hekmat-e eshraq va falsafeh-ye Iran-e bastan: Moharrekha-ye Zartoshti dar falsafeh-ye eshraq* (Zoroastrian themes in the philosophy of Shahaboddin Sohravardi). Translated by Ahmad Fardid and Abdolhamid Golshan. Tehran: Anjoman-e Iranshenasi.

———. 1980. *Avicenna and the Visionary Recital.* Translated by William R. Trask. Irving, Tex.: Spring Publications.

Dabashi, Hamid. 1993. *Theology of Discontent: The Ideological Foundation of the Islamic Revolution in Iran.* New York: New York Univ. Press.

D'Amico, Robert. 1990–91. "Karl Popper and the Frankfurt School." *Telos,* no. 86:33–48.

Davari-Ardakani, Reza. 1354/1975a. *Falsafeh-ye madani-ye Farabi* (The civil philosophy of Farabi). Tehran: Showra-ye Ali-ye Farhang va Honar.

———. 1354/1975b. *Farabi: mo'asses-e falsafeh-ye Eslami* (Farabi: The founder of Islamic philosophy). Tehran: Anjoman-e Shahanshahi-ye Falsafeh-ye Iran.

———. 1359/1980. *Falsafeh chist?* (What is philosophy?). Tehran: Anjoman-e Eslami-ye Hekmat va Falsafeh-ye Iran.

———. 1361/1983. *Enqelab-e Eslami va vaẓ'-e konuni-ye alam* (Islamic revolution and the present status of the world). Tehran: Entesharat-e Markaz-e Farhangi-ye Allameh Tabataba'i.

———. 1363/1984a. "Lavazem va natayej-e enkar-e Gharb" (The necessities and consequences of refuting the West). *Keyhan-e Farhangi* 1, no. 3:18–19.

———. 1363/1984b. *Shemmeh'i az tarikh-e gharbzadegi-ye ma [vaẓ'-e konuni-ye tafakkor dar Iran]* (A short account of our westoxicated history [The present status of intellection in Iran]). 2d ed. Tehran: Sorush.

———. 1364/1985. "Molahezati chand piramun-e *Jame'eh-ye baz va Doshmananash*" (Some observations on *The Open Society and Its Enemies*). *Keyhan-e Farhangi* 2, no. 10:23–26.

———. 1365/1986. "Elm va azadi ari, elteqat nah" (Yes to science and freedom, no to eclecticism). *Keyhan-e Farhangi* 3, no. 1:12–14.

———. 1369/1990. "Mi'adgah-e teknik kojast?" (Whither technology?). *Kar va Towse'eh,* 1, no. 1:34–37.

———. 1991. Correspondence with author, June.

———. 1370/1992. "Sonnat, moderniteh va post-Modernism" (Tradition, modernity and post-modernism). *Keyhan-e Hava'i,* 15 January, no. 965:12.

Derakhshesh, Mohammad. 1990. Interview by author. 10 Feb., Chevy Chase, Md.

Derrida, Jacques. 1982. *Margins of Philosophy.* Translated by Alan Bass. Chicago: Univ. of Chicago Press.

De Santillana, Giorgio. 1968. Preface to *Science and Civilization in Islam,* by S. H. Nasr, vii–xiv. Cambridge, Mass.: Harvard Univ. Press.

Diamond, Stanley. 1974. *In Search of the Primitive: A Critique of Civilization.* New Brunswick, N.J.: Transaction Books.

Djaït, Hichem. 1985. *Europe and Islam: Cultures and Modernity.* Berkeley: Univ. of California Press.

Dustdar, Aramesh. 1359/1981. *Molahezati falsafi dar din, elm va tafakkor* (Philosophical observations on religion, science, and thought). Tehran: Agah.

———. 1370/1991. *Derakhsheshha-ye tireh* (Dark sparkles). Cologne: Andisheh-e Azad.

Echo of Iran. 1977. *Iran Almanac and Book of Facts 1977.* Tehran: Echo of Iran.

Eftekharzadeh, Seyyed Hasan, comp. 2536/1977. *Fehrest-e maqalat va kotob-e fal-*

safi dar sal-e 2535 (Annual bibliography of philosophical works published in Iran, 1975–1976). Tehran: Anjoman-e Shahanshahi-ye Falsafeh-ye Iran.

Ellul, Jacques. 1964. *The Technological Society.* Translated by John Wilkinson. New York: Knopf.

Enayat, Hamid. 1962. "The Impact of the West on Arab Nationalism." Ph.D. diss., Univ. of London.

——. 1349/1970. *Bonyad-e falsafeh-ye siyasi dar Gharb* (The foundations of political philosophy in the West: From Heraclitus to Hobbes). Tehran: Farmand.

——. 1350/1972a. "Hamid Enayat va falsafeh-ye Hegel" (Hamid Enayat and the philosophy of Hegel). *Ketab-e Emruz,* no. 2:2–11.

——. 1972b. Review of *Religion and State in Iran, 1785–1906,* by Hamid Algar. *Muslim World* 62, no. 3:260–64.

——. 1973. "The Politics of Iranology." *Iranian Studies* 6, no 1:2–20.

——. 1974. "The State of Social Sciences in Iran," *Middle East Studies Association Bulletin* 8, no. 3:1–12.

——. 1354/1975a. *Eslam va Sosiyalism dar Mesr* (Islam and socialism in Egypt). 3d ed. Tehran: Mowj.

——. 1353/1975b. *Jahan-i az khod biganeh: Majmu'eh-ye maqalat* (An alienated world: Collection of essays). 2d ed. Tehran: N.p.

——. 1358/1979. *Seyri dar andisheh-ye siyasi-ye Arab* (A survey of Arab political thought). 2d ed. Tehran: Amir Kabir.

——. 1980. "The Resurgence of Islam." *History Today* (Feb.): 16–22.

——. 1982. *Modern Islamic Political Thought.* Austin: Univ. of Texas Press.

——. 1983. "Revolution in Iran 1979: Religion as Political Ideology." In *Revolutionary Theory and Political Reality,* edited by Noel O'Sullivan, 191–206. New York: St. Martin's Press.

——. 1986. "Iran: Khumayni's Concept of the 'Guardianship of the Jurisconsult.'" In *Islam in the Political Process,* edited by James Piscatori, 160–80. Cambridge: Cambridge Univ. Press.

——. 1369/1990. *Shesh goftar dar baray-e din va jame'eh* (Six essays on religion and society). 2d ed. Tehran: Daftar-e Nashr-e Farhang-e Eslami.

Encyclopedia of Philosophy. 1972. S.v. *positivism, historicism.*

Eslami-Nadushan, Mohammad-Ali. 2536/1977. *Azadi-ye mojassameh* (Liberty of the statue). Tehran: Tus.

E'temadzadeh (Behazin), Mahmud. 1349/1970. *Mehman-e in aqayan* (Guest of these gentlemen). Tehran: Nil.

Fanon, Frantz. 1967. *Black Skin, White Masks.* Translated by Charles Lam Markmann. New York: Grove Press.

——. 1979. *The Wretched of the Earth.* Translated by Constance Farrington. New York: Grove Press.

Farda-ye Iran. 1360/1981. "Fehrest-e asami kotob-e mozerreh'i keh montasher shodehand" (List of harmful books that have been published). *Farda-ye Iran* 1, no. 5:462–78; no. 6:548–55.

Fardid, Ahmad. 1350/1971. "Chand porsesh dar bab-e farhang-e Sharq"

(Some questions on the culture of the Orient). Transcribed by Reza Davari. *Farhang va Zendegi,* no. 7:32–39.

———. 1352/1974. "Soqut-e Hedayat dar chaleh-ye harz-e adabiyyat-e Faranse" ([Sadeq] Hedayat's descent into the cesspool of French literature). *Ettela'at,* 24 Feb., 19.

Farhang, Mansour. 1979. "Resisting the Pharaohs: Ali Shariati on Oppression." *Race and Class* 21, no. 1:31–40.

Felstiner, Mary L. 1980. "Seeing the Second Sex Through the Second Wave." *Feminist Studies* 6, no. 2:247–76.

Fischer, Michael M. J. 1980. *Iran: From Religious Dispute to Revolution.* Cambridge, Mass.: Harvard Univ. Press.

———. 1984. "Towards a Third World Poetics: Seeing Through Short Stories and Films in the Iranian Cultural Area." *Knowledge and Society* 5:171–241.

Floor, Willem M. 1983. "The Revolutionary Character of the Ulama: Wishful Thinking or Reality?" In *Religion and Politics in Iran,* edited by Nikki R. Keddie, 73–97. New Haven, Conn.: Yale Univ. Press.

Foucault, Michel. 1965. *Madness and Civilization: A History of Insanity in the Age of Reason.* New York: Pantheon Books.

———. 1972. *The Archaeology of Knowledge.* Translated by A. M. Sheridan Smith. New York: Pantheon Books.

———. 1975. *The Birth of the Clinic: An Archaeology of Medical Perception.* New York: Vintage Books.

———. 1977a. *Language, Counter-Memory, Practice: Selected Essays and Interviews.* Edited by Donald F. Bouchard. Ithaca, N.Y.: Cornell Univ. Press.

———. 1977b. *Power/Knowledge: Selected Interviews and Other Writings 1972–1977.* Edited by Colin Gordon. New York: Pantheon Books.

———. 1979a. *Discipline and Punish: The Birth of the Prison.* New York: Vintage Books.

———. 1979b. "L'Esprit dans un monde sans esprit." In *Iran: La Révolution au nom de Dieu,* edited by Claire Briere and Pierre Blanchet, 227–41. Paris: Seuil.

———. 1980. *The History of Sexuality.* Vol. 1: An Introduction. New York: Vintage Books.

———. 1988. "Technologies of the Self." In *Technologies of the Self: A Seminar with Michel Foucault,* edited by Luther H. Martin, Huck Gutman, and Patrick H. Hutton, 16–49. Amherst: Univ. of Massachusetts Press.

Friedman, Jonathan. 1987. "Beyond Otherness: The Spectacularization of Anthropology." *Telos,* no. 71:161–70.

Frye, Richard N. 1984. Interviewed by Shahla Haeri. 10 Oct., Cambridge, Mass. *Iranian Oral History Collection.* Harvard Univ., Houghton Library, Cambridge, Mass.

Ganji, Akbar. 1365/1986. "Gharbsetizi, dindari va . . ." (Anti-Westernism, religiosity and . . .). *Keyhan-e Farhangi* 3, no. 5:11–16.

———. 1366/1987. "Falsafeh-ye tarikh e Hegel" (Hegel's philosophy of history). *Keyhan-e Farhangi* 4, no. 2:10–14.

Ghaffari, Hoseyn. 1368/1989. *Naqd-e Nazariyyeh-ye shari'at-e samet* (Critique of the theory of a silent shari'ah). Tehran: Hekmat.

Ghani, Qasem. 1361/1983. *Zendegi-ye man* (My life). Tehran: Entesharat-e Aban.

Gheissari, Ali. 1989. "The Ideological Formation of the Iranian Intelligentsia (From the Constitutional Movement to the Fall of the Monarchy.)" Ph.D. diss., Oxford University. Forthcoming as "Iranian Intellectuals in the Twentieth Century."

————. Forthcoming. "Hamid Inayet [Enayat]." In *Islam Ansiklopedisi* (Encyclopaedia of Islam). Istanbul, Turkey.

Ghiyasi, Mohammad-Taqi. 1367/1988. "Chehel va shesh sal zendegi, si sal neveshtan" (Forty-six years of living, thirty years of writing). *Adineh*, no. 27:40–42.

Goethe, Johann Wolfgang von. 1976. *Faust, Part I.* Translated by R. Jarrell. New York: Farrar, Straus and Giroux.

Gregory, Donna U. 1989. "Forward." In *International/Intertextual Relations: Postmodern Readings of World Politics,* edited by James Der Derian and Michael J. Shapiro. Lexington, Mass.: Lexington Books.

Guénon, René. 1962. *The Crisis of the Modern World.* Translated by M. Pallis and R. Nicholson. London: Luzac.

Habermas, Jürgen. 1987. *The Philosophical Discourse of Modernity.* Translated by Frederick Lawrence. Cambridge, Mass.: MIT Press.

Haj-Bushehri, Mohammad-Taqi. 1368/1989. "Az *Kashf- al-asrar* ta *Asrar-e hezar-saleh*" (From *Kashf al-asrar* [secrets unveiled] to *Asrar-e hezar-saleh* [thousand year old secrets]). *Cheshmandaz*, no. 6:14–26.

Haj-Seyyed-Javadi, Ali-Asghar. 1984. Interviewed by Zia Sedghi. 1 Mar., Paris. *Iranian Oral History Collection.* Harvard Univ., Houghton Library, Cambridge, Mass.

Hakamizadeh, Ali-Akbar. 1369/1991. "Gozidehha'i az *Asrar-e hezar-saleh*" (Selections from *Asrar-e hezar-saleh*). *Cheshmandaz*, no. 8:65–79.

Hanafi, Hasan. 1991. *Muqaddima fi ilm al-istighrab* (An introduction to occidentalism). Cairo: Ad-Dar al-Fanniya lil-Nashr wa-l-Tauzi.

Hartley, L. P. 1984. *The Go-Between.* New York: Stein and Day.

Heidegger, Martin. 1976. "Only a God Can Save Us: Der Spiegel's Interview with Heidegger." *Philosophy Today* 20, no. 4:267–84.

Hempel, Carl G. 1945. "Studies in the Logic of Confirmation," *Mind* 54, no. 213:1–26; no. 214:97–121.

————. 1369/1990. *Falsafeh-ye olum-e tabi'i* (Philosophy of natural sciences). Translated by Hoseyn Ma'sumi-Hamadani. Tehran: Markaz-e Nashr-e Daneshgahi.

Hezarkhani, Manuchehr. 1984. Interviewed by Zia Sedghi. 1 June, Paris. *Iranian Oral History Collection.* Harvard Univ., Houghton Library, Cambridge, Mass.

Hillmann, Michael Craig. 1987. Iranian Nationalism and Modernist Persian Literature," *Literature East and West* 23:69–89.

Hobsbawm, Eric. 1959. *Primitive Rebels: Studies in Archaic Forms of Social Movement in the 19th and 20th Centuries.* Manchester, England: Manchester Univ. Press.

Holzner, Burkart, Donald T. Campbell, and Muhammad Shahidullah. 1985. "Introduction: The Comparative Study of Science and the Sociology of Scientific Validity." *Knowledge: Creation, Diffusion, Utilization* 6, no. 4:307–28.

Homayun, Daryush. 1982. Interviewed by John Mojdehi. 21 Nov., Washington, D.C. *Iranian Oral History Collection.* Harvard Univ., Houghton Library, Cambridge, Mass.

Honarmandi, Hasan. 1366/1987. Poem cited in Ali-Akbar Kasma'i, "Esalat-e farhangi va qofl-e basteh-ye Gharb" (Cultural authenticity and the closed lock of the West). *Keyhan-e Hava'i,* 7 Oct., 18.

Hutton, Patrick H. 1988. "Foucault, Freud, and the Technologies of the Self." In *Technologies of the Self: A Seminar with Michel Foucault,* edited by Luther H. Martin, Huck Gutman, and Patrick H. Hutton, 121–44. Amherst: Univ. of Massachusetts Press.

Issawi, Charles. 1978. "The Iranian Economy 1925–1975: Fifty Years of Economic Development." In *Iran under the Pahlavis,* edited by George Lenczowski. Stanford, Calif.: Hoover Institution Press.

Jalili, Abolhasan. 1348/1969. "Sharqshenasi va jahan-e emruz." (Orientalism and the contemporary world). *Olum-e Ejtema'i* 1, no. 2:52–56.

Jameson, Fredric. 1986. "Third-World Literature in the Era of Multinational Capitalism." *Social Text,* no. 15:65–88.

Kant, Immanuel. 1963. "Perpetual Peace." In *Immanuel Kant: On History,* edited by Lewis White Beck, 85–135. Indianapolis, Ind.: Bobbs-Merrill.

Karimi, Ata'ollah. 1369/1990. *Faqr-e tarikhinegari: Barresi-ye enteqadi-ye maqalat-e qabz va bast-e shari'at az doktor Sorush* (The poverty of historiography: A critical appraisal of Dr. Sorush's articles on the constriction and expansion of shari'ah). Tehran: Allameh Tabataba'i.

Karimi-Hakkak, Ahmad. 1977. "A Well amid the Waste: An Introduction to the Poetry of Ahmad Shamlu." *World Literature Today* 51, no. 2:201–6.

———. 1985. "Protest and Perish: A History of the Writers' Association of Iran." *Iranian Studies* 18, nos. 2–4:189–229.

Katouzian, Homa. 1981. *The Political Economy of Modern Iran: Despotism and Pseudo-Modernism, 1926–1979.* New York: New York Univ. Press.

Kazemi, Farhad. 1980. *Poverty and Revolution in Iran.* New York: New York Univ. Press.

Kazemi, Farhad, and Ervand Abrahamian. 1978. "The Non-revolutionary Peasantry of Modern Iran." *Iranian Studies* 11:259–304.

Kazemiyyeh, Eslam. 1983–84. "The Reminiscences of Eslam Kazemiyyeh." Interviewed by Shirin Sami'i. Transcripts of tape recording, 3 Oct. and 8 May, Paris. *Oral History of Iran Collection.* Foundation for Iranian Studies, Bethesda, Md.

Keddie, Nikki R. 1981. *Roots of Revolution: An Interpretive History of Modern Iran.* With a section by Yann Richard. New Haven, Conn.: Yale Univ. Press.

———. 1995. *Iran and the Muslim World: Resistance and Revolution.* New York: New York Univ. Press.

Keyhan-e Farhangi. 1371/1992. "Tahajom-e farhangi va vaz'iyyat-e tafakkor"

(Cultural invasion and status of intellection [a roundtable discussion]). *Key-han-e Farhangi* 9, no. 6:5–16.

Khamenei, Seyyed Ali. 1365/1986. *Gozareshi az sabeqeh-ye tarikhi va owzaʿ-e ko-nuni-ye Howzeh-ye Elmiyyeh-ye Mashhad* (A report on the historical background and the present status of Mashhad's Theological Seminary). Mashhad: Kon-gereh-ye Jahani-ye Hazrat-e Reza.

Khanbaba-Tehrani, Mehdi. 1368/1989. *Negahi az darun beh jonbesh-e chap-e Iran: Goftogu ba Mehdi Khanbaba-Tehrani* (An insider's look into the Left movement in Iran: Interview with Mehdi Khanbaba-Tehrani). Edited by Hamid Shaw-kat. 2 vols. Saarbrücken, Germany: Baztab.

Khomeini, Ruhollah. 1350/1971. *Hokumat-e Eslami* (Islamic government). 3d ed. N.p.

———. 1981. *Islam and Revolution: Writings and Declarations of Imam Khomeini.* Translated and annotated by Hamid Algar. Berkeley, Calif.: Mizan Press.

Khorramshahi, Baha'oddin. 1361/1983. *Pozitivism-e manteqi* (Logical positiv-ism). Tehran: Markaz-e Entesharat-e Elmi va Farhangi.

Kia, Mehrdad. 1986. "Toward a Theory of Intellectual Formation: The Case of Iranian Intellectuals 1850–1900." Ph.D. diss., Univ. of Wisconsin, Madison.

Knysh, Alexander. 1992. "*Irfan* Revisited: Khomeini and the Legacy of Islamic Mystical Philosophy." *Middle East Journal* 46, no. 4:631–53.

Lakatos, Imre. 1978. *The Methodology of Scientific Research Programmes.* Cambridge: Cambridge Univ. Press.

Lambton, Ann K. S. 1964. "A Reconsideration of the Position of the *Marjaʿ al-taqlid* and the Religious Institution." *Studia Islamica,* no. 20:115–35.

Landgrebe, Ludwig. 1966. *Major Problems in Contemporary European Philosophy: From Dilthey to Heidegger.* Translated by Kurt F. Reinhardt. New York: Fred-erick Ungar.

Larijani, Sadeq. 1368/1989. "Naqd-e naqd va ayar-e naqd" (Critique of criti-cism and the assay of criticism). Pts. 1, 2. *Keyhan-e Farhangi* 6, no. 1:6–12; no. 2:8–13.

Liberman, Kenneth. 1989. "Decentering the Self: Two Perspectives from Philo-sophical Anthropology." In *The Question of the Other,* edited by Arleen B. Dal-lery and Charles E. Scott, 127–42. Albany: State Univ. of New York Press.

Lloyd, Genevieve. 1984. *The Man of Reason: "Male" and "Female" in Western Phi-losophy.* Minneapolis: Univ. of Minnesota Press.

Looney, Robert E. 1977. *A Development Strategy for Iran Through the 1980s.* New York: Praeger.

Lukacs, Georg. 1971. *History and Class Consciousness: Studies in Marxist Dialectics.* Cambridge, Mass.: MIT Press.

Magee, Bryan. 1359/1980. *Poper* (Popper). Translated by Manuchehr Bozorg-mehr. Tehran: Kharazmi.

Mahdavi, Hossein. 1970. "The Patterns and Problems of Economic Develop-ment in Rentier States: The Case of Iran." In *Studies in Economic History of the Middle East: From the Rise of Islam to the Present Day,* edited by M. A. Cook, 428–67. New York: Oxford Univ. Press.

Mahdavi-Damghani, Ahmad. 1990. Interview by author. 24 Mar., Philadelphia, Pa.

Mahfuzi, Ali-Reza. 1984. Interviewed by Zia Sedghi. 7 Apr., Paris. *Iranian Oral History Collection.* Harvard Univ., Houghton Library, Cambridge, Mass.

Makarem-Shirazi, Naser. 1348/1969. *Asrar-e aqabmandegi-ye Sharq* (Secrets of the Orient's backwardness). Qom: Entesharat-e Nasl-e Javan.

———. 1367/1989. "Feqh va ma'aref Eslami dar keshakesh-e efrat va tafrit" (Jurisprudence and Islamic knowledge caught in the battle of extremes). *Keyhan-e Farhangi* 5, no. 11:7–9.

Maktab-e Eslam, Editorial Committee. 1337/1958. "Hadaf-e ma" (Our goal). *Maktab-e Eslam* 1, no. 1:2–5.

Mardin, Şerif. 1962. *The Genesis of Young Ottoman Thought.* Princeton, N.J.: Princeton Univ. Press.

Mashayekhi, Mehrdad. 1987. "Dependency as a Problematic: A Study in the Political Implications of the Dependency Perspective." Ph.D. diss., American Univ.

Mashhad University. 1351/1972. *Rahnama-ye Daneshgah-e Mashhad: Sal-e tahsili-ye 1349–1350* (A guide to the University of Mashhad: 1970–1971 academic year). Mashhad: Entesharat-e Daneshgah-e Mashhad.

Matin-Daftari, Ahmad. 1930. "La Suppression des capitulations en Perse: L'Ancien Régime et le statut des étrangers dans l'empire du 'Lion et Soleil.'" Ph.D. diss., Univ. of Lausanne.

Mehta, Jarava L. 1985. *India and the West: The Problem of Understanding.* Chico, Calif.: Scholars Press.

Menashri, David. 1992. *Education and the Making of Modern Iran.* Ithaca, N.Y.: Cornell Univ. Press.

Milani, Abbas. 1374/1995. "Seyyed Fakhroddin Shadman va mas'aleh tajaddod" (S. F. Shadman and the question of modernity). *Iranshenasi* 7, no. 2:261–79.

Milani, Farzaneh. 1985. "Power, Prudence, and Print: Censorship and Simin Daneshvar." *Iranian Studies* 18, nos. 2–4:325–47.

Miller, Eugene F. 1972. "Positivism, Historicism, and Political Inquiry." *American Political Science Review* 66, no. 3:796–817.

Millward, William G. 1975. "The Social Psychology of Anti-Iranology." *Iranian Studies* 8, nos. 1–2:48–69.

Mir-Ahmadi, Maryam. 1357/1978. "Ta'sir va nofuz-e mazhab dar asar-e Jalal Al-e Ahmad" (Effect and influence of religion in Al-e Ahmad's works). *Sokhan* 26, no. 10:1077–81.

Mirzazadeh, Ne'mat [M. Azarm, pseud.]. 1977. "Statue of Liberty." *Review of Iranian Political Economy and History* 1, no. 2:78–79.

———. 1984. Interviewed by Zia Sedghi. 25 May, Paris. *Iranian Oral History Collection.* Harvard Univ., Houghton Library, Cambridge, Mass.

Mo'azzen, Naser, ed. 1357/1978. *Dah shab: Shabha-ye sha'eran va nevisandegan dar anjoman-e farhangi-ye Iran va Alman* (Ten nights: The nights of poets and writers at the Iran-Germany cultural association). Tehran: Amir Kabir.

232   *Works Cited*

Moghadam, Val. 1985. "Against Eurocentrism and Nativism: A Review Essay on Samir Amin's *Eurocentrism* and other Texts." *Socialism and Democracy*, no. 9 (Fall/Winter): 81–104.

Mojtahed-Shabestari, Mohammad. 1365/1986. "Masihiyyat-e Qorun Vosta va zamineha-ye peydayesh-e sekolarism" (Christianity in the Middle Ages and the backdrop to the emergence of secularism). *Keyhan-e Hava'i*, 30 July, 19.

———. 1366/1988. "Din va aql" (Religion and intellect [pt. 3]). *Keyhan-e Farhangi* 4, no. 12:10–11.

———. 1371/1992. "Din va modernism dar jahan-e Eslam" (Religion and modernism in the Islamic world). *Keyhan-e Hava'i*, 29 Apr., 12.

Mo'meni, Baqer. 1364/1985. "Al-e Ahmad sisad sal aqab bud" (Al-e Ahmad was three hundred years behind). In *Yadnameh-e Jalal Al-e Ahmad* (Jalal Al-e Ahmad commemoration volume), edited by Ali Dehbashi, 644–52. Tehran: Pasargad.

Monshizadeh, Davud. 1328/1949. "Sharqshenasan va sharqshenasi dar Alman" (Orientalists and orientalism in Germany). *Yadegar* 5, nos. 8–9:73–81.

Motahhari, Morteza. 1341/1963a. "Mazaya va khadamat-e marhum Ayatollah Borujerdi" (Advantages and services of the late Ayatollah Borujerdi). In *Bahsi dar bareh-ye marja'iyyat va ruhaniyyat* (A discussion on the principle of emulation and the religious establishment). 2d ed., 233–49. Tehran: Sherkat-e Sahami-ye Enteshar.

———. 1341/1963b. "Moshkel-e asasi dar sazman-e ruhaniyyat" (The central problem in the organizational structure of the religious establishment). In *Bahsi dar bareh-ye marja'iyyat va ruhaniyyat*. 2d ed., 165–98. Tehran: Sherkat-e Sahami-ye Enteshar.

———. 1366/1987. *Khadamat-e motaqabel-e Eslam va Iran* (Mutual services of Islam and Iran). 13th ed. Tehran: Sadra.

Mottahedeh, Roy. 1985. *The Mantle of the Prophet: Religion and Politics in Iran.* New York: Pantheon Books.

Naess, Arne. 1353?/1974?. *Rudolf Karnap* (Rudolf Carnap). Translated by Manuchehr Bozorgmehr. Tehran: Kharazmi.

Na'ini, Ayatollah Mohammad-Hoseyn. 1344/1955. *Tanbih al-umma va tanzih al-milla* (The admonition and refinement of the people). Introduction and annotations by Seyyed Mahmud Taleqani. N.p : Chapkhane-ye Ferdowsi.

Najmabadi, Afsaneh. 1987. "Depoliticisation of a Rentier State: The Case of Pahlavi Iran." In *The Rentier State: The Political Economy of Public Finance in the Arab Countries*, edited by Hazem Beblawi and Giacomo Luciani. London: Croom Helm.

Nameh Farhang. 1371/1992. "Goftoguy-e adyan va tafahom-e howzehha-ye farhangi" (Interreligious dialogue and mutual understanding in cultural fields [a roundtable discussion]). *Nameh Farhang* 2, no. 4:6–23.

Nandy, Ashis. 1983. *The Intimate Enemy: Loss and Recovery of Self under Colonialism.* Delhi: Oxford Univ. Press.

Naraqi, Ehsan. 1347/1969. *Olum-e ejtema'i va seyr-e takvini-ye an* (The genesis of the social sciences). 2d ed. Tehran: Chapkhane-ye Pars.

———. 1353/1974. *Ghorbat-e Gharb* (The alienation of the West). Tehran: Amir Kabir.

———. 2535/1976a. "Ab'ad-e farhangi dar tahqiqat-e elmi va ejtema'i" (Cultural dimensions in scientific and social research). *Rahnama-ye Ketab* 19, nos. 3–6:267–74, 573–86.

———. 2535/1976b. *Ancheh Khod dasht* . . . ([Cherishing] one's own trove . . .). Tehran: Amir Kabir.

———. 2536/1977. *Tamaᶜ-e kham* (Raw greed). Tehran: Tus.

——— [Naraqi]. 1994a. *From Palace to Prison: Inside the Iranian Revolution.* Chicago: Ivan R. Dee.

———. 1994b. Interview by author. 7 June, Paris.

———. 1374/1996. "Goftogu ba doktor Ehsan Naraqi" (Discussion with Dr. Ehsan Naraqi). *Kelk* 71–72:483–569.

Nasr, Seyyed Hossein [Hoseyn]. 1964. *Three Muslim Sages: Avicenna, Suhrawardi, Ibn ʿArabi.* Cambridge, Mass.: Harvard Univ. Press.

———. 1966. "The Immutable Principles of Islam and Western Education," *Muslim World* 56, no. 1:4–9.

———. 1972. *Islamic Philosophy in Contemporary Persia: A Survey of Activity During the Past Two Decades.* Research monograph no. 3. Salt Lake City: Univ. of Utah Middle East Center.

———. 1975a. *Islam and the Plight of Modern Man.* New York: Longman.

———. 1354/1975b. "Preface." *Javidan kherad (Sophia Perennis),* no. 1:7–8.

———. 1976a. *Man and Nature: The Spiritual Crisis of Modern Man.* London: Unwin.

———. 1976b. *Western Science and Asian Culture.* New Delhi: Indian Council for Cultural Relations.

———. 1982–83. "The Reminiscences of Seyyed Hoseyn Nasr." Interviewed by Hoseyn Ziya'i. Transcripts of tape recording, Oct. and Jan., Boston. *Oral History of Iran Collection.* Foundation for Iranian Studies, Bethesda, Md.

———. 1987. *Traditional Islam in the Modern World.* London: Kegan Paul.

———. 1989. *Knowledge and the Sacred.* Albany: State Univ. of New York Press.

———. 1990. Interview by author. 9 Feb., Washington, D.C.

———. 1372/1993. "Goft va shonud [Shiva Kaviyani] ba Seyyed Hoseyn Nasr" ([Shiva Kaviyani's] conversation with S. H. Nasr). *Kelk* 43–44:177–97.

———. 1994. "In Quest of Eternal Sophia." In *The Complete Bibliography of the Works of Seyyed Hossein Nasr From 1958 Through April 1993,* edited by Mehdi Aminrazavi and Zailan Moris, xxvii–xxxii. Kuala Lumpur, Malaysia: Islamic Academy of Science.

Nateq, Homa. 2536/1977. "Farang va farangima'abi va resaleh-ye enteqadi-ye sheykh va shukh" (The West and Westernization, and the critical essay of the cleric and the joker). *Alefba* (Tehran) 1st ser., no. 6:56–72.

Nazari, Ali-Asghar. 1368/1989. *Joghrafiya-ye jamʿiyyat-e Iran* (Population geography of Iran). Tehran: Sazman-e Gitashenasi.

Nikitine, Basile. 1956. "Farangshenasi ou L'Europe vue de Téhéran." In *Char-*

isteria Orientalia: Praecipue ad Persiam pertinentia, edited by Felix Tauer, Vera Kubickova, and Ivan Hrbek, 210–26. Prague: Nakladtelstvi Ceskoslovenske Akademie Ved.

Ogburn, William F., and Meyer F. Nimkoff. 1958. *Sociology.* 3d ed. Boston: Houghton Mifflin.

Oparin, Aleksandr I. 1961. *Life, Its Nature, Origin and Development.* Translated by Ann Synge. New York: Academic Press.

Pakdaman, Naser. 1984. Interviewed by Zia Sedghi. 26 May, Paris. *Iranian Oral History Collection.* Harvard Univ., Houghton Library, Cambridge, Mass.

———. 1994. Interview by author. 7 June, Paris.

———. 1995. "Dah shab-e she'r: Barrasi va arzyabi-ye yek tajrebeh" (Ten nights of poetry readings: A review and evaluation of an event). *Kankash,* no. 12:125–70.

Parham, Baqer. 1347/1968. "Pay-e sohbat-e filsuf: Gozareshi az falsafeh-ye daneshgahi" (Confabulation with the philosopher: A report on [the teaching of] philosophy at the universities). *Jahan-e Now* 23, nos. 10–12:4–11.

———. 1367/1988. "Negahi beh nazariyyat-e Na'ini dar bab-e hokumat va bonyad-e mashru'iyyat-e qodrat-e siyasi" (A look at [Ayatollah] Na'ini's views on government and the foundations of the legitimacy of political power). *Cheshmandaz,* no. 5:48–77.

———. 1368/1989. *Tajareb-e gozashteh-ye Kanun-e Nevisandegan-e Iran va zaruratha-ye konuni* (Past experiences of the Writers' Association of Iran and present necessities). Paris: author.

Parsa, Misagh. 1989. *Social Origins of the Iranian Revolution.* New Brunswick, N.J.: Rutgers Univ. Press.

Paz, Octavio. 1985. *One Earth, Four or Five Worlds: Reflections on Contemporary History.* Translated by Helen R. Lane. San Diego: Harcourt Brace Jovanovich.

Pazhum, Ja'far, ed. 1370/1991. *Yadnameh-ye ostad Mohammad-Taqi Shari'ati-Mazinani* (Mohammad-Taqi Shari'ati-Mazinani commemorative volume). Qom: Khorram.

Pessaran, M. H. 1982. "The System of Dependent Capitalism in Pre- and Post-Revolutionary Iran." *International Journal of the Middle East Studies* 14, no. 4: 501–22.

Popper, Karl. 1959. *The Logic of Scientific Discovery.* London: Hutchinson.

———. 1350/1971. *Faqr-e tarikhigari* (The poverty of historicism). Translated by Ahmad Aram. Tehran: Kharazmi.

———. 1370/1991. *Manteq-e ekteshaf-e elmi* (The logic of scientific discovery). Translated by Seyyed Hoseyn Kamali. Tehran: Markaz-e Entesharat-e Elmi va Farhangi.

Popper, Karl, and Herbert Marcuse. 1358?/1979?. *Enqelab ya eslah* (Revolution or reform). Translated by Hushang Vaziri. Tehran: Kharazmi.

Puyan, Amir-Parviz. 1973. *Zarurat-e mobarezeh-ye mosallahaneh va radd-e te'ori-ye baqa* (The necessity of armed struggle and refutation of the theory of survival). Beirut: Sazman-e Jebheh-ye Melli-ye Kharej az Keshvar.

Rahimi, Mostafa. 1347/1968. "Melat va rowshanfekran" (The nation and the intellectuals). *Jahan-e Now* 23, nos. 7–9:29–39.

Rajavi, Mas'ud. 1358/1979. *Tabyin-e jahan* (Comprehending the world). Vol. 1. Tehran: Sazman-e Mojahedin-e Khalq-e Iran.

———. 1984. Interviewed by Zia Sedghi. 29 May, Paris. *Iranian Oral History Collection.* Harvard Univ., Houghton Library, Cambridge, Mass.

Rasekh, Shapur. 1351/1972. "Ertebat-e tahqiqat-e Iranshenasi ba neyazha-ye jame'eh-ye konuni" (The relation between Iranology research and the needs of contemporary society). *Sokhan* 22, no. 2:114–26.

Richard, Yann. 1981. "Contemporary Shi'i Thought." In *Roots of Revolution: An Interpretive History of Modern Iran.* Nikkie R. Keddie, with a section by Yann Richard, 202–30. New Haven, Conn.: Yale Univ. Press.

———. 1988. "Shari'at Sangalaji: A Reformist Theologian of the Rida Shah Period." In *Authority and Political Culture in Shi'ism,* edited by Said Amir Arjomand, 159–77. Albany: State Univ. of New York Press.

Rodinson, Maxime. 1980. *Europe and the Mystique of Islam.* Translated by Roger Veinus. Seattle: Univ. of Washington Press.

Rokni, Mohammad-Mehdi. 1366/1987. "Cheraghi keh dar kanun darakshid" (The lamp that glowed in the foyer). *Majalleh-ye Daneshkadeh-ye Adabiyyat va olum-e Ensani Daneshgah-e Ferdowsi-ye Mashhad* 20, nos. 1–2:5–29.

Rorty, Richard. 1985. "Solidarity or Objectivity?" In *Post-Analytic Philosophy,* edited by John Rajchman and Cornel West, 3–19. New York: Columbia Univ. Press.

Sabbagh, Suha. 1982. "Going Against the West from Within: The Emergence of the West As an Other in Frantz Fanon's Work." Ph.D. diss., Univ. of Wisconsin.

Sadri, Ahmad. 1992. *Max Weber's Sociology of Intellectuals.* New York: Oxford Univ. Press.

Sa'edi, Gholamhoseyn. 1984. Interviewed by Zia Sedghi. 7 June, Paris. *Iranian Oral History Collection.* Harvard Univ., Houghton Library, Cambridge, Mass.

Said, Edward W. 1978. *Orientalism.* New York: Vintage Books.

———. 1985. "Orientalism Reconsidered." *Race and Class* 27, no. 2:1–15.

———. 1987. "Foucault and the Imagination of Power." In *Foucault: A Critical Reader,* edited by David Couzens Hoy, 149–55. New York: Basil Blackwell.

———. 1993. *Culture and Imperialism.* New York: Knopf.

———. 1994. *Representations of the Intellectual.* New York: Pantheon Books.

Salehi-Najafabadi, Ne'matollah. 1364/1985. *Shahid-e javid* (Eternal martyr). 14th ed. Qom: Sadra.

Sanasarian, Eliz. 1983. *The Women's Rights Movement in Iran: Mutiny, Appeasement, and Repression from 1900 to Khomeini.* New York: Praeger.

Sartre, Jean-Paul. 1972. *Plaidoyer pour les intellectuels.* Paris: Gallimard.

———. 1979. Preface to *The Wretched of the Earth,* by Frantz Fanon, 7–31. New York: Grove Press.

Sazman-e Barnameh va Budjeh. 1357/1978. *Shakhesha-ye ejtema'i-ye Iran 1357: Barresi moqaddamati* (Social indicators of Iran in 1978: A preliminary investigation). Tehran: Sazman-e Barnameh va Budjeh.

Sazman-e Mojahedin-e Khalq-e Iran. 1358/1979. *Tahlil-e amuzeshi-ye bayaniyyeh-ye oportunistha-ye chapnama* (Instructive analysis of the manifesto of the pseudo-leftist opportunists). Tehran: Sazman-e Mojahedin-e Khalq-e Iran.

Sepanlu, Mohammad-Ali. 1366/1988. *Nevisandagan-e pishrow-e Iran az Mashrutiyyat ta 1350: Tarikhcheh-ye roman, qesseh-ye kutah, namayeshnameh va naqd-e adabi dar Iran-e mo'aser* (Progressive Iranian writers from the Constitutional Revolution to 1971: A brief history of the novel, the short story, drama, and literary criticism in contemporary Iran). 2d ed. Tehran: Negah.

Shadman, Seyyed Fakhroddin. 1937. "Education in Iran." *Asiatic Review* 33, no. 113:165–73.

———. 1939a. "Muhammad and His Mission." *Islamic Review* 27:64–73.

———. 1939b. "The Relations of Britain and Persia, 1800–1815." Ph.D. diss., Univ. of London.

———. 1326/1948. "Taskhir-e tamaddon-e farangi" (The conquest of Western civilization). In *Arayesh va pirayesh-e zaban* (Beautification and purification of language). Tehran: Chapkhane-ye Iran.

———. 1335/1956. *Dar rah-e Hend* (On the road to India). 2d ed. Tehran: Ebn Sina.

———. 1342/1964. "Zaban-e dastan" (The language of fiction). *Rahnama-ye ketab* 6, nos. 10–11:703–20.

———. 1344/1965. *Tariki va rowshana'i* (Darkness and light). Tehran: Ketabkhaneh-ye Sana'i.

———. 1346/1967. *Terazhedi-ye Farang* (The tragedy of the West). Tehran: Tahuri.

———. 1347/1968. "Shenakht-e melal" (On knowing other nations). Pts. 1–3. *Yaghma* 21, no. 3:118–24; no. 7:356–58; no 8:425–27.

Shahdadi, Hormoz. 1982. "The Iranian Intelligentsia and Political Development: 1900–1953." Ph.D. diss., Massachusetts Institute of Technology.

Shakeri, Khosrow. 1983. Interviewed by Zia Sedghi. 27 July, Cambridge, Mass. *Iranian Oral History Collection.* Harvard Univ., Houghton Library, Cambridge, Mass.

Shanehchi, Mohammad. 1983. Interviewed by Habib Ladjevardi. 4 March, Paris. *Iranian Oral History Collection.* Harvard Univ., Houghton Library, Cambridge, Mass.

Sharabi, Hisham. 1988. *Neopatriarchy: A Theory of Distorted Change in Arab Society.* New York: Oxford Univ. Press.

Shari'ati, Ali. N.d. *Tashayyo'-e Alavi va Tashayyo'-e Safavi* (Alavid Shi'ism and Safavid Shi'ism). Collected Works, no. 9. Tehran: Office for Compiling and Organizing the Collected Works of Dr. Ali Shari'ati.

———. 1356/1977. *Haft nameh az mojahed-e shahid doktor Ali Shari'ati* (Seven letters from the martyred warrior Dr. Ali Shari'ati). N.p.: Abuzar.

———. 1979. *On the Sociology of Islam.* Translated by Hamid Algar. Berkeley, Calif.: Mizan Press.

———. 1980. *Marxism and Other Western Fallacies: An Islamic Critique.* Translated by R. Campbell. Berkeley, Calif.: Mizan Press.

————. 1360/1981a. *Az koja aghaz konim?* (From where shall we begin?). Collected Works, no. 20. Tehran: Office for Compiling and Organizing the Collected Works of Dr. Ali Shariʿati.

————. 1360/1981b. *Rowshanfekr va masʾuliyyat-e u dar jameʾeh* (The intellectual and his responsibilities in society). Collected Works, no. 20. Tehran: Office for Compiling and Organizing the Collected Works of Dr. Ali Shariʿati.

————. 1361/1982. *Ari inchonin bud baradar* (Yes, brother, this is how it was). Collected Works, no. 22. Tehran: Entesharat-e Sabz.

————. 1361/1983a. *Bazgasht* (Return). Collected Works, no 4. Tehran: Office for Compiling and Organizing the Collected Works of Dr. Ali Shariʿati.

————. 1361/1983b. *Chahar zendan-e ensan* (The four prisons of mankind). Collected Works, no. 25. Tehran: Entesharat-e Qalam.

————. 1361/1983c. *Eslamshenasi* (Islamology). Collected Works, no. 16. Tehran: Entesharat-e Qalam.

————. 1362/1983d. *Tarikh va shenakht-e adyan* (History and recognition of religions). Collected Works, no. 14. Tehran: Sherkat-e Sahami-ye Enteshar.

————. 1364/1985. *Barkhi pishtazan-e "bazgasht beh khish" dar Jahan-e Sevvom* (Some of the pioneers of "Return to Self" in the Third World). Collected Works, no. 31. Tehran: Office for Compiling and Organizing the Collected Works of Dr. Ali Shariʿati.

————. 1986. *What Is to Be Done: The Enlightened Thinkers and an Islamic Renaissance.* Edited and annotated by Farhang Rajaee. Houston: Institute for Research and Islamic Studies.

Sharify, Nasser. 1959. *Cataloging of Persian Works Including Rules for Transliteration, Entry, and Description.* Chicago: American Library Association.

Shayegan, Daryush. 1346/1967. *Adyan va maktabha-ye falsafi-ye Hend* (Indian religions and philosophical schools of thought). 2 vols. Tehran: Entesharat-e Daneshgah-e Tehran.

————. 2535/1976. *Botha-ye zehni va khatereh-ye azali* (Idols of the mind and eternal memory). Tehran: Amir Kabir.

————. 2536/1977a. *Asiya dar barabar-e Gharb* (Asia facing the West). Tehran: Amir Kabir.

————. 2536/1977b. "Din va falsafeh va elm dar Sharq va Gharb" (Religion, philosophy and science in East and West). *Alefba* (Tehran), 1st ser., no. 6: 101–9.

————. 1982. *Qu'est-ce qu'une révolution religieuse?* Paris: Les Presses d'aujourd'hui.

————. 1989. Interview by author. 27 June, Bethesda, Md.

————. 1990. *Henry Corbin, La Topographie spirituelle de l'islam iranien.* Paris: Editions de la Différence, 1990.

————. 1992a. *Cultural Schizophrenia: Islamic Societies Confronting the West.* Translated by John Howe. London: Saqi Books.

————. 1992b. *Sous les ciels du monde: Entretiens avec Ramin Jahanbegloo* (Under the world's skies: Interviews with Ramin Jahanbegloo). Paris: Editions du Félin.

————. 1373/1994. *"Zir asmanha-ye jahan: Goftoguy-e Ramin Jahanbeglu ba Dar-yush Shayegan"* (Under the world's skies: Ramin Jahanbeglu's interview with Daryush Shayegan). *Kelk* 53:271–303.

Shils, Edward. 1957. "Primordial, Personal, Sacred and Civil Ties." *British Journal of Sociology* 8:130–45.

Sho'a'iyan, Mostafa. 1975. *Enqelab* (Revolution). N.p.

————. 1976a. *Chand neveshteh* (Few articles). Florence, Italy: Mazdak.

————. 1976b. *Pasokha-ye nasanjideh be "qadamha-ye sanjideh"* (Injudicious replies to "Judicious Steps"). Florence, Italy: Mazdak.

Siassi [Siyasi], Ali-Akbar. 1931. "La Perse au contact de l'Occident (étude historique et sociale)." Ph.D. diss., Univ. of Paris.

Skocpol, Theda. 1982. "Rentier State and Shi'a Islam in the Iranian Revolution." *Theory and Society* 11, no. 3:265–83.

Sobhani, Ja'far. 1367/1988. "Tahlil'i az qabz va bast-e te'orik-e shari'at ya Nazariyyeh-ye takamol-e ma'refat-e dini" (An analysis of the theoretical constriction and expansion of shari'ah, or the theory of evolution of religious knowledge). *Keyhan-e Farhangi* 5, no. 9:10–16.

Sorush, Abdolkarim. 1977. *Nahad-e na'aram-e jahan* (The tumultuous nature of the universe). Solon, Ohio: N.p.

————. 1980. *Az tarikhparasti ta Khodaparasti* (From worshipping history to worshipping God). Tehran: N.p.

————. 1365/1986. "Ba mas'ulin-e *Keyhan-e Farhangi* dar bab-e gezafeh-forushi" (To the editors of *Keyhan-e Farhangi* concerning idle talk). *Keyhan-e Farhangi* 3, no. 2:35.

————. 1366–67/1987–88. "Mahak-e tajrebeh" (The touchstone of experience). Pts. 1, 2. *Farhang*, no. 1:21–48; nos. 2–3:43–77.

————. 1366/1988a. *Tafarroj-e son': Goftarhayi dar Maqulat-e akhlaq va san'at va elm-e ensani* (Essays on human sciences, ethics, and arts). Tehran: Sorush.

————. 1367/1988b. *Tamsil dar she'r-e Mowlana* (Allegory in Rumi's poetry). Tehran: Barg.

————. 1368/1989. *Elm chist, falsafah chist?* (What is science, what is philosophy?). Tehran: Mo'asseseh-ye Farhangi-ye Sarat.

————. 1369/1990. "Se farhang" (Three cultures). *Ayeneh Andisheh*, nos. 3–4:50–59.

————. 1991a. Correspondence with author.

————. 1370/1991b. *Qabz va bast-e te'orik-e shari'at* (The theoretical constriction and expansion of the Shari'ah). Tehran: Mo'asseseh-ye Farhangi-ye Sarat.

————. 1371/1992. "Paradoks-e modernism" (The paradox of modernism). *Keyhan-e Hava'i*, 1 Apr., no. 975:12.

Spengler, Oswald. 1939. *The Decline of the West.* New York: Knopf.

Tabari, Azar, and Nahid Yeganeh, eds. 1982. *In the Shadow of Islam.* London: Zed Press.

Tabataba'i, Allameh Mohammad-Hoseyn. 1332–50/1953–71. *Osul-e falsafeh va ravesh-e re'alism* (The principles of philosophy and the method of realism).

Introduction and annotations by Morteza Motahhari. 5 vols. Tehran: Mohammad Akhundi.

Tabataba'i, Allameh Mohammad-Hoseyn, and Henry Corbin. 1339/1960. *Mosahebat-e Allameh Tabataba'i ba ostad Korban* (Interviews of Allameh Tabataba'i with Professor Corbin). Tehran: Maktab-e Tashayyu'.

Taleqani, Seyyed Mahmud. 1983. *Islam and Ownership.* Translated by Ahmad Jabbari and Farhang Rajaee. Lexington, Ky.: Mazda.

Tehran University. 1342/1963. *Majmu'e maqalat-e tahqiqi-ye khavarshenasi ehda be aqa-ye Profosor Hanri Mase* (Henri Massé Commemoration Volume). Tehran: Tehran Univ. Press.

———. 2536/1977. *Jashnnameh-ye Hanri Korban* (Henry Corbin Commemoration Volume). Edited by S. H. Nasr. Tehran: McGill University, Tehran University, and the Imperial Iranian Academy of Philosophy.

Tehranian, Majid. 1980. "Communication and Revolution in Iran: The Passing of a Paradigm." *Iranian Studies* 13, nos. 1–4:5-30.

Times (London). 1982. 3 Aug., 10.

Todorov, Tzvetan. 1984. *The Conquest of America: The Question of the Other.* Translated by Richard Howard. New York: Harper and Row.

Tonokaboni, Fereydun. 1356/1978. *Dah dastan va neveshtehha-ye digar: Zamimeh-ye maqalati dar bareh-ye sansur dar Iran va list-e ketabha-ye mozerreh* (Ten stories and other writings [of Fereydun Tonakaboni] plus an appendix on censorship and the list of unauthorized books). 2d ed. Berkeley, Calif.: Sazman-e Daneshjuyan-e Irani dar Amrika.

Turner, Bryan S. 1988. "Religion and State-Formation: A Commentary on Recent Debates." *Journal of Historical Sociology* 1, no. 3:322–33.

Vali, Abbas, and Sami Zubaida. 1985. "Factionalism and Political Discourse in the Islamic Republic of Iran: The Case of the Hujjatiyeh Society," *Economy and Society* 14, no. 2:139–73.

Varedi, Ahmad. 1992. "Muhammad 'Ali Furughi, Zuka al-Mulk (1877–1942): A Study in the Role of Intellectuals in Modern Iranian Politics." Ph.D. diss., Univ. of Utah.

Vezarat-e Olum va Amuzesh-e Ali [Ministry of Science and Higher Education]. 1350/1971. *Amar-e daneshjuyan-e e'azami beh kharej az keshvar dar sal-e 1349* (Statistics on students sent abroad in 1970). Tehran: Vezarat-e Olum va Amuzesh-e Ali.

———. 2535/1976. *Rahnama-ye a'za'-ye hey'at-e elm-yi daneshgahha va mo'assessat-e amuzesh-e ali-ye keshvar: Sal-e tahsili-ye 2534–35* (A guide to the faculties of universities and institutions of higher learning: 1975–76 academic year). Compiled by Ali-Akbar Beyhaqi. Tehran: Vezarat-e Olum va Amuzesh-e Ali.

Walicki, Andrzej. 1979. *A History of Russian Thought From the Enlightenment to Marxism.* Translated by Hilda Andrews-Rusiecka. Stanford, Calif.: Stanford Univ. Press.

Weber, Max. 1981. *From Max Weber.* Edited by H. H. Gerth and C. Wright Mills. New York: Oxford Univ. Press.

Williams, Patrick, and Laura Chrisman, eds. 1994. *Colonial Discourse and Post-Colonial Theory: A Reader.* New York: Columbia Univ. Press.

Wolf, Eric R. 1973. *Peasant Wars of the Twentieth Century.* New York: Harper and Row.

Index

Abadan Oil College, 55
Abbasid dynasty, 86
Abedzadeh, Haj Ali-Asghar, 103, 185
Adabiyyat-e mota'ahhed, 43
Adams, Charles J., 125n. 21
Adib-Soltani, Mir-Shamsoddin, 148
Adorno, Theodore, 164
Afghani (Asadabadi), Seyyed Jamal al-
  Din, 144n. 22, 185; *Rejection of Mate-*
  rialists, 130
Afghanistan, 74
Afshar-Naderi, Nader, 138, 185
Agricultural Bank, 138
Agricultural sector, 27
Ahmadi, Abdolrahim: *Nahamahangi-ye*
  Roshd-e Eqtesadi va Ejtema'i dar Donya-
  ye Mo'aser, 71n. 24
Ahmadzadeh, Mastureh, 101, 186
Ahmadzadeh, Mas'ud, 34, 35, 37, 101,
  117, 186
Ahmadzadeh, Taher, 101, 102, 186
Akhavan-Sales, Mehdi, 44, 104, 186;
  Zemestan, 48
Akhbari-Usuli dispute, 128
Akhundzadeh, Mirza Fath-Ali, 75, 186
Alavi, Bozorg, 43, 44, 186
Alavi, Reza, 148, 186
Alavi schools, 92, 93, 116
Al-e Ahmad, Jalal, xvi, 44, 49, 65, 70,
  73–76, 102, 106, 132, 134n. 6, 138,
  145n. 23, 152, 186–87; *Dar khedmat*
  va khiyanat-e rowshanfekran, 71–72, 73;
  Gharbzadegi, 53, 66–69, 71, 72, 146
Algar, Hamid, 142n. 19
Algeria, 35, 36, 39, 56, 113, 117
Alibaba'i, Ahmad, 84n. 5, 187

Al-Salafiyya movement, 144n. 21
American University in Cairo, 144
American University of Beirut, 120
Amini, Ali, 67, 187
Amini, Yadollah (Maftun), 50n. 41, 187
Amir-Kabir, Mirza Taqi Khan, 54n. 3,
  187
Anatomy of Revolution, The (Brinton), 33
Ancheh khod dasht (Naraqi), 138
Anderson, Benedict, 15
Andisheh-ye Eslami (journal), 168
Anglo-Iranian Oil Company, 54, 55
Anjavi-Shirazi, Seyyed Abolqasem, 187
Anjoman-e Hojjatiyyeh, 96, 103, 217
Anjoman-e Qalam, 44
Anjoman-e Shahanshahi-ye Falsafeh-ye
  Iran, 45n. 36, 120, 124–25
Anjomanha-ye tafsir-e Qur'an, 93, 217
Anti-Baha'i Society, 96
Anticolonialism, 73, 109, 113, 117
Anti-communism, 137
Anti-Duhring (Engels), 145n. 24
Antiorientalism, 132, 144–45
Arab world, 74, 80, 144
Arafat, Yasir, 15
Aram, Ahmad, 145n. 24, 187
Arani, Taqi, 75, 187
Aristotle, 96, 122, 132n. 2, 164; *Politics,*
  141
Arman-e Khalq Organization, 37
Aron, Raymond, 106
Aryamehr University of Technology,
  120
Aryan, Sa'id, 37, 188
Aryanpur, Amir-Hoseyn, 145n. 24, 188;
  Zamineh-ye jame'ehshenasi, 118